Social Economies

Lester Hadsell

Social Economies

How Society Shapes and is Shaped by Economic Thinking

palgrave
macmillan

Lester Hadsell
Department of Economics
University at Albany, State University
of New York
Albany, NY, USA

ISBN 978-3-032-21915-2 ISBN 978-3-032-21916-9 (eBook)
https://doi.org/10.1007/978-3-032-21916-9

This Palgrave Macmillan imprint is published by the registered company Springer Nature Switzerland AG
The registered company address is: Gewerbestrasse 11, 6330 Cham, Switzerland

To Chris. The story of my life.

Preface

The author and literary critic Dorothy Parker once suggested, "If you have any young friends who aspire to become writers, the second greatest favor you can do them is to present them with copies of The Elements of Style. The first greatest, of course, is to shoot them now, while they're happy." Replace "writers" with "economists" and "The Elements of Style" with "the leading introductory economics textbooks" and you get a sense of why I wrote this book.

What's wrong with typical introductions to economics? They're too narrowly focused—often ignoring the many economic subfields that overlap with social and biological sciences. They miss much of the interesting research taking place there that is uncovering hidden truths about how economies interact with society. They tend to be heavy on formalization and theory, abstracting from what is most useful about economics for non-economists. Abstraction and simplification have their place but something is lost in the process—there's an opportunity cost.

This book can serve as an introduction to a broader economics, one that is multidisciplinary, with a strong social science influence. We are not alone in taking this path—leading economists are publishing cutting edge research in top journals, using ideas and techniques from a host of related disciplines (just as they borrow from economics), research that is cited liberally throughout this book.

My focus is on the intersections of economics with a range of social sciences—sociology, psychology, philosophy—and biological science.

Taking this approach improves our understanding of how economies work, and how they can best serve individuals and society. It also brings economics closer to its roots—after all, economics began with a professor of moral philosophy.

So, maybe the greatest thing you can do for your friend—and yourself—is study economics from a social science perspective. If you want to know what economies are about, why economies work the way they do, then study the overlap of economics with related disciplines. In other words, take a liberal arts approach. Then pick up a leading economics textbook.

Troy, USA Lester Hadsell

Contents

About the Author

Lester Hadsell's current research and teaching interests focus on the interdisciplinary nature of economics, with recent publications examining religion's role in shaping individual economic preferences and public policies, the size of government, and satisfaction with life. His research has appeared in journals such as the *American Economic Review*, *Economics Letters*, *Journal of Comparative Economics*, *Eastern Economic Journal*, and *American Journal of Economics and Sociology*, among others. He has served in editorial capacities for several journals, including the *Journal of Education for Business*. He currently teaches economics at the State University of New York at Albany and previously held teaching positions at the University of North Carolina Wilmington and at other colleges and universities.

List of Figures

List of Tables

PART I

Values and Views

CHAPTER 1

An Expanded View

Economics: Supply and Demand. That's it.
—Father Guido Sarducci

We all know that economics is all about supply and demand. Father Guido Sarducci of late 1970s Saturday Night Live fame tells us so in his comedy skit, The Five-Minute University.[1] I chuckle every time I watch. But some people seem to take it almost literally. Nearly everyone who has completed a semester of introductory economics remembers being inundated with supply and demand graphs that were said to illustrate a range of economic truths. But of course there is so much more to the story. Those graphs represent a simplified reality, often devoid of the many complications inherent in a social world. The abstraction is valuable but there's a cost to simplification. Economies are social constructs and are best viewed from that angle, with insights from a variety of disciplines that enrich our understanding of the economic choices we make as individuals and collectively as a society.

With a few notable exceptions, introductions to economics, from mass market works to textbooks, tend to explain economics from a perspective

[1] "The idea is that in five minutes, you learn what the average college graduate remembers five years after he or she's out of school."

L. Hadsell, *Social Economies*,
https://doi.org/10.1007/978-3-032-21916-9_1

that is much too narrow. And though most include references to influences from other disciplines (such as with behavioral economics), they mostly neglect much that is new and exciting. My approach is different. This book is for readers who want more from economics, readers who are interested in how economies are connected to other areas of life, readers who want a broader perspective.

My emphasis is on the interconnectedness of economics with other disciplines, a liberal arts approach—a feature of economics that was present with the discipline at its origin, with the professor of moral philosophy Adam Smith. Recent incorporation of insights from psychology, leading to the new field of behavioral economics, is an example of how cross-over with other disciplines is enhancing understanding of economies. Nobel prizes in economic science have been awarded to psychologist Daniel Kahneman (2002) and economist Richard Thaler (2017) for contributions in behavioral economics. More recently, interest has greatly expanded to other areas so that new technologies, methods, and multidisciplinary collaborations are producing interesting insights from biology, sociology, and a range of other disciplines. These areas are also being recognized for their contributions, including with Nobel prizes.

We are learning, for instance, of the deep connection between human biology (DNA and hormones, in particular) and economic-related outcomes such as educational attainment, levels of income and wealth, and preference for risk-taking (e.g., starting a business, investing money, or applying for a promotion). Economic sociology provides insights into the importance of social networks in employment patterns and productivity. Ecological economics is expanding our understanding of the importance of the environmental context in which economic activity takes place, from source (of raw materials) to sink (destination for waste), including feedback loops and ecological limits. I elaborate on each of these, and others, in the chapters that follow.

Many of the insights are being put to use in public and business policy, and in reformulation of economic systems and economic thinking. Consider one example: As explained in detail in Chapter 2, a simple change to how retirement investment options are presented to employees has led to higher individual savings rates and more appropriate investment choices. The changes benefit not only the individuals who are saving more for retirement but also society, as those individuals will be less reliant on public financial support in old age and, in the more immediate term, with more savings available today to lend to borrowers (to expand businesses, for example), the higher rate of saving will also lead to higher economic growth—i.e., higher standards of living. A small nudge, as it's called, can make a big difference.

A theme running throughout this book is that economics cannot be separated from other disciplines. Economics is concerned with two questions, (1) How best to produce what members of society want and (2) How best to distribute those goods and services. Much of the (long and complicated) answer to these questions can be technical and mathematical, often abstract. But much of the answer also concerns questions of relationships, ethics, and values. After all, they involve choices and priorities. As such, insight—ideas, tools, methods—from a range of disciplines is helpful.

This book has three parts. In Part I, I describe the economic setting, for every economic system has a context in which it operates. Capitalism is the world's dominant economic system today, but the varieties of capitalism are many, and each economic system (including varieties of capitalism) has pluses and minuses. In Chapter 2, I emphasize that how economic relationships are structured is the result of choices made by society, individually and collectively. Different societies make different choices, often leading to significant differences across economies. I also describe some of the approaches economists take in understanding those decisions, focusing on psychology, sociology, biology, and philosophy, as each plays a significant part in the rest of the book.

Chapter 3 explains why economists sometimes disagree about the answers to the two economic questions noted above—and about how to interpret economic events or policy. Chapters 4 and 5 present alternative ways of thinking about economic relationships: Marxist, Buddhist, Feminist, and Ecological. Each offers a critique of today's dominant economic way of thinking that involves power and perspective and is necessary reading for a better understanding of our world as it is—and how it could be. Continuing the exploration of values, Chapter 6 examines rights and obligations in market settings, asking questions such as What obligations do businesses and individuals have to each other? What rights? Do these obligations and rights extend beyond our time (to past or future generations)? Ethics and economic choices cannot be separated. Chapter 7 rounds out Part I, exploring where and when market forces should be applied, discussing the benefits as well as the costs to non-economic values.

Part II looks at goals for economic systems. What could we, as a society, hope to achieve in our economic interactions? How should our resources be directed to get the greatest benefit for society, broadly defined? Far too much focus today is placed on Gross Domestic Product (GDP). This is partly due to the limited notion of what economics is and what economic systems are meant to achieve, as briefly described in Part I. The misplaced emphasis on GDP is not just a shame, it is actually becoming dangerous, for economic systems form only a small, albeit important, part of the human experience. A significant amount of economic activity occurs outside of formal markets (e.g., unpaid work), meaning a significant amount of economic activity is ignored when calculating GDP, which is based on formal market (paid) work only. This exclusion tends to undercount the work of economically marginalized populations and neglects social and ecological contexts which are central to proper functioning of economies: much of what we value—family, social connections, community, the environment—is often ignored in calculations of GDP, and market activity that adds to GDP sometimes negatively affects those things we care about outside the market. In short, the good life includes more than a narrow measure of economic value such as GDP. This is the argument in Chapters 8, 9, and 10, focusing on alternatives to GDP, sustainable prosperity, and meaningful employment. Multiple perspectives and research findings are brought to bear in considering each goal.

The next three chapters of Part II are all about hot button issues in the U.S. and many other countries. How much choice should be permitted in economic settings—and how much do we actually want—is the subject of Chapter 11. Multiple perspectives on economic freedom are examined, ranging from Nobel recipients Milton Friedman and Amartya Sen to President Franklin Roosevelt and pop icon Janis Joplin. The issues raised are practical as well as philosophical and lie at the heart of today's substantial social and political discord. Chapter 12 discusses the purpose of business: is their *raison d'être* to serve customers and society or to make profit for shareholders/owners? (Perhaps there is no conflict between the two?) Chapters 13 and 14 combine freedom and purpose in an extended discussion of economic inequality. A range of economic, social, and biological factors that contribute to inequality is considered. Philosophical perspectives, combined with empirical observations, shape the debate about how much inequality is necessary and fair.

Part III examines social influences on our economic participation and the structure of economies and society. Norms and customs are the focus of Chapter 15. These cultural influences act to limit our self-interest in economic interactions, encouraging cooperation, honesty, trust, and a respect for fairness. Specific examples are provided, from price gouging laws to provision of public goods. Not only are influences like these common, but well-functioning economies benefit in demonstrable ways. Chapter 16 examines the long and well-documented role of religion in shaping individual and societal economic choices and possibilities. Sunday baseball (once banned) and Chick-fil-A (closed on Sunday to observe the Christian Sabbath) are examples. So, too, are findings that belief in Hell is a force for economic growth and that religious Christians (though not others) on the whole favor market-oriented approaches over government intervention.

The connection between marriage, children, and economic growth is the topic of Chapter 17. We see that a confluence of social, technological, and economic forces has led to dramatic changes in family structure over the past century-plus in the U.S. and other western developed economies. Those same changes are currently occurring in developing economies such as China, where population is projected to decline over the next century. Chapter 18 presents research findings about the role parents have in shaping their children's economic success, through the dual pathways of nature and nurture. Community (Chapter 19) closes out this section and the book, looking at the roles of social capital, community organizations, and participation in determining The Good Life.

This book provides an overview of economics from a social sciences perspective. Much is necessarily excluded or abbreviated, as my goal is to introduce perspectives and recent research that can serve as a jumping off point for those who wish to know more. Extensive footnotes with references are included for that purpose. The emphasis is breadth rather than depth. Many resources exist exploring all the topics in greater detail. Here I seek to bring them together in a single space, allowing the reader to see the whole, based on the belief that too narrow a focus is worse than one that is too broad.

CHAPTER 2

Society Decides

> The number of shops closed in Paris in August astonished me. When I mistakenly attempted to laugh at this with my (French) boyfriend, he responded with: "Do we not…" – and his lips seemed to curl with disdain around the shape of 'not' – "have the right to vacations?"[1]

> Complex issues surround workforce shortages [in the U.S.] … resulting in workers questioning their work conditions and wages. An unpleasant side effect has been the rise of entitled attitudes from workers.[2]

In 1970, workers in France and the U.S. worked about the same number of hours per year, 1990 and 1920, respectively. Fifty years later, French workers have reduced their time at work by 30%, to 1400 h annually. Americans have reduced theirs as well, but by just eight percent, to 1770 h. These very different outcomes, essentially ten 37-h work weeks, resulted from a series of choices made by French and American workers, individually and collectively. Fundamentally, the former chose to take most of the benefits of its increased productivity since 1970 in the form of reduced work hours rather than increased income, while the latter chose

[1] Craig (2014).
[2] Miller (2022).

L. Hadsell, *Social Economics*,
https://doi.org/10.1007/978-3-032-21916-9_2

increased pay over reduced hours. Average income today is much higher in the U.S. than in France, about $69,000 per year per full-time worker versus $46,000. But the GDP per hour worked, productivity, is similar ($73/h in the U.S. versus $68/h in France). In fact, between 1970 and 2020, productivity increased at a significantly faster pace in France than in the U.S.[3] In a way, the French chose to eat their cake and have it too. True, the French have lower income, but more importantly, to them at least, they have more time outside of work to enjoy life.[4] Economists cannot tell you which path is better, only that different paths exist, and it is up to all of us to decide what is best for us.

The two quotations at the beginning of this chapter, both written by Americans, exemplify the contrasting views that French and Americans tend to have regarding work–life balance. They represent the wide cultural differences that have led to vastly different forms of capitalism, as seen throughout the economy, not just in number of hours worked per year. Economic systems are social constructs, meaning they are created from explicit and often implicit agreement among members of society, individually and collectively through institutions such as labor unions, business groups, community and social organizations, and the political system. These agreements cover concrete measures such as work hours, as well as such things as acceptable forms of behavior, motivations, and goals within the economic system. Because economic systems are social constructs, society decides which relationships and behavior in the production and distribution processes are acceptable. This book explores those choices within this broader social context.

2.1 The Purpose of Economic Systems

Economic systems are designed to solve two basic problems:

i. How best to produce what members of society want, and
ii. How best to distribute those goods and services.

[3] 104% vs 78%. In 1970, French productivity was 70% of the American level. In 2020, that ratio was 92% (OECD n.d.).

[4] French workers are entitled by law to twenty-five days vacation per year—in addition to 11 paid holidays. U.S. workers typically get 10 vacation days per year, plus 11 paid holidays.

Proof that each society chooses their economic system—and, hence, often answer these two questions differently—is seen in the variety of economic systems operating around the world today, and in the fact that economic systems change over time. Capitalism as practiced in the U.S. today, for example, is different from the capitalism currently seen in France or Germany or Japan; and it is also different from the form of capitalism seen in the U.S. in the late 1800s. The forces that lead to such differences across space and time are an important element of understanding for society in determining how their economic relationships are structured.

The choices for how best to produce are many but fall into two broad categories: Technical and Social. The technical aspects address how much of each different input to use, and which tools and methods are employed. Economic science emphasizes efficient use of scarce resources. Even within this narrow criteria, different economies will arrive at different solutions. The particular technical approach taken depends on the circumstances. Compare the U.S. economy, with its heavy use of technology and resultant high wages for skilled workers, to China or Mexico, where production—often of the same goods—is more labor-intensive and wages are lower. Or compare production in most industries in the U.S. today to similar production just thirty or forty years ago: production methods in nearly every sector have changed, as new materials, technology, and techniques are implemented. Recent advances in and widespread adoption of artificial intelligence promises a continued, perhaps even accelerated, change in how the question "how best to produce" is answered. Economics provides wonderful tools for analyzing and solving much of the technical aspect. And while many technical details exist, we must recognize that technical choices occur within non-technical settings—namely, society, culture. This context increases the difficulty of identifying and applying appropriate solutions.

As important and interesting as the technical side is, I'm rather more interested in focusing instead on the social aspects. Though the social portion may be harder to model and often is less precise, I will show that attempting to understand economies without study of the wider social and environmental context is to identify the part without knowing the whole. To further this understanding, economists are working in areas of common interest to other disciplines, returning economics to its social science roots, as economists are complementing their significant cache of technical tools by incorporating insights from these disciplines into analysis of economic problems.

From psychology and sociology, for example, we are now taking quite seriously a broader understanding of motivation and incentives, separating intrinsic (internal) from extrinsic (external). Instead of focusing solely on extrinsic motivations/rewards—money—as economists have been prone to do previously, we recognize that culture and community are important considerations. As such, we gain insights into organizations within social structures and relationships, between employer and employee, buyer and seller, community and economy. Throughout this book, I highlight recent insights such as these that economists are finding relevant to explaining economic behavior.

For the second question, How to Distribute, consider the following. In the aftermath of a hurricane, many items, such as ice, building supplies, and gasoline are in short supply. I know this from personal experience (Hurricane Florence, 2018). In such situations, prices tend to shoot up, as rising demand far exceeds limited supply. Individuals may feel a sense of desperation, as they seemingly have no choice but to pay—if they can even afford to. After one recent hurricane in North Carolina, a couple of enterprising young men in a nearby unaffected area loaded up their pick-up truck with bags of ice they had purchased for $2 a bag and headed into the center of destruction, selling the ice for $8. Customers formed a long line, and though most were upset at the high price—after all, ice normally sold there for around $1.75—they purchased multiple bags. Nevertheless, because North Carolina has a price gouging law, restricting price rises in the aftermath of a natural disaster, the police were called and the men arrested. Demonstrating the importance placed on the notion of fair pricing and equitable distribution, buyers, including those still waiting in line, clapped as the police carted away the entrepreneurs—and the unsold ice.[5]

Alternatively, consider concert tickets for the hugely popular pop star Taylor Swift. Demand for tickets and everything that goes with attending a concert has been the subject of intense international attention. During her recent Eras tour, some tickets in Stockholm cost more than $1500 each and hotel rooms in Dublin were 40% more expensive at concert

[5] Munger (2007).

times than normal.[6] Accusations of high ticket prices and exorbitant fees in Texas led to the unusual bipartisan tandem of Sens. John Cornyn (R-Texas) and Amy Klobuchar (D-Minn.) introducing the "Fans First Act." Cornyn, normally a strong supporter of free-market principles, argued, "The current ticketing system is riddled with problems and doesn't serve the needs of fans, teams, artists or venues. This legislation would rebuild trust in the ticketing system by cracking down on bots and others who take advantage of consumers."[7] One senator claimed, "Fans have become increasingly frustrated with how difficult it has been to obtain affordable tickets to see their favorite artists perform." Even so, venues are sold out, concert after concert.

Should market forces always be allowed to work, even in emergencies which typically see drastic price rises, bringing demand in line with supply? Or should legal limits on price increases be implemented? Economic theory (and observation) is clear regardless of the circumstances: Limiting price rises will likely lead to shortages, long lines of customers, and unmet needs. Such shortages would be especially problematic in the aftermath of natural disasters. In other cases, such as concert tickets for Taylor Swift, the consequences are less dire, and specific action to curb prices depends on the level of competition among sellers. But in either case, limiting prices will often be seen as fairer, more acceptable, even if it does create other problems.

In a world of scarcity, where unlimited demand exceeds supply, the method of distribution can take many forms, from free markets to authoritarian command, and trade-offs—pros and cons—are present in each. Which way is "best" is subjective, based on how much value is placed on each of those pros and cons. Thus, the question of how best to distribute society's produce is ultimately quite complex. Competing interests, rights, and obligations are part of the relationships that bind participants in any economy, regardless of its organization. Some people seek fairness as a primary goal. Others value efficient use of resources. Some insist that competition leads to the preferred result. Others contend that competition puts some at unfair disadvantage. Many put a premium on property rights and freedom—an individual's prerogative to do what

[6] Black (2023).

[7] USA Today (2023). In June 2024, the Department of Justice filed an antitrust lawsuit against the ticket distributor, arguing that Ticketmaster used its market power to unfairly raise prices.

they want with their property and labor and the resultant produce. Others prefer collective approaches (e.g., government or some other centralized decision-making authority).

All economies are a mix of these approaches. The price system is dominant in the U.S. and most developed economies, as decentralized, competitive markets determine the distribution of most goods and services. But no one can deny the influence of command, social networks, and even tradition. Differences between countries—especially the U.S. and many in Europe—are often measured by the level of government involvement in the predominantly market-oriented economy via regulation, taxes, spending, and ownership. Government is the typical image of command, but corporations and families are in nearly every respect command structures as well, with top-down decision-making as a key feature.

Social networks are active when employees refer friends to their employer. Tradition is evident in the predominance of women in certain professions such as nursing, elementary school teaching, and administrative assistants, while men are predominant in construction, surgery, and… economics, where two-thirds of economists are men, roughly the same percentage as 40 years ago. Does it matter? In surgery, where, according to the American Association of Medical Colleges, more than 80% of surgeons are men, it does: "compared with women who had a female surgeon, women with a male surgeon had an 11% higher rate of readmission to a hospital, a 16% higher rate of complications, and a 32% higher risk of death."[8] We will see later the fact that two-thirds of economists being men makes a great deal of difference, too.

Each method has merit, each has faults, depending on your perspective. Later I explore them in more detail, but for now a summary: Economists—and most non-economists—generally prefer the price system: markets, based on the pursuit of self-interest because under most circumstances this leads to the most efficient use of resources and distribution of goods and services. Command, even under democratic leadership, suppresses freedom of choice and lacks the information necessary to

[8] As of 2021. Shmerling (2022). Though the reasons for the disparity were not part of this research, potential reasons pointed to by the authors include differences in care, patient-surgeon relationships, measures of trust, styles of communication between the four patient groups, and the possibility that female surgeons follow standard guidelines more closely than their male counterparts.

adequately reflect the wishes of millions of consumers and producers, but can often address (to varying degrees of success) "market failures" such as externalities (e.g., pollution), monopoly pricing, and unequal market power. Social networks are helpful in obtaining employment and information, but they can also block opportunity by perpetuating homogeneous grouping. Tradition tends to lack innovation, as methods and ways are propelled from past to future by virtue of being (although, as discussed in a later chapter, a slow pace of innovation is not to everyone undesirable). A lottery provides greater equality of opportunity but is inefficient in the sense that it is blind to the varying levels of value consumers place on products.

Deciding which method of organization is "best" is a value judgment and that decision takes place over time among members of society through social, political, and economic institutions.

2.2 A Further Question: How Far?

Societies make additional choices, often implicitly, about *what* is subject to market forces. Application of economic principles to more and more areas of life is not new. Markets that we think are normal today were at one time new and controversial. Surrogate motherhood, sperm and egg banks, even lending money for interest are examples, as are labor and real estate markets. And life insurance. When first introduced, each of these met with widespread resistance and yet when raised today they elicit a ho-hum response—we take them as given.

Prediction markets, which focus on the probability of a specific event occurring, are a recent example of a new application of market principles.[9] Prediction markets rely on the "wisdom of the crowd"—that is, the clearer consensus obtained by aggregating views of many diverse individuals. How many beans are in a jar? Ask a group of 30 or 40 and the average of those responses will likely be closer than all but a few of the individual responses.[10] Asking people to place money on their view focuses their attention, leading to better results. Prediction markets have developed for estimating demand for new products, forecasting movie success, and assessing the need for health services. People participating

[9] Also known as "event futures" or "information markets."

[10] Treynor (1987).

in the Hollywood Stock Exchange, for example, use money to speculate on movie-related questions like opening weekend performance, total box office returns and who will win Oscars.[11] You might imagine how such "focus groups" are valuable to businesses deciding on large investments whose success depends on popular demand.

Similarly, the Iowa Electronic Markets (IEM) allow participants to wager on the outcomes of various political events, elections typically, often providing better forecasts of winners than the much more publicized polls.[12] More controversially, prediction markets have been applied to terrorism futures in which participants wager on potential terrorist attacks, much like an office pool for picking the birth date of a colleague's baby. Someone wins a financial reward for correctly identifying the occurrence (or lack thereof) of a certain specific terrorist event (for example, an attack on the U.S. during a given period of time, perhaps in a certain location). First broached in 2004, "It was feared that [terrorism] markets would create the opportunity for a terrorist to profit from an act of terrorism or an assassination... An alternative view holds that such trade is actually a good thing to the extent that trading ultimately reveals previously secret information about the intentions of terrorist groups."[13]

Potentially controversial markets are developing elsewhere. Prisoners in Santa Ana, California, who can afford to pay $82 per night can upgrade to a better jail cell; anyone can now buy life insurance on unrelated individuals with a payoff upon that person's death (a $40 billion per year business in the U.S.); contrary to what one might infer from the college admissions scandals in the news in recent years, selling admission to elite universities is common practice—in the form of above-board payments rather than secretive deals; and some countries, including the U.S., sell fast-paths to citizenship to foreigners willing to pay (e.g., by promising to invest in U.S. business and hire a certain number of American workers).[14] In a later chapter, I examine a proposed new market with widespread support among economists: one that trades human kidneys. Such a market would

[11] Wolfers and Zitzewitz (2004), Wolfers et al. (2008).

[12] Iowa Electronic Markets (n.d.).

[13] Wolfers and Zitzewitz (2004).

[14] For differing views, on these and related markets, one from a Nobel Laureate economist and another from an ethicist, see Roth (2007) and Sandel (2012).

supplement the current system of organ donation run by the non-profit UNOS—and is projected to save thousands of lives each year.

Moral questions are raised when putting a price on something that previously had not been valued in such a way. Ethicist Michael Sandel argues that this "erodes certain moral and civic goods worth caring about." And that "some market transactions are objectionable on moral grounds." Clearly such questions are worthy of consideration to anyone studying the pros and cons of markets. We return to this topic in Chapter 6.

2.3 Social Science Influence

The best way to understand the complex nature of society's choices about the primary economic questions is to take a multidisciplinary view. That is, to consider multiple perspectives and multiple ways of knowing. Economic thought has benefited from the incorporation of a range of other disciplines which are playing an increasingly important role in understanding economic systems.

The multidisciplinary approach has a rich history in economics. Adam Smith, whom many consider the founder of economics, was a professor of moral philosophy and referenced conscience, principle, and morality in his *Wealth of Nations* and *Theory of Moral Sentiments*. Alfred Marshall, a titan of the profession around 1900, wrote of custom, cooperation, fairness, friendship, and dishonesty in trade in his principles textbook—the most used economics text of the time. Even the American Economic Association, the leading professional organization for economists today, was founded upon religious precepts, by a leading proponent of the Social Gospel Movement in America in the late 1800s, with the express intention of greatly influencing government economic policy in a range of areas, from labor markets to food safety. In fact, many disciplines are of interest to economists. The way I think of this overlap is as a Venn diagram with economics at the center (of course) and other disciplines represented by the overlapping circles, each overlap representing an area of common interest. Incorporation of a multidisciplinary perspective allows one to better see how parts of a very complicated social system interact. Here I think of the parable of the blind men and the elephant.

> It is a story of a group of blind men who have never come across an elephant before and who learn and imagine what the elephant is like by

> touching it. Each blind man feels a different part of the elephant's body, but only one part, such as the side or the tusk. They then describe the elephant based on their limited experience and their descriptions of the elephant are different from each other. In some versions, they come to suspect that the other person is dishonest and they come to blows. The moral of the parable is that humans have a tendency to claim absolute truth based on their limited, subjective experience as they ignore other people's limited, subjective experiences which may be equally true.[15]

Too narrow a focus will lead to a misreading of the evidence and mistrust among those with differing views. A multidisciplinary approach, a wider angle, then, with exposure to numerous ideas and areas within and related to economics, is ideal. Four disciplines prominent in the understanding discussed in this book are:

- Psychology, the science of individual choice;
- Sociology, the science of group interaction;
- Philosophy, examining the moral basis for actions; and
- Biology, the study of under-the-hood.

Though many other disciplines, ranging from mathematics to history, are valuable companions to economics, I focus on these four as representing expanding areas of knowledge, catching the attention of economists tackling some of the most pressing questions facing society. Consider a couple of examples from each to illustrate how they shed light on society's choices in economic realms.

2.4 Psychology: Behavioral Economics

Before the incorporation of psychology in the form of behavioral economics, a basic assumption in economics was that how choices were presented did not matter—an individual's preferences were not influenced by such esoterica. Now we know—as psychologists, pollsters, and marketers learned long ago—that framing, how choices are presented, matters a great deal. Decisions can be substantially influenced by ordering

[15] Wikipedia (n.d.). David Epstein argues in his fascinating book *Range* that developing a broad range of interests and skills is the key to success "in a specialized world" Epstein (2019).

of choices, or even inclusion of clearly inferior choices. Furthermore, decisions can be influenced by anchoring—the selection of the starting, or reference, point. Real estate agents anchor when they choose a listing price and retailers anchor when they choose an introductory price for a new product. In each case, the initial price creates a perception in the minds of potential buyers as to the product's value. When the price is subsequently lowered, buyers perceive a deal is at hand. We prefer discounts, after all—the higher initial price creates the perception of such.

Recent Nobel prizes have been awarded to economists incorporating insights from psychology, including Richard Thaler for his work on nudges. When the wording or ordering of the options is changed so as to improve the chances of achieving a desired outcome, we are "nudging" choosers. Thaler and colleague Cass Sunstein provide examples of nudges, including arrangement of food in a school cafeteria: healthy foods at eye level and less healthy foods in more difficult to see (and reach) places.[16] Diners can still choose the less healthy food, but they are less likely to do so. Sunstein and Thaler have called the use of nudges *libertarian paternalism* because it preserves the freedom of choice while at the same time either steering choosers to a "better" option or helping them avoid common psychological pitfalls. Both conservatives and liberals generally prefer nudging to other approaches such as taxes or regulation. And studies show the overwhelming effectiveness in achieving desired outcomes—healthier diets, for instance.

Another example of nudging has tremendously important economic implications: Because of the prevalence of defined-contribution retirement plans, most working Americans will have to choose for themselves where to invest their retirement monies and how much of their salary they wish to contribute. Consider the following alternative statements illustrating what a new hire might see (either Statement A or Statement B):

STATEMENT A
Our company offers a pension plan. We will match your contributions, up to 3% of your salary. So, for example, if you contribute 2% then we will also contribute 2% and your total will be 4% of your salary. If you contribute 3% then we also contribute 3%, etc. **You currently are not enrolled (your**

[16] Sunstein and Thaler (2008).

current contribution is 0%). What percent of your salary would you like to contribute?

STATEMENT B
Our company offers a pension plan. We will match your contributions, up to 3% of your salary. So, for example, if you contribute 2% then we will also contribute 2% and your total will be 4% of your salary. If you contribute 3% then we also contribute 3%, etc. **You currently are enrolled with a contribution of 3%.** Would you like to keep this or change your contribution rate?

Statement A represents an opt-in (the starting point is 0%) and statement B an opt-out (the starting point is 3%). Both allow the employee to freely change their allocation. Rationally, the two statements are equivalent and should lead to exactly the same contributions. Yet, in real-life situations (economists working with human resource officers at private companies, and without the **bolding**) the second phrasing leads to significantly higher average contribution rates. In one study of a large company in the U.S., the enrollment rate for new hires was about 35 percentage points higher under an opt-out plan (or ***default-in setting***) versus previously used opt-in plans: before, with the opt-in implementation, about 60% of new hires chose to contribute to a retirement plan; after the choice was changed to opt-out (with a 3% default contribution in one case, 6% in another), the rate was 95%.[17] The difference waned some over time, but even after two years (during which employees had time to change) the opt-out plan had about 25 percentage points higher participation. Similar findings reported by other researchers explain why organizations offering defined-contribution retirement plans are changing their initial presentation of such choices to new hires. Those employees will benefit as will society: at a macro level, greater saving leads to greater investment, productivity, and economic growth. In a country with a low saving rate this is welcome news. And it's all brought about through private, individual choice—no new heavy-handed government regulation, no changes to the tax code.[18]

[17] Beshears et al. (2009).

[18] Nudging is such a powerful concept that the White House created a "Social and Behavioral Sciences Team" in 2015 (disbanded in 2017). It consisted of behavioral scientists and was charged with recommending policy that nudge individuals to subconsciously make better choices. Some criticize the approach as heavy-handed government interference

2.5 Economic Sociology: Group Dynamics

If behavioral economics is primarily about individual decision-making, then economic sociology concerns itself with groups and group interactions. Sounds pretty useful to economists. After all, individuals are members of various groups. Employees and employers; consumers and producers; private sector and public; family, associations, and clubs. And economists are interested in the interaction of those groups—for example, in things like how they create trust, influence productivity, and encourage information flows. While economics and sociology share a significant overlap, they have different centers of attention and different understandings of the world, leading to unique insights within the overlap of economic sociology. Illustrating how different disciplines may approach a question with their own focus, consider the minimum wage. A mainstream economist may focus on employment, income effects, and prices (inflation). A sociologist, on the other hand, may think primarily about:

> How much of an impact would a minimum wage raise have for a single mother? Some might study the economic effects, such as her ability to pay bills and keep food on the table. Others might look at how reduced economic stress could improve family relationships. Some sociologists might research the impact on the status of small business owners.[19]

Others questions that economic sociologists are interested in might include: How does the economy affect family structure? And vice versa? What impacts on relationships (in families, social circles, at work) has the increased female labor-force participation had?[20] What is the relationship between economic circumstances and crime? What effect does incarceration have on future earnings potential? What are the consequences of incarceration on the social and economic welfare of families and community? What is the extent of racial disparities in health status and access to healthcare?[21]

with personal freedom of choice paternalism (though the practice is already employed extensively by business). Regardless of one's views, the research clearly shows the power of framing.

[19] Conerly et al. (2021).

[20] Greenwood et al. (2016).

[21] Yearby (2018).

Research may focus on gender differences for why individuals become self-employed. One study finds that "women – especially women with young children – are more likely than men to cite flexibility of schedule and family-related reasons for becoming self-employed" while "Men's reasons for becoming self-employed show little association with their parental status." The findings suggest that employers wishing to attract women employees should consider family obligations as part of the employment package, perhaps offering alternatives to the traditional, forty-hour-per-week on-site jobs with hours set by the employer.[22]

Other economic sociologists are taking a new look at social networks in employment. A firm's decision to pay referral bonuses to current employees who recommend an eventual new hire provides an example. From the firm's perspective, such an arrangement provides significant tangible benefits in the form of lower hiring costs and reduced risk of an unsuccessful hire. On the other hand, firms will also tend toward greater worker homogeneity, as social networks typically consist of others who are like us, with similarity measured many ways, including race, gender, age, and social class. The less diverse hiring pool resulting from existing employee referrals can have real costs for individuals outside of those social networks and for the business as well: we know from other research that diversity of views, skills, and backgrounds tends to promote better business decisions, increased productivity and creativity, and profitability. One study suggests, for example, that women on corporate boards of directors typically have distinct types of expertise relative to men, thereby expanding the board's skillset when they are added to existing boards (which still tend to be comprised primarily of men). The greater diversity of skills is directly associated with higher firm value.[23] Benefits of diversity appear in other areas. Business innovation, for example, appears to be fostered by greater diversity of education level and gender.[24] In the classroom, a greater racial diversity among college students increases GPA at graduation, improves first year grades of female students, and affects white students' choice of major, according to one study.[25]

[22] Boden Jr. (2006).

[23] Kim and Starks (2016), Alsan et al. (2019), Hossain et al. (2020).

[24] Østergaard et al. (2011).

[25] Lau (2022).

2.6 Philosophy

We all, including economists, make value judgments when we choose which economic goals are preferable, model human behavior, and interpret research findings. Philosophy and ethics are central to understanding differing views of such choices, and of economic systems more broadly. Far from being extraneous to the real business of economics, philosophy helps us understand the muddy environment in which economic activity takes place. Adam Smith was a professor of moral philosophy, and economics as a discipline evolved through the 1800s and early 1900s within this frame of thinking. Early economists were not shy about considering the ethical implications of theories and policies, they were part and parcel to economic thinking. Many mainstream economists today reject the notion that economics is laden with value judgments. But others disagree. Ethicist Michael Sandel contends that economics cannot be separated from ethical concerns, as what is valued determines which goals, policies, and actions are pursued.[26] Judgments are made, for instance, when arguing for the primacy of efficiency over equity (or vice versa). Similarly, focusing on profit maximization or economic freedom above alternative goals requires that those goals be valued more highly than the alternatives. Choosing markets as an economic system over other possibilities values some outcomes over others, often undermining non-market values (e.g., civic virtue) in the process, a discussion which I revisit in Chapter 7.

Principles from philosophy are especially helpful for thinking about the second "big question" of economics—distribution. How should goods and services be distributed? What is the best way? "How" and "best" are subjective, value laden. These questions cannot be answered without considering the ethical implications of the various options. In fact, philosophers such as John Rawls have developed approaches to thinking about such questions that can inform the debates surrounding distribution of income and wealth, debates that economists are often at the center of. (Rawls' approach is discussed in Chapter 14.) When it comes to markets, rather than simply assuming that they are "free" and "fair" we must examine the trade-offs inherent in any such endeavor, the value each of us place on various outcomes. We might also consider the

[26] Sandel (2012). See also Jackson (2013)

moral obligations of business entities, beyond their legal concerns (which we will explore in Chapter 12).

Philosopher Elizabeth Brake provides an example in addressing the practice of charging drastically higher prices for necessities such as ice, generators, gasoline, and the like during times of shortages following a natural disaster, what some call price gouging. Defenders of free markets maintain that allowing large price rises in such instances elicits an increase in supply of scarce necessities. Brake argues that such price increases are morally wrong as they violate a "duty of easy rescue"—a moral obligation to prevent harm to others so long as the costs of doing so are low.[27] Just asking questions concerning obligation and duty lead to a fuller appreciation of the implications of actions.

2.7 Biological Sciences

The fourth overlap is with biological sciences. Economists have long used the language of evolutionary biology in its descriptions of certain economic fundamentals. We talk of survival of the fittest, for example, as a justification for *laissez-faire* policies; we speak of the evolution of economies or industries—birth, growth, maturity, decline. This reflects the coevolution, if you will, of theories about the natural world (e.g., by Charles Darwin) and economics beginning in the mid-eighteenth century. In describing the operation of markets in terms of natural forces a certain scientific aura is created, and market processes are defended as inevitable, natural, and perhaps divinely inspired.

Fortunately, recent work in economics has moved beyond the mere adoption of terminology to a much more promising use of principles, insights, and technologies from biological sciences to address a wide range of questions of economic interest. For instance, economists working in the overlap called Genoeconomics are studying the role of genetics in shaping economic outcomes. They are shedding light on questions related to income and wealth inequality, labor markets and employment, economics of the family, and health economics, among a wide range of areas. Research suggests that one's genes appear to play about as big a role in shaping economic outcomes and preferences as they do shaping

[27] Brake (2021).

many medical conditions and personality traits.[28] We know, for example, that DNA strongly influences a range of physical characteristics and health measures, such as height, cancer, mental health, obesity, and diabetes.[29] We also now have evidence that educational attainment, employment, and levels of wealth at retirement are strongly correlated to one's genetic makeup. That is, just as with a variety of health factors, we can estimate your chances of getting a college degree or having a certain level of wealth by knowing your genetic makeup. Most importantly, this knowledge can inform public policy (as described in Chapter 18).

Stress is an interesting mitigator limiting the power of genetics. Stress can occur in many forms: uncertainty over employment or income; poverty; or food insecurity, all of which, when experienced during childhood, are linked to poor physical and mental health, and reduced educational achievement, with effects extending into adulthood.[30] Economists are now analyzing biological markers of stress such as cortisol levels to see how economic outcomes are related. Stress, even of the mother while the child is in utero, reduces the child's early cognitive skills and increases later socio-emotional problems.[31] These negative impacts cut across economic class, occurring among both low and high-income children. We are learning that the influence of genetic factors may depend substantially on environmental exposures—as true for economic outcomes as for health outcomes.[32]

The influence of genes on economic outcomes is complicated and not yet well-understood; it is worth studying given the implications for understanding a variety of economic outcomes. We all inherit a mix of DNA, but the eventual economic consequences depend not only on our initial starting point but also on our environment, especially our early years,

[28] Benjamin et al. (2012).

[29] To predict the adult height for an offspring, add the parents' heights, then, for boys add five inches and for girls subtract five inches, then divide by two. It's possible to be far taller or shorter than the predicted height, but larger and larger differences from the expected are less and less likely. Most people will be near the predicted value. We commonly accept that genetic makeup plays a role in health outcomes. The BRCA gene is known to be predispose one to breast cancer. Other markers are linked to heart disease and diabetes. Genetic differences account for between 35 and 86% of the variance in heaviness of smoking (Bierut et al. 2023).

[30] Santaularia et al. (2023).

[31] Berthelon et al. (2021).

[32] Bierut et al. (2023).

beginning in utero. Negative environments (such as those brought about by stress) and positive (such as early childhood education enrichment) can alter a trajectory. The economic implications of genoeconomics are wide ranging and are revisited later in multiple chapters (particularly 13, 14, and 18).

2.8 Concluding Comments

The choices we make as individuals and collectively as a society are influenced in myriad ways. A multidisciplinary social science perspective is the best way to fully appreciate those influences—and to make sense of the diversity of actions and outcomes we see in economies all across the world. Such an approach reflects the direction of twenty-first-century economists who are engaging with researchers from related disciplines to uncover previously hidden truths.

I begin in the next few chapters with a brief examination of how economists think about economies. Their perspectives, varied as they are, provide a basis for society's understanding. You will see there is no single economics just as there is no single "best" way to organize economic activity. This is followed by a discussion of the moral foundations of markets and the application of market principles to previously unaffected areas.

What we as a society might strive for in our economic endeavors follows in Part II, where I show how culture, family, and community influence economic goals. Here, the rich research findings from economists and others in the multidisciplinary space discussed in the present chapter are further detailed. Social norms and customs, family, and community are further explored in Part III.

References

Alsan M, Garrick O, Graziani G (2019) Does diversity matter for health? Experimental evidence from Oakland. Am Econ Rev 109(12):4071–4111

Benjamin DJ, Cesarini D, Chabris CF, Glaeser EL, Laibson D et al (2012) The promises and pitfalls of genoeconomics. Annu Rev Econ 4:627–662

Berthelon M, Kruger D, Sanchez R (2021) Maternal stress during pregnancy and early childhood development. Econ Hum Biol 43 (December), Article 101047. https://doi.org/10.1016/j.ehb.2021.101047

Beshears J, Choi JJ, Laibson D, Madrian BC (2009) The importance of default options for retirement saving outcomes: evidence from the United States. In: Brown J, Liebman J, Wise DA (eds) Social security policy in a changing environment. University of Chicago Press

Bierut A, Biroli P, Galama TJ, Thom K (2023) Challenges in studying the interplay of genes and environment: a study of childhood financial distress moderating genetic predisposition for peak smoking. J Econ Psychol 98, 102636.

Black R (2023) Hotels accused of 'rampant price gouging' on Taylor Swift tour dates. Independent. 28 June. Available at: https://www.independent.co.uk/news/uk/taylor-swift-tour-hotel-prices-dublin-b2365929.html

Boden RJ Jr (2006) Flexible working hours, family responsibilities, and female self-employment: gender differences in self-employment selection. Am J Econ Sociol 65(2):279–303

Brake E (2021) Price gouging and the duty of easy rescue. Econ Philos 37(3):329–352

Conerly TR, Holmes K, Tamang A (2021) Introduction to sociology. Openstax available at: Introduction to Sociology 3e - OpenStax

Craig J (2014) My French life: nailing the work-life balance—is the French work ethic the best in the world? MyFrenchLife.org, 23 October. Available at: https://www.myfrenchlife.org/2014/10/23/french-work-ethic/. Accessed on 2 July 2025

Epstein D (2019) Range: why generalists triumph in a specialized world. Riverhead Books, New York

Greenwood J, Guner N, Vandenbroucke G (2016) Family economics writ large. Federal Reserve Bank of St. Louis Working Paper 2016-026A. Available at: http://research.stlouisfed.org/wp/2016/2016-026.pdf. Accessed on 2 July 2025

Hossain M, Atif M, Ahmed A, Mia L (2020) Do LGBT workplace diversity policies create value for firms? J Bus Ethics 167(4):775–791

Iowa Electronic Markets (IEM) (n.d.) Available at: https://iem.uiowa.edu/iem/. Accessed on 2 July 2025

Jackson M (2013) Market reasoning as moral reasoning: why economists should re-engage with political philosophy. J Econ Perspect 27(4):121–140

Kim D, Starks LT (2016) Gender diversity on corporate boards: do women contribute unique skills? Am Econ Rev 106(5):267–271

Lau Y (2022) Does racial diversity improve academic outcomes? A natural experiment in higher education classrooms. Labour Econ 78:1–13

Miller R (2022) Entitled workers challenge employers. Albany Times Union, 7 January, p D1

Munger M (2007). They clapped: can price-gouging laws prohibit scarcity?" Econlib. https://www.econlib.org/library/Columns/y2007/Mungergouging.html
Østergaard CR, Timmermans B, Kristinsson K (2011) Does a different view create something new? The effect of employee diversity on innovation. Res Policy 40(3):500–509
Roth AE (2007) Repugnance as a constraint on markets. J Econ Perspect 21(3):37–58
Sandel MJ (2012) What money can't buy: the moral limits of markets. Farrar, Straus and Giroux, New York
Santaularia J, Kunin-Batson A, Sherwood NE, Gunnar MR, French SA, Mason SM (2023) Is economic hardship associated with young children's cortisol levels? Dev Psychobiol. https://doi.org/10.1002/dev.22390
Shmerling RH (2022) Does the sex of your surgeon matter? A new study says yes. Harvard Health Blog. Available at: https://www.health.harvard.edu/blog/does-the-sex-of-your-surgeon-matter-a-new-study-says-yes-202202172691. Accessed on 2 July 2025
Sunstein CR, Thaler RH (2008) Nudge: improving decisions about health, wealth, and happiness. Yale University Press, New Haven
Treynor J (1987) Market efficiency and the bean jar experiment. Financ Anal J 43(3):50–53
USA Today (2023) Eras tour: Taylor Swift ticketmaster fiasco inspires bills, inquiries. USA Today, 14 December. Available at: https://www.usatoday.com/story/entertainment/music/2023/12/14/eras-tour-taylor-swift-ticketmaster-fiasco-inspires-bills-inquiries/71921029007/. Accessed on 2 July 2025
Wikipedia (n.d.) Blind men and an elephant. Available at: https://en.wikipedia.org/wiki/Blind_men_and_an_elephant. Accessed on 2 July 2025
Wolfers J et al (2008) The promise of prediction markets. Science 320(5878):877–878
Wolfers J, Zitzewitz E (2004) Prediction markets. J Econ Perspect 18(2):107–126
Yearby R (2018) Racial disparities in health status and access to healthcare: the continuation of inequality in the United States due to structural racism. Am J Econ Sociol 77(3–4):1113–1152

CHAPTER 3

One-Handed Economists: Paradigms and Ideologies

> Give me a one-handed Economist. All my economists say, 'on one hand…' Then 'but on the other…'[1]

Economists are famous for hedging their bets. Forecast a particular outcome or a specific time for an event but never both. George Bernard Shaw once said, if all the economists were laid end to end, they would not reach a conclusion. It seems Harry Truman is not alone in wishing (in the above quote) for a one-handed economist.

Economics is not the only profession with disagreement among its members. In spring 2022, near the end of the worst of the COVID pandemic, the FDA approved a second booster shot. Still, even after this approval, experts disagreed about whether getting the booster was a good idea.[2] The constantly changing understanding of a complex environment was one reason for the disagreement. As Markham Heid reported in the New York Times, "The lack of expert consensus may seem perplexing — or even discouraging — to people who want forthright answers. But tidy solutions are the province of salespeople, not scientists." And just as in economics, "people on both sides of the booster debate say that

[1] Harry Truman.
[2] Heid (2022).

L. Hadsell, *Social Economics*,
https://doi.org/10.1007/978-3-032-21916-9_3

there are several considerations, all valid, that are nonetheless at odds with one another." Lack of good data, methodological differences, and the absence of a controlled environment, all hamper understanding, and hence encourage disagreement among experts.

Economists reach varying conclusions in part because the models they use are based on varying assumptions, not too dissimilar to weather forecasts. You likely are familiar with the predictions of multiple hurricane paths shown on The Weather Channel each time one of the storms approaches the U.S. Different understanding (modeling) of the effects of ocean temperatures, wind speed, humidity, and other variables is the main culprit. Economists must make assumptions about how people respond to incentives, or how trade policy or interest rates affect other things such as consumer spending or government budgets. They do this with limited knowledge, limited understanding, limited data, and in one-shot "experiments" that can never be repeated exactly. There is no laboratory where economists can re-run events to get a clear handle on what is a very complex system.

So, science is full of uncertainty. And as a social science, economics contains even more uncertainty than physical sciences like physics or chemistry, which have (mostly) known laws of nature. Economics is complicated by having to model human behavior—and people are not as well behaved as atoms. They are not as predictable and can also react to the economic forecasts themselves in ways that the weather does not. In such circumstances, providing a range of outcomes based on a given range of assumptions is only wise.

Still, economists like to stress the scientific nature of the discipline, placing great emphasis on objectivity (*positive* as opposed to *normative* analysis, as they say). That is, economists generally pride themselves on being unbiased and value free, offering observations based on pure science, without influence from personal values. But even here, individuals bring their own limited experiences, knowledge, and understanding to bear on problems confronting them, as they do in every discipline. Even the most well-rounded, well-read, experienced economist knows only a small subset of economic knowledge.[3] And the realm of what is known is itself a subset of all that is knowable.

[3] Of the thousands of research papers published in economics each year, the typical economist likely reads only a very small fraction. Many economists likely read very little academic work outside of economics.

Professional knowledge and personal experiences play large roles in the formation of individual beliefs. Examples of the role of personal experiences are easy to find. Take people's views of climate change. Many studies find that such views depend on one's own weather experiences: Recent much hotter (colder) than normal temperatures elicit stronger (weaker) belief that climate change is a problem.[4] In finance, we similarly find that past investment returns shape investors' future return expectations, risk perceptions, and risk tolerance.[5] We also know that differences in experiences strongly predict differences in expectations of inflation, affecting young and old individuals differently, helping to explain household borrowing and lending behavior, including the choice of mortgages: for example, people with past exposure to high inflation are more likely to use fixed-rate rather than variable-rate mortgages.[6] Economists are no different, and as such are likely to be influenced by their personal as well as professional experience.

Beyond personal and professional experiences, sources of differing philosophies and models are often related to interpretation of research findings, or even data, and what they mean, all of which leads to different assumptions about how the world works. Consider as an example multiple understandings of labor markets, as told by British economist Roger Blackhouse:

> Some economists take the view that the only legitimate way to model labour supply is as the result of rational choice in a competitive market, which means that unemployment must be voluntary. Other economists take involuntary unemployment as a reality and consider it better to make a seemingly ad hoc assumption, such as that wages do not fall in response to unemployment, as a better way to describe how the labour market works. Models often require mathematical rigor that compel unrealistic assumptions that some see as so unrealistic that the model is unacceptable even as others see those same assumptions as similarly unrealistic but worthy of acceptance because of the analytical gains available from the use of mathematics. These different views not only lead to alternative models but also, quite naturally, to different policy prescriptions.[7]

[4] Egan and Mullin (2012), Sugerman et al. (2021).

[5] Hoffmann and Post (2015).

[6] Malmendier and Nagel (2016).

[7] Blackhouse (2010, p. 169).

And it is true: we see very different policy prescriptions from economists at the University of Chicago and the University of Massachusetts at Amherst. Consequently, I'll argue that although having a one-handed economist might make life less confusing, it is an unrealistic expectation and would be detrimental to our goal of understanding the economy.

3.1 Paradigms

All this is to say that economics, like other social sciences, has paradigms, or schools of thought: different philosophies or ways of thinking about economic systems, based on one's understanding of a subject. Psychology provides a nice comparison. Multiple schools of thought exist today and have existed since the emergence of psychology as a distinct discipline more than a century and a half ago. As psychologist John Benjafield explains, each school in psychology has different views concerning the proper subject matter and research methods. Some schools examine subjective experience and experimental methods while others reject this approach and instead focus on objective methods. Functionalism was inspired by Darwin's evolutionary theory—much like economics, with its "survival of the fittest" mantra applied to market competition—and was open to using a variety of methods. Psychoanalysis was a theory of development and personality based largely on clinical experience. Cognitive psychology incorporates views and methods from multiple paradigms. In the end, "many psychologists are flexible enough to tailor their approach to the problem on which they are working rather than use the same approach regardless of the nature of the problem."[8]

Multiple paradigms typically co-exist, representing disagreement within a discipline, and paradigms can overlap. But the dominant paradigm is the one that is accepted by the majority of practitioners. Dominant paradigms can change over time, as new information arrives or society changes. Adam Smith, for example, led the introduction of capitalism in late 1700s' England. The market-based approach he advocated was built on individual choices, a radical philosophy that eventually became a paradigm shift away from previous thinking that emphasized hierarchical direction and centralized decision-making. This early formulation

[8] See Benjafield (2019).

Table 3.1 Paradigms summary

Paradigm	*Emphasis on*
Neo-classical (mainstream)	Private ownership, free markets, self-determination
Marxist	Power, coercion, inequality
Buddhist	Process rather than output
Feminist	Gender inclusion
Ecological economics	Environmental and social contexts

of economics was eventually replaced by a more formalized, mathematical version: neo-classical economics, today's mainstream economics, the dominant paradigm in most developed economies. Several challenges to the neo-classical paradigm offer options for those who disagree with the validity of key assumptions underlying the neo-classical models, or who interpret data and research findings differently, or who simply conceive of economic systems in a different way.

In this chapter, I provide an overview of a subset of notable paradigms, beginning with the dominant neo-classical. Beyond the neo-classical perspective, I examine prominent alternatives (Marxist) and less well-known approaches (Buddhist, Feminist, and Ecological economics). Table 3.1 provides a reference for the top-line differences. Non-mainstream paradigms represent fairly small subgroups of economists, particularly in the U.S. And many other paradigms are not included in the discussion below. But I have chosen paradigms that I think provide the most interesting contrast to mainstream economics. Agree or disagree with their fundamental views but be open to their insights. Knowing the differences tells us a lot about the nature of economics as a social science.

3.2 Ideology

Before turning to these individual paradigms, note that substantial disagreement can exist within each, providing another reason for the differing views of two-handed economists. That is to say, not all main stream economists, for example, are the same. Ideologies reflect disagreement among individuals who share common beliefs within a certain paradigm.[9] Thus the labels "conservative" and "liberal" in the U.S. are often placed on adherents to the dominant paradigm: both are considered mainstream, as they support the same neo-classical approach to economics even as they disagree on some of the details. Paul Krugman and Milton Friedman are neo-classical economists. They agree on certain foundational assumptions—markets are generally the best approach to solving economic problems, people are (and should be) self-interested maximizers, and trade is generally good, for example. They disagree on the details. Krugman is a liberal economist, supporting government intervention to correct market shortcomings (e.g., advocating government deficit spending during a recession). Friedman is a conservative, even libertarian, strongly preferring less government, once declaring that one could choose any three letters and with them form the name of a government agency that was not needed. Clearly, he was a believer that markets should be left alone. Their policy prescriptions sometimes differ greatly, and yet both are esteemed economists and Nobel recipients.

Understanding paradigms and ideology is important to understanding why economists differ in their views of certain fundamental economic issues. In this way, economics is like other sciences, both "hard" and "soft." With this in mind, the remainder of this chapter explores the primary facets of the dominant mainstream paradigm and the multiple perspectives/ideologies within it. The next two chapters move on to alternative perspectives. An appreciation of multiple perspectives will build trust of two-handed economists, even as it promotes a wary consumer of economic advice.

3.3 Neo-classical, Mainstream Economics

The neo-classical paradigm emphasizes private ownership, property rights and individual autonomy. Self-interest is seen as the primary motivator, in the context of markets with free exchange unhindered by government interference. Control over one's own decisions and resources is key. For the firm, the overarching goal is to maximize profit; and for individuals it is to maximize utility (or satisfaction). Price, determined in markets with abundant sellers and buyers, is the mechanism that determines allocation. Markets are efficient, in the sense that no individual buyer can affect

[9] Riddell (2005, p. 11) define economic ideology as "a set of ideas and beliefs that tend to justify morally a society's social and economic relationships."

price, and competition among the many suppliers pushes price down, both ensuring that resources are put to their most desired use. Consumers who are not willing to pay market price do not get the product. Firms that are not able to match other suppliers' lower price are driven from the market: a survival of the fittest. This competitive process leads to maximum economic benefit for society, even though no individual aims to achieve such a goal, focusing instead on their own interests.

Within the neo-classical paradigm, everyone agrees with the general principles of markets and individual choice, but not with all of the details. Some mainstream economists place emphasis (to varying degrees) on the impediments to free exchange or the pitfalls of reliance on self-interest.[10] Some readily acknowledge shortcomings of human decision-making. Consequently, ideologies within the neo-classical paradigm range from libertarian (strongly pro-market; anti-government) on one end to very liberal (strongly favoring government intervention) on the other. The practical implication of these differences is mostly about the proper amount of government oversight of markets: primarily the extent of regulation and taxes. Government ownership of productive resources typically is not broached by neo-classicals—that's the purview of Marxists. If you think of paradigms as conceptualization and ideology as implementation, the neo-classical paradigm serves as the basis for capitalist systems around the world, with the strength of support unfettered markets versus government intervention serving as the measure of one's ideology within this paradigm. Because it is the dominant paradigm and most economists are mainstream, neo-classical economics is the focus of nearly all major economics textbooks and formal classes.

Assessment of one's placement on the ideological spectrum of the neo-classical paradigm is imperfect. It's not like taking one's blood pressure or measuring the speed of light. Nevertheless, colleagues and I developed the following set of statements in an attempt to create such a measurement.[11] Take a couple minutes to respond to the statements before reading on. (Instructions for scoring your responses are included at the bottom of the survey.)

[10] Such as information asymmetry or large, dominant producers.

[11] Hadsell et al. (2013), Jones et al. (2019). Note the survey is less useful for measuring other paradigms/belief structures as the statements' primary assumption is that markets generally work well. Note, too, that this is just one potential measure of economic ideology. Others may produce somewhat different results.

Capitalism Index Survey
Use the following scale to indicate how strongly you agree or disagree with each statement.

Strongly Agree	Agree	Slightly Agree	Neither Agree nor Disagree	Slightly Disagree	Disagree	Strongly Disagree
1	2	3	4	5	6	7

1. *If people are poor, it is mostly because of their own actions.
2. The price of pharmaceutical drugs should be regulated by the government.
3. *Within the US, at birth, everyone has an opportunity to become rich.
4. *Tax money should NOT be used to subsidize the development of technologies designed to be environmentally friendly.
5. People with high incomes and wealth should be heavily taxed.
6. The government should ensure that all people are provided with basic housing.
7. The government should provide benefits and training to help the unemployed get back on their feet.
8. The government should help the poor.
9. Health care is a basic human right that must be guaranteed by the government.
10. High levels of income inequality are bad for society.

Agreement with statements without an * indicated a more laissez-faire, free-market view whereas agreement with statements with an * [not shown to surveytakers] indicate a less laissez-fire, free-market view. We characterize the former as capitalist/pro-market (i.e. conservative) and the latter as less capitalist/pro-market (i.e. liberal).

The Capitalism Index is scored by the first reverse coding statements with an * (that is, a response of 1 is changed to 7, 2 is changed to 6, etc.) and then summing the responses to the 10 statements. As each individual statement value can range from 1 to 7, the Capitalism index can range from 10 to 70.

Scoring your responses to the statements provides a measure of support for free markets that we call the Capitalism Index (CI), an indication of your place on the ideological spectrum within the neo-classical paradigm. People who score highest on the Capitalism Index would be called economic Libertarians (in today's American vernacular; think of the "Tea Party"). Libertarians show very strong support for markets free from government intervention—and a desire for self-determination, at least in economic settings.[12] Conservatives generally place great emphasis on freedom of choice in market settings—but perhaps not quite as strongly as libertarians, so they score a bit lower (See Fig. 3.1). As one moves along the continuum away from the high-CI Libertarian/Conservative end toward the other, support for government intervention in the market economy increases—suggesting a more Liberal view.[13] At the lowest scores on the Index, support for free markets is weakest. The lower the score on this survey, the greater the likelihood of being open to considering alternative paradigms.

Keep in mind that we are interested in economic decisions, not social decisions (such as gay marriage and abortion), so the Capitalism Index measures only economic ideology, not social ideology. Thus, one can be a conservative on social issues and a liberal on economic issues, for instance.

Figure 3.1 and Table 3.2 summarize these views. While many details may differentiate one's placement along the continuum, in practice, the single biggest factor is the level of government intervention in markets.

Anyone who generally favors markets as the preferred economic system (versus socialism, for example) has a point of view that can be summarized by the Capitalism Index. When my colleagues and I asked 2380 U.S. residents to respond to the survey, we found systematic differences in

Fig. 3.1 Capitalism Index

[12] One of the more confusing aspects of current vernacular is the conflation of social and economic ideology. To be conservative in the economic sense is to support free markets. Social conservatives also support freedom in terms of social choices: marriage, drugs, guns, and the like.

[13] Note the modern American terminology differs from earlier times and from some other places currently. The meaning of "Liberal" in America today is much different than "Classical Liberalism" of earlier times. In fact, Classical Liberalism is what Americans would today call Conservatism.

Table 3.2 Summary of the neo-classical ideologies

←*More liberal (lower score)*	*More conservative (higher score)*→
Markets are often efficient: though often there is not enough competition Market failures require government intervention	Government intervention makes things worse: Summed up in Milton Friedman's quip that "think of any three letters and you will identify a government program that is not needed"
Governments are not perfect, but neither are markets	Individuals are better decision makers for themselves than governments on their behalf
Fairness is not ensured by markets—different "starting points"	Fairness is ensured by markets—with its emphasis on individual freedom, choice
Unequal outcomes reflect unequal opportunities, as well as different choices	Unequal outcomes largely reflect different choices, although unequal opportunities may be present
Imbalance of power in the labor market. Coercion is possible	Voluntary transactions

free-market ideology for a range of characteristics. In particular, women, Blacks, and individuals with a BA as their highest degree, were all significantly less pro-market (lower CI). We might naturally think that women and Blacks would be less pro-market and more pro-government intervention, given the levels of discrimination historically present in the U.S. economic system, though we did not seek reasons for the respondents' views, so we can only suppose this point. That college graduates favor more government intervention likely does not surprise many, given the criticism often leveled on higher education as a bastion of liberal thought. Alternative explanations may exist—such as more liberal minded high school students attend college—but given data limitations, we did not examine these.

We found that older and higher income respondents were on average more pro-market, as were individuals who had completed a college economics class, suggesting that college economics instruction is either pro-market-oriented or that students with pro-market tendencies self-select into economics classes. In connections that will be explored in a later chapter, we also found that religious Christians were significantly more pro-market than both adherents to other religions and non-religious respondents.

We also see differences by state: not surprisingly, residents of New York and California, two states with relatively heavy government intervention in economic choices (via regulation, taxes, and spending), had the lowest average scores among residents while states with lower levels of government intervention, such as Arizona and Florida, had higher average scores. It is the last part, "average," that provides the basis for a critical observation from our survey: Nearly the entire continuum is represented in each state, as seen in Fig. 3.2, showing the distribution of responses in California and Florida.

What are some implications? In a subsequent paper, we showed that individual happiness is linked to one's placement on the continuum relative to other residents of their state, particularly for liberals. In short,

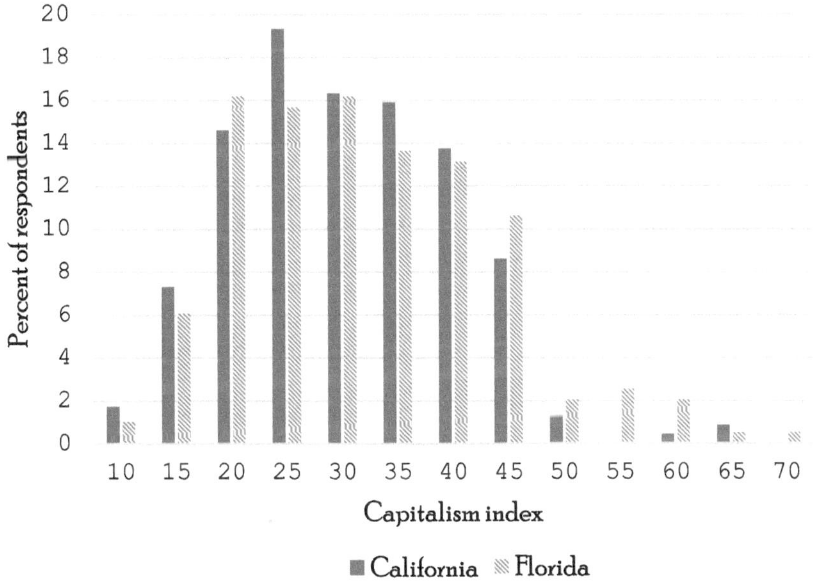

Fig. 3.2 Distribution of self-reported economic ideology (Though Florida and California have quite different government economic policies, reflecting preferences of its voters, each state has wide distribution of views on markets amongst its residents, as evidenced by scores on the Capitalism Index. The graph shows the distribution of self-reported economic ideology (Capitalism Index) from 'liberal' (left, lowest) to 'conservative' for residents of the two states; *Source* Based on data from Hadsell and Jones [2020])

liberals living in a conservative state are less satisfied with life than others, even conservatives living in a liberal state. We suggest that liberals feel worse off living in a state without much of a government safety net while conservatives in a state with an extensive safety-net are happy to have one when they need it (as during the COVID pandemic or a recession?) and are unaffected (in terms of their own happiness) by it otherwise.

We have not administered our survey to economists, but other surveys suggest that economists are similarly varied in their views on a range of economic questions.[14] Economists disagree to differing extents, for example, that tariffs and quotas lower society's general welfare and that federal government deficit spending during a recession stimulates the economy and reduces unemployment. Disagreement, in fact, abounds on many issues. A seemingly settled issue such as the effects of minimum wage laws is another example. As typically presented in most economics textbooks, minimum wage laws lead to more unemployment among the lowest skilled. But even here disagreement exists about the proper models and real-world effects, as one-quarter of economists disagree that minimum wage laws "increase unemployment among young and unskilled workers." Certain theory suggests that minimum wage laws may *increase* employment levels in certain circumstances.[15] And, in fact, empirical evidence supports a range of claims, depending on the place, the period, the size and timing of the minimum wage increase, and techniques used to evaluate the data. Similarly, the negative incentive effects of high income tax rates are generally presented in textbooks as clearly negative—reducing incentive to work, lowering employment. Tax cuts are promoted as growth-inducing. Yet, some controversy about the effects exists within the profession, where one-third of economists are not convinced that lower income tax rates increase work effort. Such views as these naturally inform the economist's economic ideology in terms of degree to which s/he favors government intervention in markets.

A survey by the Wall Street Journal highlights the disagreement about recent (2024) public policy proposals among economists *and* between economists and the public: issues with the strongest agreement among economists were the same issues where economists differed most from public opinion (eliminating taxes on tips and social security benefits;

[14] Fuller and Geide-Stevenson (2007).

[15] In labor markets with one (or only a few) employers, called monopsony markets.

imposing 20 percent across-the-board tariffs; penalizing price gougers).[16] While economists generally think these are bad economic policy, the public overwhelmingly supports them.

3.4 Concluding Comments

The take-away from all this is that there's widespread disagreement in the U.S. about the specifics of the dominant economic system, both among economists and the public. Some economists and members of the public are dissatisfied with the mainstream: the unquestioned material gains brought about by capitalism have not been without great cost. Those gains are vastly unevenly distributed, and the nature of markets has changed how humans interact, and how they view their world. Details are subjects of later chapters. Alternative paradigms (summarized in Table 3.1) that confront these shortcomings head on are examined in the next two chapters, beginning with Marxist economics.

References

Benjafield JG (2019) Major paradigms and approaches in psychology. In: The Cambridge handbook of the intellectual history of psychology. Cambridge University Press, Cambridge. Available at: https://www.cambridge.org/core/books/abs/cambridge-handbook-of-the-intellectual-history-of-psychology/major-paradigms-and-approaches-in-psychology/5E3585AA0353B433AD5D866389C6316B. Accessed on 2 July 2025

Blackhouse R (2010) The history of the social sciences since 1945. Cambridge University Press, Oxford

Egan PJ, Mullin M (2012) Turning personal experience into political attitudes: the effect of local weather on Americans' perceptions about global warming. J Polit 74(3):796–809

Fuller D, Geide-Stevenson D (2007) Consensus on economic issues: a survey of republicans, democrats and economists. East Econ J 33(1):81–94

Hadsell L, Jones AT (2020) The company you keep: satisfaction with life, economic freedom, and preference-policy mismatch. J Comp Econ 48(3):642–657

Hadsell L, McAvoy M, McGovern J (2013) Promoting economic literacy and self-awareness through an understanding of economic ideology. N Y Econ Rev 44(1):54–76

[16] Kiernan (2024).

Heid M (2022) Why experts can't seem to agree on boosters. The New York Times, 13 April. Available at: https://www.nytimes.com/2022/04/13/opinion/covid-booster-shot.html. Accessed on 2 July 2025

Hoffmann AOI, Post T (2015) How return and risk experiences shape investor beliefs and preferences. https://doi.org/10.1111/acfi.12169

Jones AT, Hadsell L, Burrus RT Jr (2019) Capitalist views and religion. East Econ J 45(3):384–414

Kiernan P (2024) Voters, economists diverge on policy. Wall Str J, 23 September, p A4

Malmendier U, Nagel S (2016) Learning from inflation experiences. Q J Econ 131(1):53–87

Riddell T (2005) Economics: a tool for critically understanding society. Pearson Addison Wesley

Sugerman ER, Li Y, Johnson EJ (2021) Local warming is real: a meta-analysis of the effect of recent temperature on climate change beliefs. Curr Opin Behav Sci 42:121–126

CHAPTER 4

Power and Purification: Marxists and Buddhists

"Thinking like an economist" is not easy. First you need to know what type of economist.

Some economists like to argue for universal adoption of "the economic way of thinking." But, of course, there is no such universal approach. Beyond neo-classical are many other ways of thinking about economic activity. Paradigms range from Austrian (which also emphasizes individual action) to Keynesian (which emphasizes the need for government intervention) to Behavioral (with its influence from psychology). In this chapter I present outlines of two alternatives which provide heavy critiques of markets, Marxist and Buddhist. Two more are presented in the next chapter. Though their perspectives are quite different they all share a common foil, neo-classical economics.

4.1 Marxist Economics

Just outside central London, north of Regents Park and east of Hampstead Heath, with its clear views of the London skyline, lies Karl Marx. You can visit Marx's grave in Highgate Cemetery but be forewarned, you'll have to pay an entry fee. And the price does not follow his famous dictum "From each according to his abilities, to each according to his needs" but rather is a fixed rate. Ironic, isn't it? You and I will pay the

L. Hadsell, *Social Economies*,
https://doi.org/10.1007/978-3-032-21916-9_4

same five pounds as would Elon Musk—assuming the ultimate capitalist would ever visit a memorial to the ultimate anti-capitalist.

A central assertion of Marx was that distributions of income and wealth are determined by the power structure within the economic system. That is, in contrast to the neo-classical view, income and wealth disparities, rather than reflecting differences in market value produced, reflect differential power between business owners and workers. Karl Marx identified, in the midst of the nineteenth-century Industrial Revolution, class and power as primary manifestations of the capitalist system. In short, the class structure, based on separation by ownership of productive assets, creates power and power leads to coercion which in turn leads to inequality.

"Class" is defined by the terms of relationships in the production process. The capitalist class is dominant. These are the owners of businesses who control the tools of production: factories or offices, machines, technology. Workers (labor) are subordinate—they are dependent on the capitalist class for their livelihood in the sense that workers have to sell their labor to capitalists to survive. Marx asserted, in an interesting turn of phrase, that labor was "free"—free of ownership and control of the tools necessary to earn a living independently: "Workers of the world unite; you have nothing to lose but your chains." This conception contrasts sharply with the neo-classical view expressed by Milton Friedman who asserted that individuals could leave the labor market, and indeed the entire economic system, if they wished, simply by producing for themselves all they needed.[1] In other words, workers are under no obligation to work in formal markets. Marx's view also contrasts with Adam Smith's capitalism as "benignly competitive." Marx recognized the influence of economic systems on society: "economic organization ... is the most powerful factor in determining social structure."[2]

According to Marx, class hierarchy creates a power differential. In a relationship between two individuals, Alice has power over Ben if by imposing costs on Ben (or threatening to do so) Alice can cause Ben to act in a way that is to Alice's advantage.[3] Power is enhanced, in concrete terms, in that capitalists can survive a shutdown of production while labor cannot, as labor needs to work to earn income to survive. Thus, the

[1] Friedman (1962).

[2] Sackrey et al. (2016, p. 56).

[3] Sackrey et al. (2016, p. 55).

consequence of class and power is the potential for a coercive relationship between employer and employee. Coercion occurs when "the conditions under which people make trades affect the outcome of those trades."[4] So, for example, facing the armed robber's ultimatum, "Your money or your life!" presents the target with a choice only in theory, as compliance with the assailant is assured.[5] Or, continuing with Alice (as owner) and Ben (as worker), if Alice "asks" Ben to work beyond his scheduled hours, for example, there are situations in which Ben has little choice but to comply.

Likewise, many goods and services traded in markets—health care, food, housing—are necessities, required not just for good living but for sustaining life. Going without them is a choice only in a very narrow sense. Marxists contend that leaving these necessities of life to markets imposes undue coercion on those who are "free"—that is, who do not own their own means of production and therefor are unable to choose in a meaningful way—as they have no real choice but to accept work and pay under conditions set by capitalists.[6] Other examples occur when large businesses interact with smaller ones, or when a monopoly exists. Unequal relationships create the opportunity for one party to use their greater power over the other. Unequal education, knowledge, skills, and so on are other bases for coercion—people who lack those things are at a disadvantage in many settings. As many of these settings are features of markets it is the market system itself that serves as the root of coercion.

Consider the potential for differential power and coercion in labor markets in the context of a recent report by the Federal Reserve. Two-fifths (41%) of all U.S. hourly workers surveyed said they were not given more than one week notice of their work schedule and half said they have little or no say in that schedule. A survey of British workers produced similar results.[7] Presumably many of these workers would prefer more input in the determination of their work so they can, for example, better

[4] Bowles et al. (2005, p. 76).

[5] The concern with coercion and freedom of choice is raised in the discussion of extension of market principles to new areas, in Chapter 6.

[6] A critique is that businesses/capitalists must compete with one another, thereby lessening their power.

[7] Partington (2021). "Short-notice periods were even more pronounced for those in jobs with variable hours or shift work built into their contracts, with 62% having less than a week to prepare for their schedule. At the extreme, 12% of this group – amounting to 7% all working adults– had less than 24 hours' notice."

plan childcare, arrange transportation, attend classes or other regularly scheduled events, or hold a second job elsewhere. A conservative neoclassical economist might wonder why workers would agree to such arrangements if the arrangements were not desirable. To them workers are free to work elsewhere if they choose. For Marxists, the answer lies in the coercive nature of the limited choices for workers resulting from their relationship to employers. Many workers have few opportunities to easily move to new employment and fear creating a work history (such as from switching jobs) that future potential employers might view negatively. Freedom to work elsewhere or to obtain additional skills is often not a viable option due to cost or time constraints (rent must be paid, food purchased, children cared for), or even cognitive or physical limitations of the individuals. Marxists would say it illustrates class, differential power, and coercion as dominant features of capitalist economies.

In the Marxist view unequal bargaining power results from the unequal distribution of ownership of the tools of production. Additional sources of unequal bargaining stem from information asymmetries, debt, and personality attributes. Information asymmetries occur because employers are typically more aware of available jobs and prevailing market wages than are employees, putting employers at an advantage in employment decisions. Debt obligations (rent/mortgages, student loans, auto loans) create an additional cost of failure to gain employment: An employee with high debt has a fixed payment due each month and so must work, having limited ability to adjust their expenses as their income changes. Personal bankruptcy is generally less forgiving than business bankruptcy. Personality attributes such as self-confidence and risk preference are important in selection of profession, specific jobs, decisions to apply for promotion, and generally, bargaining in employment negotiations. Some individuals are at a particular disadvantage, given high correlations that gender and socioeconomic class have with those attributes.

The extent of coercion is open to debate, given the difficulty in defining exactly what coercion is and how to measure it. One economist claims that coercive "threats of poverty, poor medical care and education (or lack of it), etc. are similar to threats of physical harm."[8] Others dismiss the idea out of hand, contending that we always have a choice. For me,

[8] Schmitt (1987, p. 80).

a world without differential power, and coercion, is hard to imagine. The only question is, how much.

With coercion comes exploitation. In addition to unequal power, Marx identified the capitalists' goal of profit as the driving force in capitalism and the root of exploitation. As profit is the difference between revenue the capitalist receives for selling a product and what the capitalist pays to the labor employed in its making (along with other costs), capitalists have an incentive to hold down labor costs by lowering wages, or by increasing productivity through a faster pace or reduced worker safety. As such, workers' incentives are directly opposed to the capitalists'. In Marx's view, the upper hand goes to the capitalists who do not have to employ their capital to survive whereas workers do have to sell their services. Workers ultimately must accept terms of employment while employers do not.

Marx and Smith agreed that one consequence of the drive for greater profit by owners and higher wages by labor is greater and greater specialization. Smith emphasized the greater productivity and higher wages brought about by such a division of labor. Marx contended that over-specialization leads to worker alienation—defined as the separation of meaning from labor's effort. Commodification, turning something into an item that is primarily bought or sold, further adds to alienation.[9] In a capitalist-dominated market economy, everything is ultimately for sale. And, of course, the target of commodification most concerning to Marx is that of labor—who become in the capitalist system simply another input in the production process, absent value other than as determined by the labor market. Thus, specialization can be a double-edged sword. True, the benefit to the worker of specialization is higher wages; but the cost is often monotonous work and repetitive tasks, absent of meaning, and a separation of the value of their production from their earnings. The commodification of people as "labor" silently permeates thought in market-oriented societies, with no better example than the pervasiveness today of the view in the U.S., even among educators and parents, of middle and high school students as workers-in-training, learning not for preservation of democracy or personal enlightenment but for future employment.

[9] Sackrey et al. (2016, p. 59).

One solution to the inequities Marx identified is for communal ownership of the means of production. Banning private ownership of productive assets (factories, offices, etc., though not other property such as homes or autos) removes the class conflict and associated exploitation. Socialism is the common name for such a system. Socialism, as an application of Marxist ideas, has not fared well in practice. Prominent failures most often cited by critics include the Soviet Union, North Korea, and Cuba. But of course, each of these states had an authoritarian political structure and international economic sanctions sometimes hindering their participation in world economies, limiting our ability to measure the functioning of the economic system independently. The example of twenty-first-century China, which also has an authoritarian political regime, is instructive: while maintaining its repressive political structure, China in recent decades has shifted away from its socialist-based economy, with its overwhelming state ownership of the means of production to much greater reliance on market forces, including entry into global trade, and the result has been tremendous economic growth, raising hundreds of millions of Chinese out of poverty.[10] There is little doubt that markets bring about greater material well-being. Marxists would contend that though this may be true, what has been surrendered in terms of autonomy and dignity is worth considering.

Marxist-type systems can exist in many shades of the same general form. State ownership is the most common conception; others include worker-owned cooperatives, in which workers participate in the governance of the business; and employee stock-ownership plans, ESOPs, in which a company's productive assets are owned by its workers. While many European countries are known for their state-operated enterprises and highly regulated and taxed economies, this has lessened over the last few decades (beginning in the 1980s, with a widespread move to deregulation), as many European countries privatized enterprises in many sectors of the economy. Airlines that used to be state-owned and operated, such as British Airways, Aer Lingus, and Air France, are now either entirely or mostly privately owned. Swedish pharmaceutical giant Pharmacia is now owned by Pfizer. Power companies, auto manufacturers, and banks have all been fully or partially privatized. This shading away from strong socialist policies toward more market-friendly systems has led to

[10] For more discussion, see Naughton (2017).

more vibrant economies, even as it has also played a part in increasing social conflict, as evidenced, in part, by recent elections of far-right candidates in many of those countries, one result of dissatisfaction with the new economic order that encompasses greater uncertainty and inequality.

Even more extensive privatization and deregulation took place in the U.S. and the U.K. Still, U.S., European (and Chinese) economies are subject to significant regulation and oversight (and sometime, direct support). Recent European history provides a vivid assessment of the economic potential of capitalism versus socialism. Perhaps an extreme, but comparison of market-oriented West Germany and socialist East Germany at the time of reunification in the early 1990s provides an interesting example. Tables 4.1 and 4.2 show the greater productivity and economic well-being in West Germany in 1990, after four decades of separation.

Of course, East Germany was not a model socialist economy and West Germany certainly was not an all-out capitalist economy, but the contrast is stark—and informative. The combination of economic and political freedom has great power. Still, present-day Europe offers an important contrast to the American form of capitalism. The former may have higher taxes, spending, and regulation, but I imagine few Europeans would prefer the U.S. system (and the majority have not, when given the choice in various referenda intended to Americanize their economic system).

Table 4.1 Percent of population (1990) with...

Good	*West*	*East*
TV set	99	96
Color TV	95	57
Telephone	99	17
Washing machine	97	99

Table 4.2 Hours of labor required (in 1990) to purchase...

Good	*West*	*East*
Men's shirt	1	7
Color TV	81	1008
Washing machine	59	491
Coffee	0.2	4
Month's rent	12	6

4.2 Buddhist Economics

How many times have you heard the advice, "Follow your passion"? Young people are especially encouraged not to focus on money when choosing a career; a job should never be "just a job." Rather, one should seek meaning and purpose from the work they get paid to do. After all, work will for many decades comprise the most significant portion of the typical person's waking hours. And, in fact, much research indicates the wisdom of following this advice: people who do are healthier and more productive—and are better for the organization for which they work.[11]

Advice to follow your passion is complementary to Buddhist Economics—an economic paradigm that emphasizes as a primary goal an economic system that purifies human character. Work for example, is seen by the Buddhist economist as integral to the development of character, in contrast to the neo-classical view of work as a disutility—something to generally be avoided. Under the Buddhist conception of labor, "properly conducted in conditions of human dignity and freedom," one is rewarded not only with one's production (or payment therefor) but also a greater sense of self-worth. According to one Buddhist economist,

> If the nature of the work is properly appreciated and applied, it will stand in the same relation to the higher faculties as food is to the physical body. It nourishes and enlivens the higher man and urges him to produce the best he is capable of. It directs his free will along the proper course and disciplines the animal in him into progressive channels. It furnishes an excellent background for man to display his scale of values and develop his personality.[12]

Rather than a means to an end, work is, to the Buddhist economist, character building, seeking to fulfill three goals:

1. development of self;
2. overcoming of egocentrism;
3. production of goods and services.

[11] Simon-Thomas (2018).

[12] Indian philosopher and economist J. C. Kumarappa, as quoted in Schumacher (n.d.)

A measure of economic success in the Buddhist view, then, is not efficiency—getting the most output per hour of work, but development of one's character.

To illustrate the primary importance of work as more than an income-producing activity, consider future work in an age of artificial intelligence. Will we be happier, more fulfilled if (when?) AI substantially supplants humans labor, even if a universal basic income is provided in its place? If work is a disutility, something to be avoided, then the answer is yes. If work has meaning, as in the Buddhist conception, then the answer is no. Clearly, some work is drudgery—and so replacing unpleasant work may improve happiness. But for the Buddhist economist, happiness is not the goal, just as consumption is not the goal. Purification of character—something much deeper than happiness—is the end point.

> To organise work in such a manner that it becomes meaningless, boring, stultifying, or nerve-racking for the worker would be little short of criminal; it would indicate a greater concern with goods than with people, an evil lack of compassion and a soul-destroying degree of attachment to the most primitive side of this worldly existence. Equally, to strive for leisure as an alternative to work would be considered a complete misunderstanding of one of the basic truths of human existence, namely that work and leisure are complementary parts of the same living process and cannot be separated without destroying the joy of work and the bliss of leisure.[13]

So even work that is drudgery has purpose and replacing such work, fully at least, goes against the Buddhist perspective. To further contrast this view with the mainstream neo-classical, note that the latter proposes that "the ideal from the point of view of the employer is to have output without employees, and the ideal from the point of view of the employee is to have income without employment."[14] This neo-classical utopia is

[13] Schumacher (n.d.).

[14] Schumacher (n.d.). From the same article is a disturbing observation by Schumacher: "The very start of Buddhist economic planning would be a planning for full employment, and the primary purpose of this would in fact be employment for everyone who needs an 'outside' job: it would not be the maximisation of employment nor the maximisation of production. Women, on the whole, do not need an 'outside' job, and the large-scale employment of women in offices or factories would be considered a sign of serious economic failure. In particular, to let mothers of young children work in factories while the children run wild would be as uneconomic in the eyes of a Buddhist economist as the

potentially attainable with AI, but completely at odds with the Buddhist conception of work as purifying.

The economic and social decline associated with deindustrialization across much of the Northeast and Midwest U.S.—evidenced by fraying communities and increases in "deaths of despair" (drug overdose, suicide, and alcohol abuse)—may demonstrate the power of work to add meaning to lives and the devastation when work disappears. As has been shown time and again, in the words of economist E. F. Schumacher, "If a man has no chance of obtaining work he is in a desperate position, not simply because he lacks an income but because he lacks this nourishing and enlivening factor of disciplined work which nothing can replace."[15] Similarly, the upending of work routines during the 2020 COVID pandemic led many to greater appreciation of the benefits of work itself beyond the monetary aspect.

Deindustrialization results from both changing trade patterns and technological change. Each are seen as avenues to higher wages and economic growth. And yet each has a cost, certainly in the short run as people who lose one job seek a replacement. Neo-classical economics tends to place greater emphasis on the aggregate economic benefits while relegating to second-tier status distributional concerns and non-monetary effects. In other words, there are winners and losers, and neo-classicals tend to look at the sum more than the parts. Buddhist economics places great emphasis on the opportunity cost of both trade and technological change, and is willing to sacrifice higher incomes and economic growth for non-monetary benefits and sustainability. When you next visit a farmers market think of Buddhist economic principles that lay behind such endeavors. Buddhist economics favors small, local production and disparages the large-scale, long-distance trade so common today. Knowing who produces your food and the methods used is important. The gains from trade noted by neo-classical trade theory are seen as illusory by Buddhist economists, because they focus on efficiency gains while leaving out important considerations such as resource depletion and long-term effects of overconsumption, including pollution from transportation over long distances.

employment of a skilled worker as a soldier in the eyes of a modern economist." Consider the good but don't forget the wrong-headed and call it out.

[15] Schumacher (n.d.).

> From the point of view of Buddhist economics, therefore, production from local resources for local needs is the most rational way of economic life, while dependence on imports from afar and the consequent need to produce for export to unknown and distant peoples is highly uneconomic and justifiable only in exceptional cases and on a small scale.... [T]he Buddhist would hold that to satisfy human wants from faraway sources rather than from sources nearby signifies failure rather than success. The [neo-classical economist] tends to take statistics showing an increase in the number of ton/miles per head of the population carried by a country's transport system as proof of economic progress, while to the ... Buddhist economist the same statistics would indicate a highly undesirable deterioration in the pattern of consumption.[16]

Social and ecological limits play a prominent role in Buddhist thinking about economic growth. The focus is on internal development (higher quality of life) rather than the external (more GDP). Implied in the Buddhist goal of maximum well-being with minimum consumption is a limitation on human desires beyond minimum material comfort. Wanting less is a key goal. In the neo-classical paradigm, limits are seldom acknowledged or are seen as an ancillary concern—growth is good (or "growth is god," according to one critic). Declines in GDP, for whatever reason, are viewed negatively. If Americans decided *en masse* that they preferred more leisure and less work, the consequent decline in GDP would rattle markets, politicians, and most economists. Great alarm would follow. Failure of the economic system would be declared by mainstream economists. The Buddhist economist would hail the development as a success.

The Buddhist economics emphasis on the opportunity cost of technological change is particularly relevant as we enter the era of AI:

> there are therefore two types of mechanisation which must be clearly distinguished: one that enhances a man's skill and power and one that turns the work of man over to a mechanical slave, leaving man in a position of having to serve the slave. How to tell the one from the other? The craftsman himself... can always, if allowed to, draw the delicate distinction between the machine and the tool. The carpet loom is a tool, a contrivance for holding warp threads at a stretch for the pile to be woven round them

[16] Schumacher (n.d.).

> by the craftsmen's fingers; but the power loom is a machine, and its significance as a destroyer of culture lies in the fact that it does the essentially human part of the work.[17]

Opportunity costs of technological change are two-sided. On the one hand, change that replaces rather than complements human skill has the cost of reducing the human experience. On the other hand, not using the new technology means lower consumption, as fewer goods and services are produced, but maintains the benefits of work. Buddhist economics places the trade-off center-stage, coming down on a clear side: against certain technological change.[18] Complementary technology, that which enhances the human experience (and perhaps increases productivity) is desired. And the loss of consumption is less of a concern, as the Buddhist goal is maximum well-being through minimum consumption. And because ensuring a minimum standard of living for everyone is a key, Buddhist economics promotes building community through genuine caring and discourages the kind of individual self-interest dominant in the neo-classical perspective.[19] Genuine caring, for others in market transactions (buyer, seller, employer, employee, animals, environment), often increases costs. Buddhist economic principles of genuine caring challenge the sometimes-cruel modern economic practices such as factory farming, noting that suffering "is universal in the realm of both human and non-human kingdoms."[20] And yet, such caring can actually be good for business and profits. Practical benefits for businesses that practice caring (discussed more in Chapter 12) developed by economist Robert Frank (2010) include avoiding opportunistic behavior between owners and managers, customer loyalty (i.e., repeat sales), and trust between the company and employees, suppliers, and community.

The overarching goal of an economic system in Buddhist economics is purification of human character. Contrast this with the Neo-classical goal: maximum utility through consumption. Table 4.3 summarizes

[17] Schumacher (n.d.)

[18] While neo-classical economics tends to acknowledge the trade-off only in passing, perhaps to be dealt with by public policy such as re-training programs. Neo-classicals also assume that in the long run unemployed individuals will find new employment.

[19] Zsolnai (2009).

[20] Zsolnai (2009).

Table 4.3 Buddhist and neo-classical paradigms

	Buddhist	*Neo-classical*
Goal of economic system	Purification of human character	Maximum utility via consumption
Consumption	Maximum well-being with minimum consumption Minimize desires	Maximum well-being via maximum consumption Maximize desires
Work	Character building, with three goals: 1. develop self, 2. overcome egocentrism, 3. produce goods and services	Pure disutility—Therefore, to be minimized. Engaged in as a means of obtaining money (for purchase of goods and services). Only a means to an end
Relationships	Community through Genuine caring	Individualism, self-interest in primary

three key points that differentiate Buddhist economics from Neo-classical economics.

Economist Clair Brown, in her excellent book-length treatment of Buddhist economic principles, provides a detailed eight-step recommendation for movement to an economy based on the Buddhist ways.[21] These include,

- Tax and transfer policies that discourage consumption (e.g., a sales tax) and environmental degradation (a carbon tax) while also providing minimum levels of material and social well-being through, for example, enhanced social programs, especially for children, and minimum basic incomes.
- Changing focus on how we measure economic activity—away from measures such as GDP.
- Sustainable food production that feeds while also protecting the environment's ability to provide nutrition far into the future.
- Corporate social responsibility (CSR) and environmental, social, and governance (ESG) policies, particularly as they apply to climate change.

[21] Brown (2016).

- Living wages and meaningful work.
- Focus on community and interconnections.

4.3 Concluding Comments

Both Marxist and Buddhist paradigms are harshly critical of mainstream neo-classical economics. Marxists contend that markets are characterized by unequal power and coercion, necessitating a role for collective ownership of productive assets and shared decision-making. Unfettered markets inevitably lead to vastly unequal incomes, and the strive for profits leads to economic and social conflict and a decoupling of meaning from work.

The Buddhist perspective also makes substantive criticism of the goals of neo-classical economics. For the Buddhist, the primary goal of economic systems is to meet material needs with minimum consumption. Notably, work is seen as a way to develop oneself and overcome egocentrism rather than simply a means to produce goods and services.

References

Bowles S, Edwards R, Roosevelt F (2005) Understanding capitalism. Oxford University Press

Brown C (2016) Buddhist economics: an enlightened approach to the dismal science. Bloomsbury Press, New York

Frank R (2010) What price the moral high ground? Ethical dilemmas in competitive environments. Princeton University Press, Princeton, NJ, Princeton and Oxford

Friedman M (1962) Capitalism and freedom. University of Chicago Press, Chicago

Naughton B (2017) Is China socialist? J Econ Perspect 31(1):3–24

Partington R (2021) Almost 40% of UK workers 'get less than a week's notice of shift patterns'. The Guardian, 15 April

Sackrey C, Schneider G, Knoedler J (2016) Introduction to political economy, 8th edn. Economic Affairs Bureau, Boston

Schmitt R (1987) Introduction to Marx and Engels. Routledge, New York

Schumacher EF (no date) Buddhist economics. Available at: https://centerfor neweconomics.org/publications/buddhist-economics/. Accessed on 2 April 2022

Simon-Thomas ER (2018) The four keys to happiness at work. Available at: https://greatergood.berkeley.edu/article/item/the_four_keys_to_happin ess_at_work

Zsolnai L (2009) Buddhist economics for business. In: Zsolnai L, Boda Z, Fekete L (eds), Ethical prospects. Springer, Dordrecht. https://doi.org/10.1007/978-1-4020-9821-5_5

CHAPTER 5

Feminist and Ecological Alternatives

> You cannot understand the economy without looking at gender relations.[1]

> Emphasis on being hard, logical, scientific, and precise has served a valuable purpose, it is true, in guarding against analysis that is weak, illogical, unscientific, and vague. But if these are the only virtues we value in our practice [as economists], we are easy prey to other vices.[2]

Here I round out the discussion of paradigms by outlining two that demonstrate the perils of a universal "economic way of thinking" based on the neo-classical mainstream approach. The first, Feminist Economics, takes a more inclusive view of economic activity—expanding beyond market-based measures and male-centric approaches. The second, Ecological Economics, further widens the interest of economics, emphasizing the ecological context of economic activity. As such, both are concerned with a wider, more inclusive view of economic systems.

[1] Economist Jayati Ghosh.
[2] Economist Julie Nelson.

L. Hadsell, *Social Economies*,
https://doi.org/10.1007/978-3-032-21916-9_5

5.1 Feminist Economics

In a recent survey of economists, women were much more likely than men to disagree with the statement "market solutions are superior to government intervention" and were much more likely to agree that "environmental protection should increase" and that "labor market opportunities are unequal."[3] Such disparity highlights a much less well-known aspect of the problem of two-handed economists (see Harry Truman's quote at the beginning of Chapter 3): a gender-based aspect of disagreement that pervades mainstream economics. Beyond having disparate theoretical and policy views, men and women economists also tend to have different research interests. Compared to men, women economists are more likely to research areas such as employment, education, and health.[4] One study of more than 1000 research papers in the field of development economics found that research on issues of gender inequality, health, international trade, migration, and education were much more likely to have women authors than papers on macroeconomics, microfinance, or agriculture, reflecting large differences between men and women economists in terms of research field choices.[5] Clearly, as two researchers put it, "men and women bring distinct perspectives to research and are interested in answering different research questions."[6]

It's hard to know what is at the root of these differences, but they surely exist. And the differences are important because the economics profession remains male-dominated, with women comprising only about one-third of the profession at all levels, from undergraduates in the economics classroom all the way to tenured professors. The economics profession has failed to attract more women professionals over the past three decades, even as other STEM fields have gained far greater female

[3] Bayer and Rouse (2016): "Relative to male economists, women economists are 21 percentage points more likely to disagree that the United States has excessive government regulation of economic activity; 32 percentage points more likely to agree with making the distribution of income more equal; 30 percentage points more likely to agree that the United States should link import openness to labor standards; and 42 percentage points more likely to disagree that labor market opportunities are equal for men and women. The prevailing range of views among economists is likely to be biased by the relative lack of women and minority economists" (p. 232).

[4] Goldin (2019).

[5] Dolado et al. (2012), Jayachandran and Daubenspeck (2018).

[6] Jayachandran and Daubenspeck (2018).

representation (and as college enrollment for women far outpaces men, with women comprising nearly 60% of overall enrollment). This lack of gender representation likely leads to differences in not just the profession's modeling and research focus but also in policy prescriptions—ideas and actions that affect each of our lives.[7] As economists Amanda Bayer and Cecilia Elena Rouse conclude, "If the ultimate goal of economic research is to develop and communicate lasting insights, this evidence suggests that the value and impact of the economics profession suffer from the lack of diversity in its ranks."[8]

Feminist economics seeks to address these shortcomings: "Much feminist economic research focuses on topics that have been neglected in the field, such as care work, intimate partner violence, or economic theories which could be improved through better incorporation of gendered effects and interactions, such as between paid and unpaid sectors of economies."[9] With regard to the latter—treatment of paid versus unpaid work—a male-centric economics profession tends to minimize the contribution of non-market work (e.g., in households and volunteer organizations), placing much more emphasis on measurable market-based transactions, partially because market-based work is easier to track and put in dollar terms: records are kept, wages are paid. But perhaps as important, because the vast majority of non-market work is performed by women.[10] It's not necessarily that men consciously exclude non-market work because it tends to be performed by women; rather, non-market work tends to be invisible to those who do not do it. Perhaps this leads to men underestimating the importance and value of such work. Just as such neglect of non-market work biases GDP (GDP includes only market-based transactions), it also skews measures of individual incomes, with practical implications for such things as credit toward Social Security benefits and unemployment insurance: work performed outside of formal

[7] Jayachandran and Daubenspeck (2018). A similar observation is made for some other disciplines. For example, "there is ample evidence on female physicians being over-represented in pediatrics or obstetrics and under-represented in surgery or orthopedics. Likewise, female psychologists are over-represented clinical and environmental psychology and under-represented in neuropsychology…" (Dolado et al. 2018).

[8] Bayer and Rouse (2016, p. 233).

[9] Wikipedia (n.d.).

[10] Brenan (2020).

markets, whether paid or unpaid, are not factored into either program; these workers simply are not eligible. They are invisible.

Also neglected or at least under-appreciated by the male-dominated discipline are notions of economic power and coercion in gender relationships, the importance of cultural norms and expectations, and gender biases, particularly in employment. Gender bias, for example, is less likely to be felt by those who benefit from the inherent bias. A survey of economists revealed that half of women economists thought that they had "been discriminated against or treated unfairly because of sex" compared to only 3% of men.[11] Men also appear to place greater focus on competition, at least in certain contexts. This naturally leads to a greater interest in the study and support of markets, where competition is viewed favorably. Cooperation, shown in many studies in economics and other disciplines to be present in abundance in the real-world, is often neglected by neoclassical economists as a substantial component of economic decisions. Such neglect leads to substandard models and explanations of economic phenomenon (such as the provision of public goods).[12] A good deal of understanding is being forsworn as a result. This may be changing, albeit slowly.

Recognizing these issues, feminist economics seeks a more inclusive and expansive definition of economics and to reshape some of the underlying assumptions of economic models and approaches. A starting point is to critique the assertion that economics engages in value-free (or "positive") analysis; that is, that economic science is completely objective, without bias one way or another in its choice of models, data, and policy prescription. The reasons for the feminist economist's objection to this assertion are clear: the differences in professional focus of men and women economists noted above; and the norms and customs of society that influence economic choices and how economists, particularly men, think about those choices.

Demonstrating the different focus of feminist economics, recent research published in the journal *Feminist Economics* includes articles investigating the effect of paid maternity leave on breastfeeding; divorce and time allocation (married women in states with unilateral divorce

[11] CBR Economics (2019).

[12] Women have been shown to exhibit more cooperative behavior than men—in settings such as the Ultimatum Game, for instance—see Chapter 15 on social norms and customs for more on the ultimatum game.

spend less time on core housework than those in states without unilateral divorce laws); and the impacts of gender inequality in education and employment. These are subjects substantially different from the typical focus of most of economics: men are less likely to study these things. And that's a problem.[13]

Feminist economists develop new measures such as the Gender Inequality Index (GII), a summary of reproductive health (maternal mortality and adolescent birth rates); empowerment (proportion of parliamentary seats occupied by women and proportion of women aged 25 years and older with at least some secondary education); and economic status (labor market participation).[14] One purpose of the GII is to bring attention to the human development costs of gender inequality. Similarly, the Gender Empowerment Measure (GEM) gauges women's share of national income, proportion of seats held by women in national parliaments, and percentage of women in economic decision-making positions. Thus, the GEM tells us "whether women and men are able to actively participate in economic and political life and take part in decision-making."[15] One might also consider the *Economist* magazine's Glass Ceiling Index, which combines measures of higher education, labor-force participation, pay, childcare costs, maternity and paternity rights, business-school applications, and representation in senior jobs. Scandinavian countries top their list of "best countries for working women," with Sweden, Iceland, Finland, and Norway in the top four spots.[16]

> The development of economics as a discipline, from Adam Smith until recently, was almost exclusively by men, with few women or racial minority voices. Several women, however, did make significant contributions. And the role of women, despite the persistent low representation, is increasing. Scan this QR code for some notable women economists.

[13] Genadek (2017).

[14] United Nations Human Development Reports (1995).

[15] United Nations Human Development Reports (1995, p. 73).

[16] The Economist (2019).

One goal of Feminist Economics is to bring more women into the economics profession. The link in the nearby Box notes some significant women economists. Many have made their impact relatively recently (1980s onward), reflecting the relative prevalence of men in the early stages of the development of economics as a science, the result of wider cultural norms, limits, and expectations at the time. Even today, rate of women representation among economics professionals, faculty, and students remains low. While women are increasing their presence in other disciplines, economics continues to stagnate: the share of undergraduate economics majors who are female (34%) is roughly the same as it was 40 years ago, even while the overall share of undergraduates who are female has hit record levels (nearly 60%). The share of economics faculty who are women (about one-quarter) is also little changed from 40 years ago. Troubling causes—and consequences—of such underrepresentation can be found in misogynistic language used by young male economists, predominance of male-centric references in textbooks, and in myriad other areas, from grading policies to content of textbooks and courses that are less appealing to women (reflecting the research focus noted earlier).[17]

The consequences of continuing female underrepresentation in the economics profession are dire. A more inclusive profession would enlarge the scope of research and teaching, model building, and data collection. The notion that diverse groups—by gender, race, socioeconomic status—produce better outcomes is pretty firmly established.[18] "Better outcomes" in economics would mean more accurate representation and measurement of economic activity (including both market and non-market work), improved public policy (as more focus is placed on topics such as child development, health care, and discrimination), and greater opportunity for all, regardless of gender, race, or socioeconomic background.

[17] See Hadsell (2020).

[18] Note that in some circumstances, for instance, when extreme prejudice exists and is allowed to work, diverse groups can do worse. See, for example, Hoff and Pandey (2006).

How much of a paradigm shift would feminist economics be from the current mainstream? Not as large as a change to Marxist or Buddhist principles. But large enough to make a difference in how we all, not just economists, think about economic systems. In terms of economic models (and policy based on those models), consider the words of feminist economist Julie Nelson (1995):

> As a specific example, [consider] the treatment of the subject of human capital [knowledge] in a standard labor economics textbook. It does not begin with a focus on nutrition, socialization, and informal and formal education of children within families and public schools, but rather with the college choice decision of the young adult. While there is, of course, some pedagogical benefit in designing textbook examples to appeal to the immediate interests of the students, there seems to be no pedagogical reason to focus so narrowly on higher education. When I teach this subject, I find it helpful to add readings about earlier human capital development and to ask students to reflect back on the creation of their abilities and aspirations, from the very start of their lives.

Today, just over a quarter century after that statement was made, economists are thinking differently, slowly making the change—and treating early childhood programs, among other things, as a key economic interest. Part of the reason for this change is the increasing prominence of ideas from feminist economics.

5.2 Ecological Economics

Nine-billion-ton hamsters? Read on.

Ecological economics (EE) places emphasis on interactions between economic activity and environmental and social realms. The EE conception of economic systems is more encompassing than the neo-classical paradigm in that EE treats economic activity as a subset of the environment and society rather than as separate from, as depicted in Fig. 5.1. For EE, "externalities," costs or benefits that fall outside the economic system (e.g., pollution), are a misnomer: there can be no externality when the economic system is enclosed within society and the biosphere. Most importantly, because economic activity is subsumed within society and environment, economic activity has natural limits, ones imposed not by economic "laws" but very real social and environmental constraints. Of the former, consider customs and norms that often govern interactions in a range of markets (discussed in detail in Chapter 15). Of the latter, consider the first law of thermodynamics: namely, energy can be neither created nor destroyed. As applied to economics: "raw material inputs to economic processes are not "consumed"; having been extracted from the environment in the first place, they eventually return to the environment as wastes."[19] The system is a closed one, with limited ability to supply resources, and, as such, limits to the economic process.

EE is transdisciplinary, with overlaps between economics and ecology, psychology, anthropology, and others. Sustainability is the key concern. The EE concept of sustainability is substantially different from the neo-classical concept. The latter typically thinks of sustainability in terms of long-term profitability, narrowly defined measures of efficiency or market dominance. For the ecological economist, sustainability takes a much wider perspective: long-term viability of economic activity within the limits imposed by the environment and society. In this way sustainability

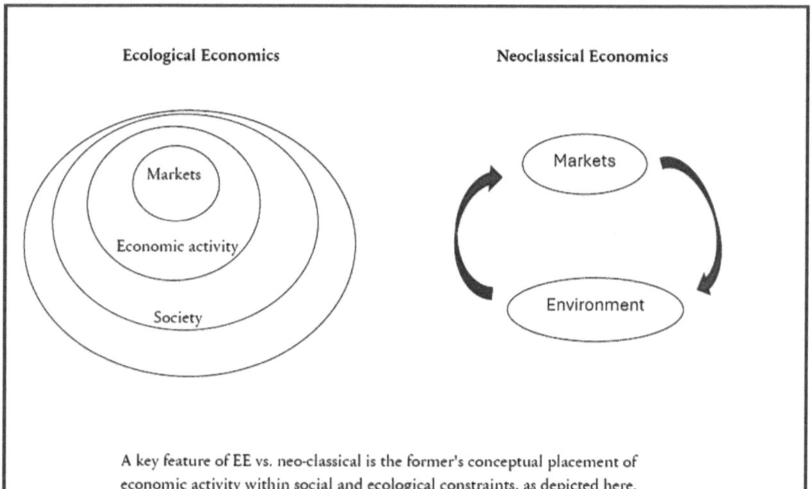

Fig. 5.1 Ecological economics paradigm

[19] Ayres (1996). The first law is the law of conservation of mass/energy and the second, the law entropy law.

considers future generations as well as the wider context of economic activity today.

Scale and capacity are central aspects of sustainability. The Indian philosopher Mahatma Gandhi once was asked if he thought Indians would one day enjoy the same level of material consumption as Americans. He replied, "How many Earths do we think we have?" His concern was capacity and scale. Nicholas Georgescu-Roegen was among the first economists to formalize such concerns. Georgescu-Roegen's primary focus was on limitations of the natural world. His work, which formed the beginning of Ecological Economics (in the 1970s and 1980s), incorporated natural resource flows into economic modeling and analysis, explicitly recognizing limits posed by nature. Following Georgescu-Roegen's lead, Herman Daly, a one-time student Georgescu-Roegen, co-founded and edited the prominent journal *Ecological Economics*. Daly's contributions to the discipline include his conception of the steady-state economy, in which economic development replaces growth as the overarching goal (discussed in further detail in Chapter 9). Criticizing our excessive focus on GDP as a measure of economic well-being, he argued that what is being measured often changes our behavior—leading to neglect of more important values.

The contention of Gandhi and Georgescu-Roegen (and Daly) is that Earth simply does not have the resources to support on a wider-scale the level of consumption enjoyed by the average American. The Sierra Club reports, for example, that the average American will drain as many resources as 35 residents of India and consume 53 times more goods and services than someone from China. According to Scientific American, "A child born in the United States will create thirteen times as much ecological damage over the course of his or her lifetime than a child born in Brazil."[20] It simply is not possible for four times as many Indians (or Chinese) to consume at the same levels as Americans (or many Europeans) currently do—the Earth has neither enough resources to supply raw materials nor the ability to absorb the waste; Americans account for only five percent of the world's population but create half of the globe's solid waste. And sadly, "U.S. consumers are among the least likely to feel guilty about the impact they have on the environment, yet they are near

[20] Scientific American (2012).

to top of the list in believing that individual choices could make a difference."[21] One can imagine the inevitable conflict that will arise in the coming decades as India and China both rapidly expand their production and consumption. One can imagine the moral questions that will arise within the EE paradigm as the distribution of a sustainable level of consumption is discussed.

According to Robert Costanza, a current leader within the EE paradigm, mainstream

> economists don't seem to understand exponential growth. Ecological economics recognizes that the economy, like any other subsystem on the planet, cannot grow forever. And if you think of an organism as an analogy, organisms grow for a period and then they stop growing. They can still continue to improve and develop, but without physically growing, because if organisms did that you'd end up with nine-billion-ton hamsters.[22]

Recognizing limits, EE points to internal development rather than external—or, in other words, "better" rather than "more."

Within this view of economic activity as a subset of society and environment, EE pays close attention to social and natural capital, in addition to the physical and human capital considered by neo-classical economists. Social capital refers to the ties that bind society—an amorphous definition for sure, but one that is meant to illustrate the complexity of the concept. Social capital will be discussed in more detail in Chapter 19; for now, consider it to be a measure of community cohesion, a representation of the ability of society (and individuals therein) to function to achieve desired goals. It can be measured by participation, membership, and relationships (in civic organizations, clubs, and other institutions). EE sees the decline of social capital in recent decades as an important shortcoming of our current economic system, with particular emphasis on the impact of rising inequality.

EE argues that economic growth can have benefits for individual and societal well-being, but that growth does not automatically ameliorate social ills. A rising tide does not lift all boats, as some contend. And for EE, social problems, rather than being a concern that should be addressed within the constraints placed on economic activity by the free market, are

[21] Scientific American (2012).

[22] Costanza (2010).

front and center, with the economic system to be adjusted so as to address these ills and achieve maximum societal well-being: the goal in EE is an economy that promotes a just society, rather than a society that promotes more economic activity. EE contends that rather than growth we should focus on development. The former is an expansion, the latter an improvement. The former increases economic activity, the latter enhances society through economic activity. For the former, the economy is the central concern, for the latter the overriding concern is society (e.g., building social capital) and individual well-being.

The other closely watched measure in EE is natural capital, the stock of environmental resources that interact with human social and economic activity, including minerals and ores, water and air, and sources of environmental services such as cleansing of water by oysters and wetlands, protection of coastal areas provided by marshes, and purifying of air performed by trees.[23] EE's view is more expansive than the mainstream view, arguing that natural capital is much less interchangeable with physical capital than mainstream economics considers; for EE, nature provides some resources and services that cannot be replicated (replaced) by technology. Think of levees around New Orleans, so devastated by Hurricane Katrina in 2005. The levees were not a viable alternative to the marshes they were meant to replace. Likewise, the protection of coastal areas and the biodiversity supported by coral reefs cannot easily be replaced with human creations. A species once extinct cannot be recovered. An atmosphere that goes beyond its capacity to hold CO_2 is not going to return to a lower state anytime soon. The global climate system will certainly survive a warming of 2 or 3°C. It has before. But the cycles that bring about moderation to more hospitable levels are millennia long. Clearly too long a time horizon for humans alive today to benefit directly. It is humans (and their economies) who are in danger.

Natural capital encompasses the EE consideration for biodiversity. Scale, sustainability, and diversity are inseparable, in both the social and natural contexts. Large-scale production implies less diversity—as economies of scale are achieved through uniformity. Diversity is directly related to sustainability. For example, we are seeing current economic forces pushing agriculture into uniform production—thousands of contiguous acres of the same crop (corn, soybeans, or wheat); and

[23] A typical oyster filters about 50 gallons of water per day, cleaning it of pollutants.

animals bred from a small genetic pool (so as to achieve the standardization helpful in processing). One prize bull, Toy Story, is reported to have sired 500,000 dairy cows.[24] Problems associated with such homogeneity are well-documented: diseases wipe out entire crops, flocks, or herds; crops and animals become increasingly vulnerable to failure; food supply becomes less secure. In 2010, an outbreak of salmonella at U.S. egg producing facilities sickened over 1000 people and led to the recall of more than 500 million eggs, including 170 million from just one Iowa supplier.[25] Eggs are produced in factory-like settings, where the emphasis on economies of scale outweighs concerns with negative consequences of that size. Likewise, fish kills and dead zones in the Chesapeake Bay and Gulf of Mexico are the result of extensive pollution of agricultural run-off from large-scale chicken and hog production. Diversity reduces risk and enhances sustainability even if it also reduces short-run production efficiency.

Put into practice, EE might promote, among other things, a transition to a more comprehensive measure of economic activity, something like the Green GDP or the Genuine Progress Indicator (GPI), discussed in Chapter 8. These alternatives to GDP consider a wide range of measures: market activity, social health, environmental conditions. The state of Maryland provides a workable example. It reports both state-level GDP and GPI. As the Maryland website explains, "GPI is designed to measure sustainable economic welfare rather than just economic activity. To accomplish this, the GPI uses three simple underlying principles for its methodology:

- account for income inequality
- include non-market benefits from the economy, environment, and society that are excluded from Gross Domestic Product (GDP) and
- identify and deduct costs such as environmental degradation, negative human health effects, and loss of leisure time."[26]

Such measures provide more comprehensive information than the simple accounting of market-based value-added provided by GDP. While not

[24] Blakemore (2015).

[25] CBS News (2010).

[26] State of Maryland (n.d.)

Table 5.1 Summary, differences between Ecological Economics and the neo-classical

	Ecological	*Neo-classical*
Goal of economic system	Creation of economic value within social and environmental limits	Maximum utility via consumption with no direct concern with limits
Key concepts	Social and natural capital; sustainability, capacity, scale, diversity	Efficiency; substitutability between physical capital and natural capital
Economic growth	Social and natural limits constrain sustainable economic activity—growth	Limits are seldom acknowledged—growth is good, "growth is god."

perfect by any stretch, they are steps in the right direction to a more comprehensive view of economic systems and their relationship to society and the natural environment.

Table 5.1 provides a summary of the differences between Ecological Economics and the Neo-classical paradigm. EE requires a rethinking of how economic systems are conceived and how economic activity is viewed. EE makes an explicit recognition of social and ecological limits, placing economic activity within very real boundaries of society and environment.

5.3 Concluding Comments

Examining alternate paradigms reminds us that economies are social constructs; that economic systems have developed over time, within and with certain historical, cultural, and geographic influences; that the discipline of economics is rife with disagreement—like any other; and that how we think about economic activity has important implications for society. An overarching theme in this regard is to question the underlying assumptions of what you know (or think you know), what you are taught, and what you see. Ultimately, each paradigm has something to offer.

References

Ayres RU (1996) Eco-thermodynamics: economics and the second law. INSEAD Working Paper

Bayer A, Rouse CE (2016) Diversity in the economics profession: a new attack on an old problem. J Econ Perspect 30(4):221–242
Blakemore E (2015) Toystory the bull fathered 500,000 cows before he died. Smithsonian Magazine. Available at: https://www.smithsonianmag.com/smart-news/bye-bye-bull-who-fathered-500000-cows-180953903/. Accessed on 29 August 2025
Brenan M (2020) Women still handle main household tasks in U.S. Available at: https://news.gallup.com/poll/283979/women-handle-main-household-tasks.aspx. Accessed on 2 July 2025
CBR Economics (2019) A climate of discrimination in economics. Available at: https://www.chicagobooth.edu/review/climate-discrimination-economics. Accessed on 2 July 2025
CBS News (2010) https://www.cbsnews.com/news/egg-recall-hits-550m-one-of-largest-in-history/
Costanza R (2010) What is ecological economics? Yale Insights. https://insights.som.yale.edu/insights/what-is-ecological-economics
Dolado JJ, Felgueroso F, Almunia M (2012) Are men and women-economists evenly distributed across research fields? Some new empirical evidence. SERIEs: J Span Econ Assoc 3:367–393
Economist, The (2019) The glass ceiling index. Available at: https://www.economist.com/graphic-detail/2019/03/08/the-glass-ceiling-index. Accessed on 2 July 2025
Genadek KR (2017) Unilateral divorce and time allocation in the United States. Fem Econ. https://doi.org/10.1080/13545701.2017.1390318
Goldin C (2019) Why are there so few women economists? Discussion with Alessandra Voena and Veronica Guerrieri. Available at: https://www.chicagobooth.edu/review/why-are-there-so-few-women-economists. Accessed on 2 July 2025
Hadsell L (2020) Not for want of trying: effort and success of women in principles of microeconomics. Int Rev Econ Educ 35
Hoff K, Pandey P (2006) Discrimination, social identity, and durable inequalities. Am Econ Rev 96(2):206–211
Jayachandran S, Daubenspeck J (2018) Gender differences in what development economists study. World Bank Development Impact Blog, March 20. https://blogs.worldbank.org/en/impactevaluations/gender-differences-what-development-economists-study
Nelson J (1995) Feminism and economics. J Econ Perspect 9(2):131–148
Scientific American (2012) Use it and lose it: the outsize effect of U.S. consumption on the environment. Available at: https://www.scientificamerican.com/article/american-consumption-habits/. Accessed on 2 July 2025
State of Maryland (n.d.) Genuine progress indicator. Available at: https://dnr.maryland.gov/mdgpi/pages/default.aspx. Accessed on 2 July 2025

United Nations Human Development Report (1995) Oxford University Press, New York

Wikipedia (n.d.) Feminist economics. Available at: https://en.wikipedia.org/wiki/Feminist_economics. Accessed on 2 July 2025

CHAPTER 6

Moral Foundations: Rights and Obligations in Markets

> Economics is a moral science.[1]

> The classical economists, going back to Adam Smith, conceived of economics as a branch of moral and political philosophy.[2]

The New York Times reported in April 2001 that pharmaceutical giant Glaxo-Smith-Kline (GSK) was selling Combivir, an AIDS treatment, for $7000 for an annual supply.[3] GSK had a patent on Combivir—giving it monopoly status and the ability to charge whatever it wanted, without fear of direct competition. Still, even with the high price, most patients who needed the drug in the U.S. could afford it, either through insurance or personal expenditures from income/wealth, so the price was not seen as an issue.[4] By 2001, nearly half a million people had died of AIDS in the U.S., but the annual number of deaths was declining (to 5000 in year

[1] Atkinson (2009).

[2] Sandel (2013).

[3] Petersen (2001).

[4] How quaint by today's standards that $7000 annually for a life-saving drug should seem "high."

L. Hadsell, *Social Economies*,
https://doi.org/10.1007/978-3-032-21916-9_6

2000, from a peak of nearly 42,000 deaths in 1995) in large part because of drugs like Combivir.[5]

The story was quite different in Africa, where about 25 million people had AIDS at the time and 3.5 million were dying each year. Combivir was too expensive for most Africans, where median income was less than $2 per day, about $700 per year. Cipla, a company based in India, seeing the dire, unmet need in Africa, reverse-engineered Combivir and began selling it in Africa for $350 per annual supply. This of course was a patent infringement by Cipla, which elicited a strong legal response from GSK. But public sentiment was not with GSK when the New York Times reported that Cipla could sell the drug for such a low price because the basic ingredients to make an annual supply of Combivir cost just $240. Thus, Cipla was selling the knock-off Combivir essentially at or just above cost (considering other expenses such as labor, packaging, and transportation).

The public's outcry was not that Cipla broke patent law but rather that GSK chose not to reduce its price for people in Africa—even though doing so would save many lives, as Cipla so clearly demonstrated. GSK argued that because of the high research and development expenditures spent creating the drug, they could not lower price below $800. GSK's principal consideration is profit, not surprisingly, and selling below cost is not good business, after all. Yet, Economics 101 tells us that R&D expenditures (paid years before) should not be part of pricing decisions today; they are sunk costs and as such cannot be recouped. Forget about it. Whether the R&D costs were $500 million or $50 is irrelevant. GSK would still have charged $7000 per year in the U.S. because that is what the market would bear. That is, $7000 was the profit-maximizing price based on current demand and current costs. And likewise, GSK could have matched Cipla's price in Africa. Similarly, Cipla's not having had to pay R&D costs is irrelevant to their pricing decision. They, like GSK, need

[5] U.S. Centers for Disease Control and Prevention (2001).

only, at minimum, to cover their current costs.[6] The big question is, what obligation did GSK have to people with AIDS?

We see similar questions raised regarding ancestry companies such as 23andme and Ancestry.com. These companies analyze DNA samples provided by customers who can then buy additional services, including genetic health markers. Suppose a woman sends DNA in and the sample indicates the presence of the BRCA1 or BRCA2 genetic mutation, indicating a greatly increased risk of breast and ovarian cancer. According to the National Cancer Institute, more than 60% of women who inherit a harmful change in BRCA1 or BRCA2 will develop breast cancer during their lifetime (compared to 13% without the mutation). If the company discovers the BRCA mutation from the sample provided, are they morally obligated to offer the additional information, even if the customer declines to buy it? Does it matter whether the person can afford to pay for the information?[7]

These examples raise several important questions concerning rights, obligations, responsibilities, and values, paralleling those asked by economist Amartya Sen more than a decade before the Combivir story broke:

- What rights does someone with a patent on a new drug that can save millions of lives have?
- Does this person (or company) have the right to set the price of this product at whatever level she/he/it wishes?
- Does this person/company have the right to withhold the product from market?

[6] R&D costs are relevant when calculating rate of profit, and all other current costs (fixed plus variable) are relevant when calculating the level of profit. Companies may want to maximize both—and this starts with maximizing profit, which Economics 101 tells us occurs at the quantity where additional revenue from sales equals additional costs of production. Price discrimination (charging a lower price in Africa while maintaining its higher price in the U.S.) was possible for GSK. In fact, if the additional revenues from sales in Africa exceed the additional costs of producing those units, such a practice increases profit. Price discrimination is a common business practice—think discounts for seniors and customer "loyalty" programs—precisely because it is good for business and consumer. The profit motive was clear, regardless of any moral responsibility one might argue GSK had; the mystery is why GSK was so reluctant to do sell its product in Africa.

[7] According to 23andme, 80% of people with a BRCA variant do not know they have one.

- What is the difference between the two previous? (E.g., if, in the extreme, the price can be set at such a price that no one can afford to buy it.)
- Are a potential buyer's rights abrogated if the patent holder does not sell to that person?[8]

In these examples, as in others, important considerations include income and wealth inequality, with both short-term and long-term ramifications. Ultimately the concerns boil down to one overarching: What rights and obligations bind market participants? Or, in a larger sense, how do we assess the moral nature of an economic system?

We should want to discuss the morality of markets because doing so allows us to explicitly recognize that economics is a normative science—that it cannot be separated from moral foundations. Some economists will protest, arguing that economists must resist the temptation, but the evidence is clear: neither economists nor anyone else is immune from social influences in the choices they make. Rather than pretending that moral considerations are absent from our decisions, we need to understand the moral bases for assumptions underlying our economic system. Furthermore, crossing disciplinary boundaries becomes so much more difficult without at least a brief discussion of ethical considerations, as related disciplines have similar concerns.[9]

A thought experiment will illustrate why this discussion is so important.[10] Consider an emergency room medical triage with 100 patients all waiting for a dose of antibiotic, which, suppose, they need to survive. Only 80 doses are available. Some patients will likely die if not given the antibiotic and some gravely ill patients will die even if given the dose. How would you decide who should get the medicine? This is a classic economic problem of allocating scarce resources. What criteria would you use when deciding? One response is to allocate the medicine to save the most lives. In this case, medical criteria—those most likely to benefit, medically—is paramount. But how is "benefit" defined. Is the number of additional years of life saved (prolonged) important? Maybe, so move younger patients closer to the front of the queue. What about someone

[8] Sen (1985).

[9] Wight (2009).

[10] Wight (2009).

in generally poor health? Move them to later... and so on. This is essentially how position on organ donation waiting lists (some of which have 100,000 names) is determined in the U.S.

An alternative to medical criteria is to sell the medicine to the highest bidder. Those who value the medicine the most will pay the most. In aggregate, benefit will be highest, at least when measured in dollars. This would be an economically efficient method, under the neo-classical paradigm, but would it be acceptable? An underlying assumption of this argument is that bidders are on equal footing, in terms of ability to express their value for the medicine. From a neo-classical economics perspective, this is a reasonable expectation (if you need more money, go get it!) and so the process is fair, accurately representing the value each participant places on saving their life. The ethical basis of neo-classical economics is utilitarianism, which argues that subjective value is what matters and those most willing to pay for something value it the most. I tend to doubt that many non-economists would favor a highest-bidder approach. And yet, the neo-classical approach is the dominant method in the U.S. to allocating scarce resources such health care, housing, and food—all necessary for existence and yet not available in markets to those who do not have the resources to pay for them. And it has been proposed as a solution to replace the current system of allocating human kidneys, as examined later. Thus, Sen's questions are applicable to a wide array of situations. Economic systems have an underlying ethical basis, no matter the exact nature of the economic system or the dominant paradigm guiding it. This fact cannot be avoided.

6.1 Morality of Markets: Three Approaches

Three major ethical approaches to addressing questions of economic rights and obligations are based on:

1. Consequences (teleology)—Utilitarian,
2. Duties/rules/rights (deontology)—Kantian,
3. Virtues—Virtue ethics.

The differences between these may not be in the outcome but in the rationale. For example,

> Suppose it is obvious that someone in need should be helped. A utilitarian will point to the fact that the consequences of doing so will maximize well-being, a deontologist to the fact that, in doing so the agent will be acting in accordance with a moral rule such as "Do unto others as you would be done by" and a virtue ethicist to the fact that helping the person would be charitable or benevolent.[11]

Utilitarian. Many economists will argue that economic systems should be based on consequentialist/utilitarian moral values: that the system's value is measured by results, in terms of consumer satisfaction and efficient use of resources.[12] Under this approach, the moral underpinnings of markets are usually evaluated by economists using the "social welfare theorem"—which focuses on outcomes: If the outcomes can be shown to be good then the mechanism is proved to be good. In other words, markets are moral if they produce good outcomes. How does one measure "goodness"? Utility was John Stuart Mill's answer: the measure of pleasure or pain resulting from an action. The aim of this philosophy, Utilitarianism, is summed up as the freedom that produces the greatest good for the greatest number. Quoting Mill from his *On Liberty*, "The only freedom which deserves the name is that of pursuing our own good in our own way, so long as we do not attempt to deprive others of theirs, or impede their efforts to obtain it." This raises one additional condition: that no one else is made worse off. In the lingo of economists: Pareto optimality. Utilitarianism is non-judgmental of values: noble or base, all that matters is utility. The easiest way to measure utility is in market settings, where the price one is willing to pay for something reflects the value placed on that object by the individual buyer.

Trade, and international trade in particular, offers an interesting example. Mainstream economists, who generally subscribe to the utilitarian approach, argue that if trade is voluntary, then those trades must be Pareto improving—that is, no one is made worse off. After all, no one would agree to something that makes them worse off. What is traded does not matter, only that both parties benefit. While some economists are concerned with power differentials and the potential for coercion leading to agreements that harm one party (as discussed elsewhere), overall, trade is seen as a bedrock of free markets. But consider trade between the

[11] Stanford Encyclopedia of Philosophy (2022).

[12] This section is based in part on Sen (1985).

U.S. and China. Here trades are not between individuals, but the same principle applies. The benefits of U.S. trade with China appear most obviously in the form of lower prices for U.S. consumers on a wide range of goods. But there are "costs," too—accruing to workers and their communities who lose their jobs as production shifts overseas. The costs are often concentrated in certain industries and geographic areas, with large local impacts on employment and wages in related businesses and the wider community, particularly in smaller cities and towns. Many, especially mainstream economists, argue that such trade is good because the aggregate benefits exceed the aggregate costs. But comparison of aggregate benefits and costs neglects the basic requirement that "no one else is made worse off." Mainstream economists deal with this contradiction by noting that the benefits *could* be distributed such that no one is worse off (i.e., workers losing their jobs could be compensated for such loss). But because this compensation is only partially made (in the form of unemployment benefits and retraining programs), the defense falls apart. All this simply illustrates the difficulty of applying ethical approaches in real-world settings.

We can further note that even if an outcome where no one is made worse off can be achieved it can still be highly objectionable. Consider an initial distribution of assets and abilities that leads to wide inequality, perhaps such that most wealth is controlled by a tiny fraction of the population which lives quite luxuriously, while the vast masses struggle to survive. Under the "no one else is made worse off" rule, forced redistribution of any kind is unacceptable: any taxes would make some, albeit a tiny fraction, worse off. Can we truly say such an outcome is just? Economist Amartya Sen, who won the Nobel prize for his work on distribution and justice, argues that such "indifference to inequality of well-being requires some justification." And if "inequality of well-being or of resources is of no moral concern... that position has to be made and defended."[13]

Kantian. An alternative ethical approach taken by some economists is deontological, as exemplified by Kant: certain things, such as freedom, are valued in and of themselves, and so a market's value derives because markets allow these rights to be operative. What matters is not the outcome, but the freedom to express one's choices. Under the deontological approach, "the moral necessity of having markets would follow from

[13] Sen (1985, pp. 90, 92).

the status of rights and not from the efficiency or optimality of market outcomes."[14] In other words, following this approach, the outcomes are irrelevant in evaluating the economic system. Good outcome or bad, either way must be acceptable because basic rights empowered by markets are themselves so important. The Kantian approach is fair but with no particular ends, with its emphasis on "the right prior to the good." According to this view, rights "protect individuals from policies, even democratically enacted ones, that would impose a preferred conception of the good and so fail to respect people's freedom to choose their own conceptions."[15] One constraint is that actions will be evaluated on whether their universal application leads to desirable outcomes.[16] What may be good if practiced in isolation may not necessarily be good if the action becomes widespread. Do unto others as you would have them do unto you. Thus, for instance, a seller misrepresenting a product's quality is acting unethically.

We can identify two forms of the Kantian view, libertarian and egalitarian. Libertarians argue that individuals have a right to their bodies and the fruits of their labor. They strongly favor markets and private property without redistribution through taxes. Using today's terminology in the U.S., followers of this approach would be staunch conservatives, libertarians, when applied in economic settings (as discussed in Ch. 3).[17] Minimum wage laws, licensing requirements (e.g., for doctors and lawyers, no less hairdressers), and price caps are all anathema to this view.

But having a right does not necessarily mean the right can be meaningfully exercised. In contrast with libertarian supporters, egalitarians argue that "the capacity of persons to pursue their own ends requires government to assure minimal prerequisites of a dignified life." Egalitarians support government policies to this end: You are free to spend your money as you see fit but if you have no money, or there is no food to buy then what good is the right? As Amartya Sen writes, after witnessing extensive starvation in his native India,

[14] Sen (1985, p. 85).

[15] Sen (1985).

[16] Boatright (1999).

[17] Though, originally, they were called liberals (now referred to as classical liberals).

> It is not irrelevant to ask the question: If ... starvation and famine were to occur, must the results of the market operations be taken as "acceptable," simply because they have followed from people legitimately exercising the rights they have? It is not easy to understand why rules of ownership, transfer, etc., should have such absolute priority over the life and death of millions of people.[18]

Accordingly, Sen proposes a conception in which markets are moral if they allow individuals to exercise rights and freedoms to reach satisfactory outcomes. "The value of the market ... is, then, consequential, derivative, and contingent. To understand that value we have to understand the more fundamental social values of well-being, freedom, and justice."[19]

Virtue. The third major ethical approach is virtue ethics, which asks what kind of person we want to be. In this approach, the morality of an action is determined by whether it would be followed by a moral person. Is lying wrong? By, for example, misrepresenting the quality of a product one is selling? For the virtue ethicist, that is not the right question. Rather, one needs to ask, do I want to be the kind of person who lies? This approach is perhaps the least helpful in that what constitutes a "moral person" is ambiguous. Without firmer rules, agreeing on an acceptable path is difficult (Table 6.1).

Table 6.1 Summary of three ethical approaches

Approach	*Principle/Emphasis*
Consequentialist/Utilitarian	Consequences of actions are what matter, not motivation "The greatest good for the greatest number."
Duties/rules/rights/Kantian	Freedom for its own sake. Two forms: Libertarian: freedom above all else; strong supporters of free markets Egalitarian: ability to express freedoms is paramount
Virtue ethics	What kind of person do I want to be?

[18] Sen (1985, p. 87).

[19] Sen (1985, p. 89).

6.2 Obligations in Practice

Obligations in market settings create certain expectations. Companies, for example, have many obligations, including treating customers and employees fairly, assuring that their products and services are safe and effective, and abiding by the law. Those affected by a company's actions have a right to expect these duties to be fulfilled. Obligations to be honest in dealings, tell the truth, and not attempt to gain advantage through deception are paramount for there to be trust among market participants. Markets cannot work without a substantial amount of trust based on honest interactions between strangers. And empirically, trust and economic growth go hand-in-hand.

Often obligations are not clear-cut. In dealing with others, does one have an obligation to divulge information valuable to another, when one knows that the other party does not know? Such information asymmetry is present in nearly all market transactions. Doctors know more than their patients, mechanics more than their customers, used car sellers more than potential buyers. The more knowledgeable party is not generally thought to be under moral obligation to disclose the information that the other could obtain on their own, with exceptions for certain professions and situations.[20] A doctor has a duty to inform a patient about their medical condition. A lawyer must disclose relevant information to their client or the court.[21] Other examples occur in home sales or product safety, where it is only when there is a duty to the other party that one is legally required to provide all information. Duty is present when "the other party believes that I am looking out for his interests, and I deceive if I do not do so. Failure to disclose is deceptive in this instance because the relationship of trust and dependence between the parties."[22]

One might expect that the sense of duty is stronger between friends (and for repeat interactions more generally) than between strangers. Jennifer Moore uses touring Vermont for antiques as an example:

> Suppose I come across an antique blanket chest in the barn of a farmer, a chest I know could bring $2500 back in the city. I offer to buy it for

[20] Boatright (1999).

[21] The differences between doctor and the DNA company noted earlier on the chapter are slight. In both cases, someone presents with a clear need for help.

[22] Moore (1994).

> $75, and the farmer agrees. If he had known how much I could get for it back home, he probably would have asked a higher price – but I failed to disclose this information. I have profited from the information advantage. Have I been unethical? My suspicion is that most people would say I have not. While knowing how much I could sell the chest for in the city is in the interest of the farmer, I am not morally obligated to reveal it. I am not morally obligated to tell those who deal with me everything that it would be in their best interest to know.[23]

Situations such this are common in many product and service markets, including, notably, finance and real estate. Consider the responsibility of the stockbroker to protect the interest of her/his client:

> What is the obligation of brokers, agents, or other salespersons in finance to protect the interests of those who buy financial products? Certainly, a broker, for example, should not exploit a naïve or inexperienced client, but does a broker have a strong positive obligation, like that of a physician or lawyer, to act solely for the benefit of others? The responsibility of a broker to protect may not extend this far, but neither is a broker merely a salesperson. A broker may not be a shepherd protecting a flock, but the broker's role is not merely to shear the sheep.[24]

In real estate markets, agents are ethically and legally obligated to inform potential buyers of material faults with a property, but only to the extent that the information could not be easily ascertained by the potential buyers. Self-interest may preclude a real estate agent from disclosing that the family next door is often loud and obnoxious if the potential buyers are not known to the agent, but it seems unlikely that the agent would not reveal this important information if the potential buyers are friends. Thus, relationships clearly matter in how we treat others, and how we in turn expect to be treated.

A great deal of trust is required in modern markets, where transactions tend to take place between strangers. We trust that others are behaving ethically. Empirical research clearly supports the view that the level of trust in society affects economic growth. Some economists go so far as to argue that "trust and trustworthiness appear as the keystone for successful

[23] Moore (1994, p. 116).

[24] Boatright (1999, p. 70).

economic development."[25] Chapter 15 explores the importance of trust in economic settings in more detail.

How would the Vermont antiquing scenario above be viewed by the three ethical perspectives? A utilitarian might argue that total well-being is maximized with the sale, even if the farmer did not know the antique chest's value in the city, as long as the farmer freely chose to sell it. If no harm was done, total well-being increases. (But if such deception becomes too widespread total well-being may decline.) The Kantian would have difficulty with the purchase. The buyer's omission of relevant information might be seen as deceptive, in which case the trade would not be fair and would be inconsistent with the idea of respect for others. Further, if such dealing became widespread, it might lead to a decline of trust—which would harm everyone. But the main Kantian criticism is that withholding information and gaining from that imbalance disrespects the seller. A virtue ethicist would likely view the opportunity as exploitative, showing excessive self-interest. Would a good person take advantage of another's ignorance? No.

What about obligations to future generations? Do we have a duty to the unborn? This question is central to the climate change threat, for instance. Are we, individually and as a society, duty bound to reduce carbon emissions, even beyond what might directly benefit us? Similarly, do we have a duty to honor obligations of previous generations? For example, when we talk of reparations for slavery. Surely obligation must work in both directions, or neither. Are we obligated to right past wrongs, especially if we have benefited (directly or even indirectly) from those wrongs? Consider the following scenario:

> Imagine that you found an original copy of Charles Darwin's "On the Origin of Species by Natural Selection" in a stack of books left to you by your aunt upon her death. You have the book appraised; it is valued at somewhere between $40,000 and $75,000. You also notice, however, that the book is embossed with the local public library's insignia and that a return slip inside the back cover indicates that it was borrowed from the local library by your aunt (and is 80 years overdue!). Clearly, the book belongs to the library. Do you keep the book and possibly sell it and keep the proceeds or do you return the book to the library, and hope that the overdue fines are waived?

[25] Algan and Cahuc (2010).

The scenario is based on actual events reported in the *Boston Globe* in summer 2001. Should the heirs return the book to the rightful owner, or sell it for a large profit? Returning the book is undoubtedly the ethically sound action (it is not yours, after all; the library's ownership is clear) while the self-interested, profit-maximizing action is to sell it for a personal profit. Once again, an ethical dilemma arises in the conflict between moral duty (and perhaps social acceptance) on the one hand and personal reward on the other. Complicating the question is the debate over whether it is the finder's responsibility to honor the promises of her forbearers. Do obligations (such as the aunt's long-ago promise to return the book) continue through generations? Does it matter how the book was obtained? How one answers this last question has implications far beyond this example.[26]

When I surveyed my undergraduate students (135 business majors; 53 non-business), almost 90% placed a premium on personal gain, replying that they would keep the Darwin book. This was two decades ago, before the current bright warning flashes of climate change and widespread discussion of such issues as reparations for society's past wrongs. I wonder if students have changed at all in how they see their responsibility in such scenarios. I suspect the forces of self-interest remain strong, despite the rhetoric often seen these days on U.S. campuses.

In the business world, a firm may be faced with deciding whether to honor prior commitments to fund retirement benefits for former workers. AT&T provides one example among many. In January 2021, it drastically reduced life insurance and death benefits for many of its 220,000 retirees.[27] Those retirees argue that the company has reneged on its promises. AT&T maintains the cuts are necessary for AT&T to stay competitive in the current economic environment. Other companies, including former segments of AT&T, have similarly reduced promised retirement benefits, including health care.[28] Each is an example of the tensions between current competitive pressures and commitment to past promises. Whether a prior commitment is sustained certainly is influenced by market forces (driven by the profit motive) and social constraints

[26] Consider Jewish assets taken by Nazis, including real estate and artwork. Or consider the distribution of wealth—does how that wealth was obtained matter when considering inequality?

[27] Francis and FitzGerald (2021).

[28] Schultz (2004).

(bound by the relative strength of the relationships being considered). We may even wonder whether markets are able to honor such commitments, given that doing so has a cost, and in a competitive environment, firms with higher costs may be driven out of business.

6.3 Concluding Comments

This is only a short overview of the many issues that arise when discussing rights and obligations in markets. Moral assessments of markets challenge our conceptions of economic systems themselves and have practical implications for how we behave and expect others to behave in market settings. Sometimes government is needed to ensure acceptable behavior. Government policy may take the form of consumer protection laws and provision of certain goods and services (such as basic education and health care). Moral questions are central to economic systems of whatever variety, as seen in detail in the next chapter, though economics can offer no definitive answer. The best it can do is be part of the conversation and help frame the discussion.

References

Algan Y, Cahuc P (2010) Inherited trust and growth. Am Econ Rev 100(5):2060–2092

Atkinson AB (2009) Economics as a moral science. Economica 76(S1):791–804

Boatright JR (1999) Ethics in finance. Blackwell Publishers, Malden, MA

Francis T, FitzGerald D (2021) AT&T slashed promised life insurance for former workers—and time runs out at year-end. Wall Str J. Available at: https://www.wsj.com/articles/at-t-slashed-promised-life-insurance-for-former-workersand-time-runs-out-at-year-end-11640544022. Accessed on 2 July 2025

Moore J (1994) What is really unethical about insider trading. In: Prindl AR, Prodhan B (eds) The ACT guide to ethical conflicts in finance. Blackwell Publishers, Cambridge, MA, p 117

Petersen M (2001) Lifting the curtain on the real costs of making AIDS drugs. New York Times, 24 April, pp C1, C10

Sandel MJ (2013) Market reasoning as moral reasoning Why economists should re-engage with political philosophy. J Econ Perspect 27(4):121–140

Schultz E (2004) Companies sue union retirees to cut promised health benefits. Wall Str J, p A1. Available at: https://pnhp.org/news/companies-sue-union-retirees-to-cut-promised-health-benefits/. Accessed on 2 July 2025

Sen A (1985) Well-being, agency and freedom. Reprinted in Clarkson MBE (ed) (1998) The corporation and its stakeholders. University of Toronto Press, Toronto, pp 87–94

Stanford Encyclopedia of Philosophy (2022) Ethics: virtue ethics. Available at: https://plato.stanford.edu/entries/ethics-virtue. Accessed on 2 July 2025

U.S. Centers for Disease Control and Prevention (2001) HIV and AIDS—United States, 1981–2000. Morb Mortal Wkly Rep 50(21):430–434

Wight JB (2009) Moral reasoning in economics. In: Colander D, McGoldrick K (eds) Educating economists. Edward Elgar, Cheltenham, pp 53–58

CHAPTER 7

Everything for Sale: New Markets

> There is nothing so hard to discover in the past as that which has subsequently become familiar.[1]

> The more markets extend their reach into non-economic aspects of life, the more entangled they become with moral questions.[2]

Each year about 4000 people die in the U.S. because they are unable to get a kidney transplant. There are simply too many people waiting for one (about 90,000), given the number of donations (just 25,000) made through the United Network of Organ Sharing (UNOS), a not-for-profit that oversees the waiting list for those who are not able to otherwise obtain a kidney.[3] To the typical economist, these deaths are easily averted by converting the current system of donation to a market in which those who need a kidney can buy one from others who want to sell one.[4] We each have two kidneys but need only one to live, so it's even possible to

[1] Joyce Appleby (1984).

[2] Michael Sandel (2013).

[3] UNOS numbers are for 2023.

[4] And in fact, many economists have said so. Nobel recipient Alvin Roth supported such a market. Even if some might find it repugnant (as he discusses), he argues the benefits outweigh the costs.

L. Hadsell, *Social Economies*,
https://doi.org/10.1007/978-3-032-21916-9_7

sell one kidney while living. And promising to offer for sale one's kidneys after death will provide money for one's family in much the same way that life insurance does, or sale of the deceased's unwanted assets. With a market in place, the number of people dying each year from lack of a functioning kidney will, in a very short time, fall to near zero as the supply of available kidneys rapidly increases to meet the demand. But is creating a market for human kidneys a good idea?

While this example is quickly becoming obsolete, with recent reports of the successful transplantation of a pig kidney into a human and laboratories growing human body parts from stem cells, it still provides a clear illustration of the potential benefits and pitfalls of adoption of market principles long advocated by many economists.[5] Markets are typically promoted as the best option for organizing economic activity. The advantages of markets are well-known: competition tends to drive down prices, increase quality, encourage innovation, and provide the goods and services that are most wanted. There is no doubt that creating a market for kidneys will entice a great many people to offer one of their own for sale. And in the process, those who desperately need a kidney will benefit from the opportunity to buy one. As Adam Smith noted more than two centuries ago, it is not out of the goodness in the hearts of the baker and the butcher that bread and meat are on your dinner table. The current system of organ donation, relying on the goodness in the hearts of all of us, is falling tragically short of meeting the needs of so many on the UNOS waiting list. But how far should market principles extend? Should we put a price—a dollar value—on human kidneys? What are the implications of doing so? Are there disadvantages, costs if you will, to using markets? Is there any downside? They must exist—they always do.

The potential pitfalls of opening new areas to market forces deserve a great deal of attention, as market principles are applied to more and more areas of life. In some ways, this discussion is a continuation of the previous chapter's focus on moral foundations of markets. Harvard ethicist Michael Sandel argues that market decisions cannot be separated from moral decisions. For many economists, though, delineation between "normative" and "positive" economics ("normative" is associated with value judgments while "positive" is without such judgment) is a hallmark of the modern economic science, which contends that economists need to

[5] Dockser Marcus (2024).

be free of value judgments if they are to offer expert advice. Others have criticized the primacy of positive analysis as mistaken: simply suggesting markets as a solution, as with the shortage of kidneys, involves value judgment. Choosing one method over others results from an ordering of desired outcomes, for example valuing efficiency or fairness or some other goal—an application of values.

Economists tend to value market efficiency above all else. In the case of a kidney market, that efficiency has a very real practical measure: saved lives. Nevertheless, valid concerns arise. This chapter further examines the applications of market principles to new areas, past and present, asking, among the many questions, is anything lost when markets are created in new areas?

7.1 Extension of Market Principles

Lest we think that a market for kidneys is so "out there" as to not be realistic consider that Iran currently operates such a market (more on that later). Similarly-out-there applications of market principles have recently formed in the U.S., including[6]:

- The Booth School of Business at the University of Chicago uses a market to allocate scarce seats to students in its MBA classes. The price of a seat in any particular section of a class being offered is determined by how much students are willing to pay in competitive bidding. As a result, seats in popular classes cost more.
- For $82 per night, a prisoner can upgrade to a better jail cell in Santa Ana, California.
- For $800,000, foreigners can obtain a green card, and hence permanent residency in the U.S., if the money is invested in a business that also creates at least 10 jobs (the EB-5 program).[7]

Other examples include markets that are now common that were once non-existent:

[6] These examples are from Sandel (2013).

[7] President Trump recently (2025) proposed a "Gold Card" program whereby wealthy foreigners can fast-track U.S. residency by paying $1 million directly to the U.S. Treasury,

- Fertility markets where eggs, sperm, and surrogate motherhood are traded.
- Life insurance. In the early 1800s life insurance was seen as gambling, and a morbid one at that, since the payoff was tied to the death of an individual. Now life insurance is viewed as an obligation of any responsible breadwinner, affording financial protection and safety for loved ones.
- Tradeable pollution permits, allowing one the right to pollute, for a price. These were seen as controversial in the late 1980s but now are widely accepted. Carbon emission trading is a prominent example: to off-set the environmental cost of carbon emissions associated with my airplane flight on British Air from Boston to London, I can purchase a carbon emission permit by adding its cost to my ticket price, with the airline buying a carbon emissions permit on my behalf. The seller of the permit agrees to reduce their carbon emissions by an amount equal to my addition.[8]

Consider markets that do not currently exist and would have to overcome strong opposition before being implemented, such as a market that pays parents who give up their child for adoption; or a market in which votes can legally be bought or sold. In such schemes, people who most want the child or the vote will compensate those who want it less. Both buyer and seller are better off. Far-fetched, of course; no one is proposing either, at least directly, but the questions are the same as for all the other potential markets, including those new markets listed earlier: why not allow it? One reason Sandel points to is that extending markets to some areas "erodes certain moral and civic goods worth caring about."[9] That is, non-market values that we care about—sanctity of human life, civic virtue, democracy—are eroded in the process of achieving gains attributable to greater efficiency. Sandel argues that we "need a public debate about where markets serve the public good and where they don't belong."[10]

To flesh out your beliefs, consider a hypothetical based on procreation rights.[11] Suppose we, as a society, want to limit population growth (as

[8] Otley (2022).

[9] Sandel (2013).

[10] Sandel (2013).

[11] As discussed in detail by Sandel (2013).

China wanted in the 1980s). Which policy would be least objectionable: a fixed quota that limits each couple to one child and fines those who exceed the limit, or a market-based system that issues each couple a tradable procreation voucher entitling the bearer to have one child? The first is a rule that applies to everyone equally, rich and poor, employed and unemployed, those seeking to have children and those who are not. The second option is more economically efficient, in the sense that anyone who wants a child, whether they are rich or poor, or it's their first or fifth, can express that desire by purchasing a permit, and those who value that additional child the most will pay the most for the permit, allowing them to have the child. Those not wanting to have children are able to sell permits. One objection to this approach is that some people who may desire another child may not have the money to express that desire by purchasing a permit. They will be denied what many of us consider a human right: to pro-create. Another is that some may feel financial pressure to sell their procreation rights (to pay rent or medical bills, for example), even though they do not want to. Further consideration may identify fear that such a market might evolve over time to one in which children themselves can be bought or sold. The procreation permits are, after all, rights to have a child. This last potential, as unlikely as it may seem to us today, reflects the evolution of markets for bodily fluids, eggs, and sperm over the last half century. (Dozens of egg and sperm banks operate across the U.S. today and nearly 500 fertility clinics reportedly account for nearly 100,000 births in 2021 alone.[12]) It also leads to another central concern: that such markets erode certain non-market values. Do we really want to place a dollar value on such things? Should such a market be allowed?

To examine the implications of extension of market principles to new areas, in the remainder of this chapter I want to expand some of the details of a market for kidneys, to see it from a mainstream economist's point of view and its critics, before turning to another market that has evolved over time.

[12] U.S. Donor Conceived Council (2023).

7.2 A Market for Kidneys

The current system of allocating kidneys, run by the non-governmental entity UNOS, uses a set of medical criteria to decide where patients are placed on its waiting list. A young non-smoker with advanced kidney disease but no other health problems will be placed higher on the list than a young person with worse overall health or a much older person with less advanced kidney disease. Use of medical criteria seems fair. Individuals could instead be placed higher or lower on the list based on a first-come, first-served basis, regardless of medical condition. But that doesn't seem quite right. Alternatively, patients could gain access to a donated kidney by lottery. But that doesn't seem quite fair, either. After all, degree of medical need is important. Someone who is close to death without a kidney should be near the front of the line, all other things being equal. Shouldn't they? No doubt other methods exist—just as they do for any "product." And as is the case for any product, some methods seem more appropriate than others.

Under the current system, UNOS essentially determines the chances an individual will get a kidney. Because UNOS acts as a centralized decision-making authority, economists would label it command-and-control, in the same category as socialism, the opposite of free markets. UNOS is an interesting, and not uncommon, example of how command-and-control organization is not the exclusive domain of government.[13] Command-and-control, whether for individual products or economy-wide, relies on a centralized decision-making authority to decide what is produced and how. Markets are quite the opposite, relying on individuals to decide what to sell or buy, using price as a signal to guide those decisions. Markets are often favored by economists because of the view that individuals have a better idea of their own needs than a centralized authority. The ultimate problem with the current system run by UNOS is that it provides weak incentives for offering a kidney, which means that not enough kidneys are available to those on the waiting list. Because direct payment for a kidney is illegal in the U.S., UNOS must rely on goodwill—which overwhelmingly takes the form of pledges to donate after death. Creating a market

[13] Some see large corporations in a similar light—decisions within the organization are made at the top and then are passed down the chain of command. Families provide a clearer comparison: parents are the decision makers and providers while children are provided for without expectation of substantial contributions (as Marx would say, from each according to his ability, to each according to his needs).

in which price is allowed to signal a need for kidneys would steer many individuals to pursue their economic self-interest and sell a kidney.

The economist's answer to just about any shortage is to allow the price to rise. The implicit price for kidneys today is zero. Creating a market where people can sell a kidney at a price greater than zero, either while living or after death, with proceeds to benefit one's estate, will more than likely elicit enough kidneys so that nearly everyone needing one can get one. The benefits of a market for human kidneys are clear: far fewer deaths and a far shorter waiting list—which in turn means far fewer people on onerous and expensive dialysis treatment. We can illustrate the basics of such a market with simple supply and demand—perhaps too simple, but valid enough to get an idea of how the market might work. The current "supply" is 25,000 donated kidneys per year. "Demand" is represented by the 90,000 people on the waiting list. There is no "price" in the UNOS system, so the shortage is 65,000. As a result, about 4000 die each year waiting for a kidney because a kidney does not become available for them.

In the market alternative, the quantity supplied (offered for sale) by people like you and me would increase as the market price rises. The quantity increase probably would not be much at low prices, but as price rises to more substantial levels people will be tempted to offer a kidney for sale. This has been easy enough to demonstrate in my classes: I ask students to raise their hand when I get to a price at which they would be willing to sell a kidney. Prices below five to ten thousand dollars elicit few responses, but $25,000 and higher is a different story. (And note that college students are young and, on average, from middle- and upper-income households.) If you could sell a kidney and pay off your car loan or a student loan, wouldn't you?

On the demand side, we might readily expect that few of the 90,000 potential buyers drop out of the market as the price rises. Even at high prices, insurance or borrowing would likely cover all or most of the price. How much might that actual market price be? One estimate from a 2005 study is that the free-market price, reflecting interaction of suppliers and demanders, might be $60,000 per kidney, in today's dollars.[14] Expensive, yes, but only a bit more than the average for a new car. Surely a life saved is worth it.

[14] This covers just the cost of the kidney, not the operation itself.

A common criticism is that some people will not be able to afford a kidney in such a market. This problem could be addressed with wider insurance coverage, grants, or a guaranteed right to borrow (such as is done with student loans). It's easy to imagine that almost everyone who needs a kidney will get one. Still, markets without such provisions face the criticism that some individuals are at a disadvantage, particularly those with lower financial resources. It's the same in almost any market—education; health care; food; housing. All are essential to a good life. And all are allocated via markets—with substantial public assistance to ensure minimal access, though many argue this falls short. But this begs the question, are all the problems addressed if we ensure equal access? Economist Alvin Roth and ethicist Michael Sandel raise three primary concerns, broadly categorized as: (1) objectification/commodification, (2) slippery slope, and (3) coercion.[15]

1. Objectification/commodification

This first concern is that placing a price on something changes how we think about it, changes its meaning. In the case of kidneys, one might argue that placing a market value of $60,000 on each kidney might lead some people to view others in terms of the market value of their kidneys (or body parts more generally). Instead of saying "there goes Lester" as I walk down Main Street, people may say (or at least think), "there goes two kidneys – worth $120,000!" Further, the positive vibe associated with donating is replaced by something harsher—gain from a market transaction. Instead of saying, "he donated a kidney, what a good chap" they might remark on my market acumen as I drive by in my new sportscar—"He sold one of his kidneys to get that! Smart!"[16] In fact, substantial research shows that money can "crowd out" non-market values.

In one experiment, for instance, a day-care that was experiencing late pick-ups of children by their parents implemented a charge of $5 for every

[15] Roth (2007). Sandel (2013). Sandel also has published several interesting books related to the concerns addressed here. See, for example, his "What Money Can't Buy."

[16] This was a concern a few years back when the federal government started offering rebates for electric vehicle purchases. Before the rebate, the buyer's motive to contribute to saving the environment was clear. After (the fear was), this motive is not as clear—they did it for the environment, sure, but also the money.

five minutes the parent was late.[17] Instead of curtailing late pick-ups, late pick-ups increased. More parents were willing to pay for being late than were willing to endure the social stigma associated with the old system. The fine was seen as a fee and was less onerous to parents than the shame associated with making their child's teacher wait uncompensated when the parent was late. In another example, Swiss residents were asked if they would be willing to vote to accommodate a nuclear waste site in their community. Some were told that accepting the site would be patriotic, for the good of the country and their fellow citizens. Fifty-one percent said yes. Others were offered monetary compensation for accepting the waste site in their community, and the percentage accepting the offer declined, to 25%. The decline can be explained by crowd-out: with no monetary reward citizens' acceptance reflected public spirit, a willingness to sacrifice for the greater good.[18] This civic duty was crowded out, however, when the monetary offer was made, changing the arrangement to a primarily pecuniary one.

The relationship between monetary incentives and non-market values is often nuanced. When labor-effort is being considered, economists Uri Gneezy and Aldo Rustichini suggest "Pay Enough or Don't Pay at All."[19] That is, given that money crowds out non-monetary values, money meant to elicit effort must be enough to off-set that loss. They write,

> In our experiments [of paying people to perform certain tasks] we find that whenever money is offered, a larger amount yields a higher performance. It is not true, however, that offering money always induces a higher performance: participants who were offered a small payoff gave a worse performance than those who were offered no compensation at all. These results suggest that the behavior of participants is influenced by their perception of the contract that is offered to them. When the contract offers money, the environment is perceived as monetary, and participants respond in a qualitatively different way in monetary and non-monetary environments.

Other studies show similar results in a multitude of settings. There are some things money can't buy. Sandel provides the example of friendship

[17] Gneezy and Rustichini (2000a).

[18] Sandel (2013, p. 133).

[19] Gneezy and Rustichini (2000b).

"If I want more friends than I have, it clearly wouldn't work to buy some. A hired friend is not the same as the real thing. Somehow, the money that would buy the friendship dissolves the good I seek to acquire."[20]

Alvin Roth, who has long advocated markets such as the one described for kidneys, was awarded the Nobel Prize in Economics in 2012 for applying market principles to new areas such as matching medical school graduates with hospitals seeking resident physicians (on "Match Day" each March) and students with high schools in New York City. Each new market (and others he has helped develop) has improved the well-being of individuals involved. Yet, Roth recognizes potential objections may be a constraint on markets. He succinctly states that "[m]any people clearly regard monetary compensation for organ donation as something that transforms a good deed into a bad one." Thus, economists do generally acknowledge the problem—it seems fair to say they typically just view the costs of crowd-out to be less than the benefits from markets.

Concern with commodification sometimes has religious origins. Pope John Paul II, for example, warned that "any procedure which tends to commercialize human organs or to consider them as items of exchange or trade must be considered morally unacceptable, because to use the body as an 'object' is to violate the dignity of the human person."[21] Islamic law similarly considers humans to be "stewards of their bodies, with a strong emphasis on preserving life and avoiding harm."[22] Although "Islam encourages organ donation without financial gain as an act of charity," Iran, with an Islamic state government, is unique in that it operates a system that compensates donors through a government-run program. After registering and undergoing medical tests, matched donor and recipient agree on a price and a transplantation is performed "overseen by the Ministry of Health. The government covers transplant costs and provides donors with one year of medical coverage and potential military exemption."[23] For Jews, reflecting "the tremendous importance that

[20] Sandel (2013, p. 121).

[21] Quoted in Roth (2007, p. 45).

[22] This and the next quotation are from Alameer et al. (2024).

[23] Siraj (2022).

Jewish law gives to saving a life… donation of organs is a good thing, and that under some circumstances, it would be allowable to offer and accept compensation."[24] (Religious influence on economic behavior is discussed more in a later chapter.)

2. Slippery slope

If a market for kidneys is created, what about a market for other organs? After all, people die each year waiting for a donated liver, lung, or heart. If someone who desperately needs a lung transplant could buy one in an open market, then shouldn't they be allowed to? We commonly assume that if the trade is mutually agreed upon it must also be mutually beneficial—so everyone is better off. As noted earlier, markets already exist for blood plasma, ovum and sperm, surrogate pregnancy, and a host of other body parts and functions. These are markets that have emerged gradually over the last few decades, one after another.

If you're struggling to draw the line that separates allowable markets from those that go just too far, you are not alone. The slippery slope fear is that the line will continually move down the list of organs and body parts, with each new market serving as a prelude to subsequent markets. The logical destination may well be that all body parts are for sale—and ultimately the entire package, the human himself. Of course, most of us will think that buying and selling humans, even oneself, is repugnant, even if both parties agree. It certainly is a test of beliefs for freedom-loving libertarians. I have to concede, though, that not all of us think so. Consider the gruesome case of Armin Meiwes, a German computer repair technician. In 2001, Meiwes posted an online advertisement for "a well-built 18- to 25-year-old to be slaughtered and then consumed."[25] In the end, he settled for a 43-year-old engineer from Berlin, Bernd-Jürgen Armando Brandes. The two met, and Brandes agreed to be killed and eaten by Meiwes. A year later, after Meiwes placed another ad, police were alerted and discovered Brandes' remaining body parts in Meiwes' freezer. Perhaps this is too far down the slippery slope to be of concern. Still, the question remains, where do we draw the line between acceptable and not?

[24] Roth (2007).

[25] BBC News (2003).

3. Coercion

Coercion is hard to define precisely. To be coerced, we normally think that someone must be forced or threatened into action. We normally do not see markets as coercive. The assumption, quite reasonable for most markets, is that individuals decide freely whether to participate, what to pay, what to charge. But what about a market for kidneys? One argument with such markets is that some people will feel much more pressure than others to sell their kidney(s). I can't imagine Bill Gates would ever need \$60,000 (or whatever the market price is) so badly that he would sell one of his kidneys. But I can imagine a sale by a poor parent with two young children who has been unemployed for some time, without prospects of gaining employment soon. Or a recent college graduate who has crushing student debt (or a current college student unable to pay next semester's tuition). In fact, businesses offering to buy blood plasma are booming around college campuses, with \$50 to \$100 paid per "donation."

On an international scale, we might easily expect the typical pattern of trade to occur: individuals in poor countries would be sellers and those in rich countries would be buyers. As comfortable as some of us may feel about employing low-wage workers in foreign lands to supply our clothing and technology, most of us are less ready to accept the same with kidneys. But we may wonder why we should feel so comfortable in the arrangement for cheap clothing or technology. Conservative mainstream economists argue that Americans buying products and services provided by workers in low-wage economies is not only ethical but that stopping would be unethical. Boycotting those products and services would deprive those low-wage workers of their livelihood. This argument rests on the assumption that all actions are freely made, without coercion. Thus, a low-wage worker must be better off in their current employment than they would be in the next best alternative; otherwise, why would they do it? Working for \$2 a day may be a hard life but working for less is even worse. Some, though, consider such decisions as Hobson's choices—choosing the best among the alternatives, sure, but within an overly restrictive choice set. In other words, not much choice at all, which might be a good working definition of coercion.

What level of pressure or force is necessary to qualify as coercion? How can decisions in which the best option is chosen from those available be a coerced choice? We might argue that an opportunity to sell a kidney for more than one's normal annual income should be viewed as a positive option; that without that opportunity, the other option is by definition worse (otherwise they would choose it over selling a kidney). But to many there also seems to be something inherently unfair in the scenario where the rich do not feel tempted to partake while the poor see it as their best option. The asymmetric nature of the weight of the choices is at the heart of coercion. One person can safely ignore the option to sell while another can hardly say no. You may notice in this scenario elements of Marx's more general concern with coercion in capitalist markets (discussed in Chapter 4).

A report in the L.A. Times about the kidney market in Iran provides an example of coercive nature of kidney markets.[26] An Iranian says, "If I could sell my kidney, I could get out of debt. I would sell my liver too." The report continues:

> "Yes, people donate because they need money, but this is a reality all over the world," said Nasser Simforoosh, chairman of the urology and kidney transplantation department at the Shahid Labbafinejad Medical Center in north Tehran. "Instead of doing something illegal to cover their debts, like stealing or smuggling, they are saving a life first," he said. "This is not exploitation. The end result is good for the recipient and the donor."
> But some international transplant leaders point to … evidence that commercializing organ donations preys on the neediest people — the very thing that laws in the U.S. and elsewhere banning organ sales aim to prevent.
> "The donors are not better off in the end," said Gabriel Danovitch, director of the kidney transplant program at UCLA and a vocal opponent of organ sales. "When you are that hopeless, giving that person a lump of money while lowering their self-esteem at the same time doesn't help them. It's an act of desperation, not an act of love."

A common refrain of desperate sellers as depicted above is "what else can I do?" The alternative might be to have a house foreclosed on, credit damaged for years, or perhaps even a prison sentence (after stealing to obtain funds, say). If a family is involved, the pain would be especially pronounced.

In every market for essential goods or services, severe inequality tends to undermine the idea that transactions are fully voluntary. The question is about the extent of the pressure to buy or sell—is it too much?

[26] Bengali and Mostaghim (2017).

How viable are the alternatives? Consider food, shelter, medical care, and education. All are overwhelmingly distributed by markets in the U.S. and yet each is vital to realizing full participation in modern American life. There really is no viable alternative to professional medical care, and choosing not to earn a college degree is paramount to choosing a poorer, shorter life. Leaving essential goods to markets raises questions of coercion, just as it would in a new market such as one for kidneys.

One last note on a market for kidneys. Clearly, additional questions would arise if such a market were created. And the role of government oversight—regulation—would be hotly debated. Do participants, both sellers and buyers, need protection from unscrupulous traders, for example? Should participation be limited? For instance, to sellers who have two viable kidneys (for live sales), or to buyers who actually need the kidney to live (and not for, say, a macabre mantel piece). Will the market create incentives for illegal or immoral behavior—such as acquisition of kidneys through nefarious means? These questions are, of course, common to many markets and must be considered when weighing benefits and costs of the market mechanism.

7.3 A Market for Military Service

Now consider another type of market: one for soldiers. Is there anything wrong with mercenary armies? Mercenaries are soldiers who fight not out of allegiance but for financial rewards. In the American War for Independence, the British hired German soldiers, Hessians, to assist the English troops in their fight with the colonists. As was the usual case for mercenaries, Hessians fought with foreign armies as entire units, under their own flags, wearing their usual uniforms. Some may think this unusual, of a bygone time, but the arrangement is commonplace today. The U.S. employed mercenaries to assist in the wars in Iraq and Afghanistan. For every American soldier in those conflicts, there was at least one contractor. Though a small fraction (maybe 15%) of contractors had fighting roles (the rest performed supporting duties such as cooking and maintenance), at the height of these wars, contractors comprised over 50% of the U.S. force in Iraq and 70% in Afghanistan.[27] Of course, the "other side," including nations and terrorist groups, are doing the same. Employment

[27] McFate (2019).

of mercenaries implies a market for warriors, and the thing about markets is, the highest bidder wins, and the rest is of little consequence.

As with a market for kidneys, the employment of mercenaries raises larger questions, ones that illustrate several important points regarding market encroachment. Mercenaries may seem to represent an extreme, but it is in many ways a natural extension of market principles. What are the implications?

The U.S. first instituted a military draft during the Civil War. In July 1863, males were notified of their conscription into the Union army with one twist: conscripts were allowed to buy their way out of service by paying a fee directly to the government.[28] Many took advantage of the opportunity: John D. Rockefeller and future president Grover Cleveland avoided military duty by paying this fee. There was such an outcry, given its obvious bent toward the financially able, with riots across New York State, from Manhattan to Buffalo, that the scheme was changed in short order.[29] The revised plan was not much different, though: recruits now had the option of finding a replacement for their service (presumably by paying the replacement, instead of paying the government).

The system evolved over the next 100 years, but exceptions were still made such that certain privileged groups benefited: One could delay military conscription during the Vietnam war, for instance, by attending college. The military draft was abandoned in the U.S. in 1974, replaced with an "all volunteer" system. In other words, a labor market. Like any other employer, the U.S. armed services now competes for employees (or recruits, if you prefer). This competition involves pay and benefits, such as bonuses and college tuition payment after a certain length of service, just as any employment might.

Now consider each of the major concerns for new markets noted in the previous pages: commodification, slippery slope, and coercion, and whether non-market values are eroded when military "service" moves closer to "employment." The overarching danger to consider is that putting a price on military service, making it subject to market forces,

[28] Also exempt were men who were "mentally or physically impaired, the only son of a widow, the son of infirm parents, or a widower with dependent children." Meier (1994).

[29] In Manhattan, casualties totaled more than 2000, including 120 deaths. Riots elsewhere led to prisoner releases (for whites, not blacks) and destruction of Republican newspapers, among other actions.

changes the nature of the service and the relationship between the parties involved, in this case, between soldiers and the rest of us.

The example of the childcare centers discussed earlier is relevant. Parents' view of their relationship with caregivers changed after implementation of a late fee: rather than lateness being an inconvenience that is socially unacceptable it becomes a service that could be purchased. The nature of the relationship between soldiers and others is similarly affected when soldiers are hired in a market-based system, rather than conscripted, which applies to everyone. A duty to serve one's country becomes, at least in part, a chance to earn a living (for some; and is ignored by others). The latter crowds out the former, though clearly not entirely, as many military personnel have a strong commitment to serving their country, in a job that is dangerous and full of hardship. And this commitment is widely recognized among the public. Still, as duty and obligation become a choice with the formation of a market for military service, some taxpayers may be led to feel absolved of any additional responsibility beyond paying taxes and, perhaps, thanking servicemen and women for their service. Enlistees choose to join (i.e., be employed there) and they are compensated fairly; what else do we owe them? Furthering the distinction, military contractors working on behalf of the U.S. are treated differently in law and there tends not to be parades or special cemeteries for them, or holidays on their behalf. The differential treatment suggests that how we think of military personnel depends on their motives and how they are employed.[30]

How far should a market for soldiers go? Already, U.S. citizenship is not required. Should membership in U.S. society even be a criterion for serving? After all, many people in much poorer countries would likely be willing to work for the wages paid U.S. service members. Currently, military service offers a "faster track" to U.S. citizenship, with shorter residency requirements and waived application fees. America could easily staff its military with recruits if it applied the same principles to hiring soldiers as it applies to hiring software engineers, doctors, college professors, and laborers in agriculture and hospitality, for whom qualified

[30] We might also ask whether abolition of the draft changes the perception of military personnel of us, the non-military public—are we now employers rather than fellow citizens, separate rather than in the same boat?

applicants from outside the U.S. are more than welcome.[31] Should the military be any different?

Still, we do appreciate the sacrifice soldiers make. Special acknowledgment, discounts, parades, and so on are expressions of this appreciation. Use of the word service suggests something more than simple market activity—we tend not to describe the garbage man's, roofer's, or cashier's work as "service." Surely military employment is more than just another job. Yet will we reach the day when the appreciation ends? After all, we have no parades for laborers in our fields and restaurants.[32] Many contend that war became easier to wage after the draft ended—the voting public simply had less skin in the game.

The point is not that military personnel should be less respected because they serve in what economists would call a labor market, but rather that in the process of making military service into a market, other civic values are eroded. The benefits of shared sacrifice of the kind experienced by draftees who come from a wide swath of the American public is hard to quantify but is surely affected.[33] At the same time, conscription has its own problems. There is no perfect solution, only trade offs.

Consider also the slippery slope argument. Initially, in the very first draft, in 1863, every man was eligible but with a buyout clause, payable directly to the government. That shifted ever so slightly with expansion of the buyout such that the recruit could pay another person to take their place. Then buyouts in other forms replaced that, including college enrollment—essentially requiring the government to find a suitable replacement. Each of these buyouts is financially based, with little difference between them. Those who desire and can afford to avoid military service can do so; others, with lower financial means, cannot. The current system is simply a modified buyout, relying on markets in which

[31] Or at least were, before 2025.

[32] The argument that conscription in which members from all strata of society serve leads to greater social cohesion and that it limits politician's desire to send troops into battle is limited. After all, the U.S. had a draft following WWII until 1973, and still that era saw conflict in two major wars, albeit officially undeclared. Perhaps community cohesion was enhanced as soldiers came from all ranks (certainly much more so than today)... but how much was attributable to shared military service?

[33] Senators Bob Dole (R) and Daniel Inouye (D), and President G.H.W. Bush (R), all veterans for WWII, attributed cross-party compromise in the U.S. Senate in the 1970s and 1980s in part to their shared military experiences.

anyone can choose to work elsewhere and pay taxes rather than serve. In many respects, it is quite like the draft of 1863.

The real slippery slope problem is captured in Libertarian thought. A libertarian would likely support a market for military service as it provides a choice about whether to participate. In the libertarian thinking conscription is equivalent to forced labor, to slavery (as is taxation, as taxes are confiscation of the fruits of one's labor). One might refer to Daniel Webster's observation in 1814, "Where is it written in the Constitution … that you may take children from their parents, and parents from their children, and compel them to fight the battles of any war in which the folly or the wickedness of government may engage it?" Milton Friedman, a more recent icon of the conservative and libertarian movement, argued that patriotism was anathema to freedom. Ask not what your country can do for you nor what you can do for your country. Every man for himself. Friedman writes:

> In a much-quoted passage in his inaugural address, President Kennedy said, "Ask not what your country can do for you – ask what you can do for your country." Neither half of the statement expresses a relation between the citizen and his government that is worthy of the ideals of free men in a free society. The paternalistic "what your country can do for you" implies that government is the patron, the citizen the ward, a view that is at odds with the free man's belief in his own responsibility for his own destiny. The organismic, "what you can do for your country" implies the government is the master or the deity, the citizen, the servant or the votary.[34]

A libertarian who is also a baseball fan, might observe that under a market system, the great Willie Mays would not have had to miss the entire 1953 season, and Red Sox star Ted Williams the 1943–1945 seasons (and again in 1953) because of military service. Not only were Mays, Williams, Joe DiMaggio, and dozens of other players deprived of their freedom by conscription into military service, so were baseball fans deprived of watching them play.[35]

[34] Friedman (1962).

[35] When Mays retired in 1973 with 660 career home runs, he was within just a season or two of breaking Babe Ruth's record of 714. In essence, military service almost certainly deprived Mays of the all-time home run record. He hit 92 home runs in the two seasons after his service.

Even under a market system, many still wonder how free a choice of joining the military is. In other words, is there coercion to join under the "all volunteer" system? The evidence does not support this contention. Recruits are evenly spread across the income distribution, with as many coming from wealthy households as coming from the poorest, suggesting that joining the military was not based primarily on economic necessity.[36]

7.4 Concluding Comments

Despite the potential pitfalls, the encroachment of markets into heretofore unchartered areas continues. With each, we must consider more than simply "Will markets work?" and "Are markets more efficient?" in some narrow sense. Because markets can erode moral and civic values, we need a public debate about where markets belong, because they serve the public good, and where they don't belong, because they erode important non-market values.[37] The question is pertinent to proposed markets, but we can also ask these same questions of some existing markets; several examples have been provided in this chapter. Many more exist—Michael Sandel's book *What Money Can't Buy* is an excellent introduction.

Scarcity is at the foundation of economics. Markets are just one way of allocating scarce resources. The system to allocate kidneys run by UNOS can be thought of as a command-and-control or centralized approach, where medical concerns, not price, are the primary criteria used to decide who gets—and who gives—a kidney. At the other end of the spectrum is a market, which would rely on individual decisions, with the interplay between buyers and sellers determining who gets a kidney. In between are myriad other methods for dealing with this scarcity. Every solution—including markets—has plusses and minuses. Some methods are more appropriate than others in any given circumstance. Society needs to decide what is acceptable. The big question here is not just "How would a market work?" but also "Should markets be chosen?" We must consider the effect of markets on social relationships and non-market values. Economics can inform the debate by explicitly recognizing the pros and cons of all proposed solutions to each problem of scarcity.

[36] Council on Foreign Relations (2018).

[37] Sandel (2013, p. 121).

Scan this QR code to listen to Ethicist Michael Sandel discuss "Moral limits to markets."

CSPAN (2012).

References

Alameer RM, Alhammadi AA, Taha Y, Al Gouf T, Almaghrabi RS (2024) Dilemma of commercial organ transplant in the Middle East. BMC Medicine 22, Article 322. Available at: https://link.springer.com/content/pdf/10.1186/s12916-024-03547-0.pdf. Accessed on 2 July 2025

Appleby J (1984) Capitalism and a new social order: the republican vision of the 1790s. New York University Press, New York, p 5

BBC News (2003) German cannibal tells of fantasy. Available at: http://news.bbc.co.uk/2/hi/europe/3286721.stm. Accessed on 2 July 2025

Bengali S, Mostaghim R (2017) 'Kidney for sale': Iran has a legal market for the organs, but the system doesn't always work. LA Times

Council on Foreign Relations (2018) Demographics of the U.S. military. Available at: https://www.cfr.org/backgrounder/demographics-us-military. Accessed on 2 July 2025

CSPAN (2012) Book TV: after words with Michael Sandel. Available at: http://www.c-span.org/video/?304720-1/words-michael-sandel

Dockser Marcus A (2024) Woman near death gets a pig kidney. Wall Str J, 21 March. Available at: https://www.wsj.com/science/genetically-modified-pig-kidney-is-successfully-transplanted-into-living-patient-0aa098c2?msockid=21e2177eb81168e92415036db99e698f. Accessed on 2 July 2025

Friedman M (1962) Capitalism and freedom. University of Chicago Press, Chicago

Gneezy U, Rustichini A (2000a) A fine is a price. J Leg Stud 29(1):1–17. https://doi.org/10.1086/468061

Gneezy U, Rustichini A (2000b) Pay enough or don't pay at all. Q J Econ 115(3):791–810

McFate S (2019) Mercenaries and war: understanding private armies today. National Defense University Press, Washington, DC

Meier MT (1994) Civil war draft records: exemptions and enrollments. Prologue Magazine 26(4). Available at: https://www.archives.gov/publications/prologue/1994/winter/civil-war-draft-records.html. Accessed on 29 Aug 2025

Otley T (2022) British Airways offers new offsetting options for passengers. Business Traveller. Available at: https://www.businesstraveller.com/business-travel/2022/10/27/british-airways-offers-new-offsetting-options-for-passengers/. Accessed on 29 Aug 2025

Roth AE (2007) Repugnance as a constraint on markets. J Econ Perspect 21(3):37–58

Sandel MJ (2013) What money can't buy: the moral limits of markets. Farrar, Straus and Giroux, New York

Siraj S (2022) How a compensated kidney donation program facilitates the sale of human organs in a regulated market: the implications of Islam on organ donation and sale. Philos Ethics Humanit Med 17:10. https://doi.org/10.1186/s13010-022-00122-4

U.S. Donor Conceived Council (2023) 2022 Sperm Bank Data Survey. Available at: https://www.usdcc.org/wp-content/uploads/2023/04/Sperm-Bank-Survey_2022.pdf

PART II

Goals

CHAPTER 8

GDP, a Cautionary Note

For those of us who are blessed to live in a society where the average standard of living is far beyond anything our ancestors historically could have imagined, the question remains: Why should we, and why do we, care about rising incomes? Why does it matter that we keep our economy producing close to the existing frontier, and, moreover, work to expand the frontier over time?[1]

'I am almost ashamed,' said Sissy, with reluctance. 'But to-day, for instance, Mr. M'Choakumchild was explaining to us about... National Prosperity. And he said, Now, this schoolroom is a Nation. And in this nation, there are fifty millions of money. Isn't this a prosperous nation? Girl number twenty, isn't this a prosperous nation, and a'n't you in a thriving state?'
'What did you say?' asked Louisa.
'Miss Louisa, I said I didn't know. I thought I couldn't know whether it was a prosperous nation or not, and whether I was in a thriving state or not, unless I knew who had got the money, and whether any of it was mine. But that had nothing to do with it. It was not in the figures at all,' said Sissy, wiping her eyes.
'That was a great mistake of yours,' observed Louisa.[2]

[1] Friedman (2006).

[2] Charles Dickens, *Hard Times*.

L. Hadsell, *Social Economies*,
https://doi.org/10.1007/978-3-032-21916-9_8

What makes a life fulfilling and meaningful? Harvard researchers sought to answer just that question when they initiated a study of 238 college sophomores in 1938. Eight decades later the study continues, with more participants added over the years, including residents from Boston's inner-city and more than 1300 offspring of the original subjects. Their conclusion:

> Close relationships, more than money or fame, are what keep people happy throughout their lives... Those ties protect people from life's discontents, help to delay mental and physical decline, and are better predictors of long and happy lives than social class, IQ, or even genes.[3]

For anyone worried about their HDL and LDL, note that according to this study, satisfaction with one's relationships at age 50 is a better predictor of physical health than cholesterol levels. If you must eat cheese, do so with friends.

The Harvard study's conclusion that social ties are more important than money provides a key to placing economic systems in proper context. The purpose of economies is to provide material well-being, often measured in the aggregate by Gross Domestic Product (GDP), while enhancing physical, social, and environmental health. As the Harvard study illustrates, material well-being is but one part of a good life. Production and consumption are not ends but means to an end. While economics focuses on production and consumption, the goals of economic activity fall more broadly under the umbrella of quality of life. As such, economics has to be concerned with the interconnections between economic, social, and ecological realms. Economies cannot be deemed successful if we are maximizing production and consumption but are unhappy, unfulfilled, and socially isolated, as many appear to be. Economies cannot be successful if incidence of physical and mental illness are rising or if water and air quality are declining. Though widely used, GDP fails to capture important economic value and effects on society, as explained in this chapter. Fixating on GDP (or income, or profits), as many are wont to do, narrows the focus of what economies and those working within them should achieve to such an extent that, if we are not careful, the rest—and more important parts—of life are neglected. We need to continually

[3] Mineo (2017), Waldinger and Schulz (2022).

ask, what are the primary goals of economic activity, and how should we measure them? GDP provides a good starting point for this inquiry.

8.1 Why GDP Is Important And why it Is Not

Growing economies have brought unparalleled gains in material quality of life to billions of people worldwide over the past two centuries.[4] In just the last three decades, consistently large annual increases in economic activity, measured by GDP, have lifted an estimated 800 million people out of poverty in China alone, with similar though more modest gains in India. In developing economies, higher GDP leads to longer life spans and, arguably, an easier life. In developed economies, the typical work week is now less than 40 h, most homes have modern conveniences for completing household chores, and the average life span typically exceeds 80 years. It is easy to see why most countries around the world focus on achieving economic growth.

But the benefits of growth max out at some point, such that high-income countries see little benefit from increases in GDP in terms of measures that matter. For rich countries, there is no correlation at the national level between GDP or growth of GDP and life expectancy, life satisfaction, or physical and mental health—or a range of other measures. Further, benefits from greater economic activity are spread unevenly—as measured by income and wealth but also life span and social measures such as community engagement, and individual happiness. But even here, consider the complicated nature of happiness. Economist Richard Easterlin identified a "paradox" in the mid-1970s, since confirmed by others: though people with higher incomes tend to be happier at any point in time, higher incomes over time do not translate to greater happiness. So even though real incomes more than tripled in the U.S. in recent decades, we are no happier as a people.

Differences exist not only across countries but also within. In the U.S., GDP has doubled since 1980, but around 50% of income from that growth has gone to the top one percent of households, with nary any for the bottom 90%.[5] People at the top of the income distribution

[4] For 1900 to today, average annual growth rates of 2–3% for western economies compares to rates near zero between the years 0 and 1000 and 0.14% in the years 1000–1820.

[5] Hanauer (2020). See also, Mishel and Kandra (2020).

live between 10 and 15 years longer than people at the bottom. In fact, individuals at the very top of the income distribution have a 50% probability of living to age 90, while those at the very bottom have just a 20% chance.[6] Perhaps none of this is surprising: more income can buy more and better health care, food, and shelter, all promoting a longer life. Life is physically easier, more stable, and less stressful for those at the upper end of the income distribution than it is for those at the bottom. But as the Harvard study described at the beginning of the chapter indicates, money isn't everything. GDP has risen dramatically in recent decades, but economic and social problems are also rising. So we see that GDP may be a useful indicator for low-income developing economies but much less so for rich developed ones.

Economist Benjamin Friedman answered his question posed at the chapter opening ("Why should we, and why do we, care about rising incomes?") in 2006, by arguing that economic growth, if it were "broadly distributed," leads to (1) greater opportunity, (2) more tolerance (especially of minorities and immigrants), (3) greater generosity to the poor, and (4) stronger democratic institutions. The most recent four decades have not provided a great deal of support for his assertion. Perhaps it was never properly tested, as gains in national income in recent decades have not been broadly distributed. For many, opportunity seems to be contracting rather than expanding, tolerance is clearly receiving a society-wide backlash, the poorest of the poor—the homeless—are expanding in number, and democratic institutions are under immense pressure, to the point where many are questioning their ability to survive. In the end, Friedman recognizes these shortcomings and the role for public policy to promote the kind of growth that achieves the outcomes he lauded. What must also be emphasized is the role that society plays in promoting those policies.

Worldwide, we are witnessing some of the dramatic impacts of economic growth—both good and bad, and little of it is new, though details differ from prior iterations. Along with tremendous wealth creation and poverty alleviation, we see social discord, global environmental degradation, and political unrest. Each is closely tied to economic activity and the worsening economic conditions for many, even as GDP increases. In the U.S., worsening economic opportunities for the non-college educated

[6] Chetty et al. (2016).

appears to be associated with what economists Angus Deaton and Anne Case term "deaths of despair"—suicides, drug overdoses, and liver failure. Donald Trump was elected president in 2016 and again in 2024 in part the result of dissatisfaction with the unevenness of the benefits of a growing economy. What all this means is that we need to examine GDP as a focal measure of our economic system and GDP growth as a panacea. I begin with a quick look under the hood of the engine of growth.

8.2 GDP, Beyond the Headlines

In simple terms, gross domestic product is the value of goods and services produced in a given geographic area during a certain period of time. GDP often is stated in per capita (pc) terms, and adjusted for purchasing power, to facilitate comparison across time and place. When we make such comparisons, we see that *real* (i.e., inflation adjusted) per capita GDP in the U.S. has risen from $15,000 in 1950 to $70,000 by 2025. This implies that in the span of just a couple of generations we produce more than four times as much (both goods and services) today as our parents or grandparents did.[7] We're four times richer. And we observe that pc GDP in the U.S. is higher than in most other countries.

Table 8.1 shows, first, that material standard of living in the U.S. is the highest of large population countries, larger than in Germany, France, and the U.K.[8] And productivity—the value of what each worker produces on average each hour—is highest in the U.S., though only slightly. We also see that U.S. workers work more hours and people of working age in the U.S. are less likely to be in the work force.

We can get a sense of what makes a higher or lower pc GDP, and why GDP may grow or decline, by considering each of its building blocks: pc GDP will rise if any of the following occur:

[7] In 1950, many families had one car, no air conditioning, and shared bedrooms. Today, the norm includes multiple cars, central AC, and larger homes, in addition to more toys, gadgets, and household appliances. Add to this more medical and dental care, visits to spas and nail salons, entertainment, and so on.

[8] The U.S. has the largest economy in the world, larger than China and India, even though those countries each have several times larger population. U.S. pc GDP is six times China's and more than 20 times India's.

Table 8.1 Gross domestic product and related measures—select countries, 2022

Measure	*Denmark*	*U.S.*	*Germany*	*France*	*U.K.*
Material living standard (GDP per person)	$78,300	$77,200	$67,900	$57,900	$57,400
Population (millions)	6	340	84	66	68
Productivity (GDP per hour)	$106	$107	$106	$100	$104
Hours at work, annual (hours per worker)	1394	1804	1347	1501	1531
Workforce participation (workers per working-age pop)	84%	78%	84%	81%	82%

1. If workers become more productive (produce more per hour of work)
2. If workers work more hours
3. If a greater share of the working-age population is employed
4. If more of the population is of working age (generally, 15–64).[9]

GDP is higher in the U.S. in small part because U.S. workers are among the most productive in the world. A more significant contributor is the longer hours U.S. workers work compared to workers in most other developed economies (though Koreans and Japanese work more). Over the past 75 years, U.S. workers have essentially maintained their focus on work while residents of many other countries, especially in Western Europe, have reduced their time at work. Consequently, U.S. workers have gained more income (and more GDP) while Europeans have gained more time off (and a smaller increase in GDP).

[9] For the mathematically inclined:

$$\begin{aligned} \text{pc GDP} &= \text{GDP/POP} \\ &= \text{GDP/Workers} * \text{Workers/POP} \\ &= \text{GDP/Hours} * \text{Hours/Workers} * \text{Workers/POP} \\ &= \text{GDP/Hours} * \text{Hours/Workers} * \text{Workers/WAPOP} * \text{WAPOP/POP}, \end{aligned}$$

where Hours = total annual hours worked; Workers = total number employed; WAPOP = working-age population; POP = total population.

A further reason for high GDP growth post WWII is the massive shift of women from informal, unpaid work, to formal, paid markets, illustrating the impact of counting only formal market (paid) work in GDP. In 1950, about one-third of working-age women were in formal labor markets. By 2010 that number was more than 60%.[10] Consequently, a significant portion of annual increases in GDP during that time was simply shifting of work from unpaid markets to paid markets. Examples include childcare, cleaning, and meal preparation—as each of these areas became more oriented to work-for-hire. The increased number of women moving from unpaid work to paid work in formal labor markets accounts for up to 25% of the growth of GDP since 1950.

The importance of the size of the working-age population (i.e., the age distribution) is highlighted in the Japanese economic slowdown since the 1990s—and foretells of the inevitable decline in GDP growth for many developed—and some developing—economies over the coming decades as their populations age (details in Chapter 17). Fewer workers mean lower GDP. One reason the U.S. economy is growing while the Japanese economy is stagnating is that the U.S. has robust immigration while Japan greatly restricts it. Japanese workers are productive and work many hours; there are simply fewer and fewer workers each year, as the average age climbs and no one replaces them, as birth rates sink. China will face a similar fate as their population has peaked and is expected to decline by 10% by 2050 and 50% by 2100. With limited immigration, productivity gains will have to exceed working-age population declines for the Chinese economy to continue to expand. Every economy with a declining population faces the same basic truth.

The bottom line is that, as with so many economic measures, there's often more to the story than the headline number. Disaggregating the components of GDP illustrates one reason to proceed with caution even when using GDP as a barometer of economic activity. Economic growth can be achieved through multiple means: increased productivity, increased hours worked (reduced leisure time), increased working-age population, and increased share of working-age population in formal markets. Additionally, GDP would get a jump-start by loosening regulations that otherwise increase producer costs such as those surrounding worker safety and pollution.

[10] For men, the corresponding figures are 86% to 72. Fullerton, Jr. (1999). Toossi and Morisi (2017).

8.3 Neglected Value

So, GDP hides a lot of information. It also neglects much. As noted, GDP, as a measure of market value, does not include non-market activity—things like volunteering but also eldercare and childcare. Thus, a parent who quits their job to stay home and care for elderly parents or children, rather than continuing to work and placing the parent or child in paid care, reduces GDP, as work shifts to outside of what is counted. Homecooked meals are not counted in GDP while restaurant meals are. Pay someone to mow your lawn and GDP rises. Mow your own and it's as if it didn't happen.

GDP also makes no account for how production and income are distributed, which is important as large economic inequality is associated with several negative economic and social outcomes (detailed in Chapter 14). Further, GDP provides incomplete accounting of the economic and social costs associated with economic activity. We see, for example, the number of beneficiaries of Social Security Disability Insurance tripling from 2.6 million in 1970 to 8.3 million in 2024, and suicides increasing 35% from 2000 to 2020.[11] While each of these measures have multiple origins, the strive for greater production and profit is arguably a contributor. As just one example, economist David Autor notes the detrimental effects of trade with China on men, including declining employment and wages, increased deaths from alcohol and drug abuse, and declines in marriage and childbearing.[12] At the same time, social fabric seems to be fraying in many western industrialized countries, with Brexit in the U.K., the rise of the far right in France, Germany, Poland, and elsewhere, and social and political polarization in the U.S. Macroeconomic indicators, such as GDP and the official unemployment rate, may be saying we're doing well, but many in our society beg to differ. According to a 2024 Pew Research poll, 36% of Americans think the country's economic conditions are poor and 41% view conditions as "only fair," in spite of near all-time low unemployment and strong GDP growth.[13] Clearly, respondents are considering more than the headline numbers, even if many policymakers (and some economists) are slow to grasp that point.

[11] U.S. Social Security Administration (n.d.), also, Garnett et al. (2022).

[12] Autor (2016). See also Case and Deaton (2020), for example.

[13] Pew Research Center (2024).

GDP also does not account for costs of environmental degradation, ranging from global climate change to pollutants such as plastics and "forever chemicals," found everywhere (including in our blood). Even improvements are not accounted for, such as the massive decline of several major pollutants from the mid-1970s, with lead and sulfur dioxide emissions down more than 90%; and yet, the regulations that make these possible are seen by many only as a drag on economic activity, lowering economic growth and GDP—as those environmental benefits are hidden behind the GDP headline number.

8.4 Alternative Measures

Much will be asked of any single statistic. The problem comes when that single statistic is misused, misread, misinterpreted, and overly relied on. GDP is not meant to be an all-inclusive measure of well-being, but it is often used that way. The problem is, we like simplicity. GDP is easy to calculate and understand. Still, the search for alternatives shifts the conversation about what's important. One option is to create a single statistic that replaces GDP. An alternative is to consider many measures and change the culture to look at all of them critically. Let's start with the first option.

The **Human Development Index** (HDI) considers life expectancy at birth, average years of schooling for adults aged 25 years, and per capita income. The Inequality-adjusted HDI (IHDI) also considers education, health, and the distribution of income. The HDI and IHDI diverge as inequality increases. HDI and IHDI for selected countries are shown in Table 8.2. The low ranking for the U.S. (20th HDI, 27th IHDI) reflects relatively low life expectancy and high inequality, partially offsetting high per capita income.

Both HDI and IHDI are subject to criticism. Each is a simple measure, capturing only a small part of human development. Like GDP, the HDI reflects data limitations and is restricted to easily measurable outcomes, thereby excluding some of the important aspects noted earlier. Ultimately, the value of such measures is not the particular score or the ranking, but the shift in focus to a more encompassing measure of the human welfare impacts of economic activity.

A similar though more expansive measure of well-being, the **Genuine Progress Indicator** (GPI), is tracked by more than a dozen U.S.

Table 8.2 Human Development Index—select countries

Measure	*Denmark*	*US*	*Germany*	*France*	*UK*
Living standard (GDP per person)	$78,300	$77,200	$67,900	$57,900	$57,400
HDI	95.2	92.7	95.0	91.0	94.0
(rank)	(5)	(20)	(7)	(28)	(15)
IHDI	89.8	82.3	88.1	82.0	86.5
(rank)	(3)	(27)	(9)	(28)	(12)
Life Expectancy at birth (years)	82	79	81	83	81

Note Not only do the Danes, Germans, French, and English work fewer hours (Table 8.1), they live longer and are generally healthier

states, including Vermont and Maryland. Published alongside traditionally used measures such as state GDP, this alternative accounts for income inequality and non-market benefits of the economy, environment, and society that are not included in GDP, plus environmental conditions, human health effects, and leisure time.[14]

The Table 8.3 from Maryland's website shows the major elements of GPI. Economists at the University of Vermont have calculated GPI for all fifty U.S. states. They place each state in one of four categories in a two-by-two matrix of high or low GPI and high or low state GDP. Cursory examination shows states with higher levels of government intervention in the economy (mandating certain labor and environmental regulations, for example) tend to score higher on GPI while states with less government intervention tend to score lower, though exceptions exist: Florida, consistently ranked among the freest from government intervention, scores high on GPI (as do Idaho and Arizona).

The **CORE score**, created by the American Academy of Arts & Sciences, is comprised of 11 measures in four categories, economic security, economic opportunity, health, and political voice.[15] After talking with hundreds of people across the U.S., members of the AAAS homed in on measures that they contend "focus on actual lives." Among the eleven measures are housing affordability, education level, healthcare coverage, life expectancy, and civic participation. Launched in 2023, the CORE score is designed with the goal to advance the "national focus from how

[14] Fox and Erickson (2018).

[15] American Academy of Arts & Sciences (2021). Hacker and Cohen (2024).

Table 8.3 Maryland GPI components

Economic	*Environmental*	*Social*
Household budget expenditures	Services from natural capital	Services from human capital
Defensive expenditures	Depletion of natural capital	Services from social capital
Household investments	Costs of pollution	Social costs of economic activity
Income inequality, public provisioning, services from physical capital		

the economy is doing to how Americans are doing." Scores are currently available at the U.S. county level beginning in 2005.

The **Happy Planet Index** (HPI) assumes that how satisfied one is with life is the best indicator of individual well-being. The HPI combines life satisfaction with lifespan and environmental health in a simple equation. Environmental health measures "whether the needs and demands of a community's activity is within or extends beyond the ability of nature to provide requisite products and services."[16] This should trigger memories of the discussion of ecological economics in Chapter 5. A similar measure, **Gross National Happiness** (GNH), is the country of Bhutan's official measure of well-being. Happiness and satisfaction with life are positively correlated with a wide range of socioeconomic variables including age, marital status, religious participation, income, economic freedom, and employment, and negatively with inflation and inequality.[17]

Consider the implications of focusing on happiness or well-being, given the recent period of high inflation in the U.S. The Federal Reserve raised interest rates significantly in 2023, trying to bring down inflation by slowing the economy. And slow the economy it did: borrowing money for costly things like buying a house became much more expensive, with median monthly payments rising 40%, from $1700 to $2500,

[16] Globally, environmental health (the Ecological Footprint) "indicates that humans are harvesting and depleting natural capital faster than earth's ability to regenerate products and assimilate pollution and waste."

[17] Di Tella and MacCulloch (2006). The most often used survey is the World Values Survey conducted every five years or so, gathering hundreds of thousands of responses from individuals across the globe. See Hadsell and Jones (2020).

for new home purchases solely due to higher mortgage rates.[18] The slowing economy eventually led to lower inflation. But as economic activity slowed, unemployment rose (slightly). The trick for the Fed was to balance the gain from lower inflation with the pain associated with additional unemployment. The key question is, how much pain is associated with inflation and how much with unemployment? Both are painful; both reduce happiness. Economist Rafael Di Tella and colleagues provide an answer, finding that a change in unemployment by one percentage point has a greater impact on happiness than the same one percentage point change in inflation. More specifically, unemployment carries about 70% more hit to happiness than does inflation.[19] Both are painful, but the pain caused by inflation and unemployment as measured by happiness is not felt equally.[20] Measures of happiness are proving to be an important part of our understanding of the success of economic actions, influencing individual choice and government policy.

8.5 Concluding Comments

Gross domestic product is a useful measure of economic activity. It is also quite limited in the information it can convey not just about the well-being of society but also the economy itself. GDP can vary over time or across countries for any number of reasons. Hidden behind the headlines are important details.

Alternatives and complementary measures attempt to account for some of GDP's shortcomings. This is necessary given that GDP and other measures of importance to us such as happiness (or satisfaction with life) and environmental health are often at odds. No better examples of the divergence between GDP and well-being exist than the harm from social

[18] For a $400,000 loan, the monthly payment on a 30-year mortgage at 3% is $1686. If the interest rate is 6.5% the payment is $2528.

[19] Part of the loss from a rise in the unemployment includes fear of unemployment (Di Tella et al. 2001).

[20] Di Tella et al. actually use "subjective well-being" rather than the term "happiness" or SWL. Though debated by academics, the terms are generally seen as interchangeable for our purposes. One implication Di Tella et al. draw for economic advisors and decision makers is that prior measures of the impact of inflation and unemployment, such as the well-known "misery index," which treats the effects of each as equal, is not an accurate representation of the data.

media and the dark side of big pharma seen in the opioid crisis still gripping this nation. On the former, we cite U.S. tech companies (the biggest seven of which have greater combined market value than the entire stocks exchanges of most other countries), including the purveyor of Facebook, which according to internal documents and employee testimony knowingly and actively peddles an addictive, harmful product tied directly to mental health decline, teen suicides, and social and political discord. With pharma, we note what economists Deaton and Case call deaths of despair, which continue to take nearly 100,000 lives annually. While alternatives to GDP have their own shortcomings, they at least move attention away from an arguably worse measure of how well the economy is serving society. This is a key concern, given that economics is about making lives better, holistically, not just in the narrow material sense.

We have been here before. In 1970, the U.S. Senate passed a bill establishing the Council of Social Advisors, to be housed in the Executive Office, as a complement to the Office of Management and Budget and the Council of Economic Advisors. The stated objective was to promote the national goal of an "opportunity to live in decency and dignity." The bill required the President to report annually on such areas as education, health, housing, alienation, political participation, personal security, and social mobility." According to its sponsor, Walter Mondale, it "would do far more than assure the publication of CSA findings and recommendations: It would guarantee such societal knowledge visibility of the sort that only presidential involvement can generate."[21] Alas, the bill did not make it through the House of Representatives and so never became law. Everything we have learned since reinforces the idea that such a change is needed, now more than ever.

References

American Academy of Arts & Sciences (2021) Core score: 2021. Available at: https://corescore.us/wellbeing-2021-usa/core_score/2021/00?demographic=geography-overall. Accessed on 2 July 2025

Autor DH, Dorn D, Hanson GH (2016) The China shock: learning from labor market adjustment to large changes in trade. Annu Rev Econ 8.205–240

Case A, Deaton A (2020) Deaths of despair and the future of capitalism. Princeton University Press, Princeton, NJ

[21] Mondale (1970).

Chetty R et al (2016) The Association between income and life expectancy in the United States, 2001–2014. JAMA. 2016 Apr 26;315(16):1750–1766. https://doi.org/10.1001/jama.2016.4226

Di Tella, R MacCulloch, R. J & Oswald, A. J (2001) Preferences over inflation and unemployment: Evidence from surveys of happiness. Amer Econ Rev 91(1):335–341

Di Tella R, MacCulloch R (2006) Some uses of happiness data in economics. J Econ Perspect 20(1):25–46

Fox MJ, Erickson JD (2018) Genuine economic progress in the United States: a fifty state study and comparative assessment. Ecol Econ 147:29–35

Friedman B (2006) Moral consequences of economic growth. Available at: https://scholar.harvard.edu/files/bfriedman/files/moral_consequences_of_economic_growth.pdf. Accessed on 2 July 2025

Fullerton Jr HN (1999) Labor force participation: 75 years of change, 1950–1998 and 1998–2025. Mon Lab Rev. December: 3–12

Garnett MF, Curtin SC, Stone DM (2022) Suicide mortality in the United States, 2000–2020. National Center for Health Statistics Data Brief No. 433, March. Available at: https://www.cdc.gov/nchs/products/databriefs/db433.htm#:~:text=Vital%20Statistics%20System-,For%20both%20males%20and%20females%2C%20suicide%20rates%20were%20lower%20in,2019%20and%205.5%20in%202020. Accessed on 29 Aug 2025

Hacker JS, Cohen JD (2024) GDP and the Dow are up but what about American well-being? Wall Str J, 27–28 April, p C4. Available at: https://www.wsj.com/economy/gdp-and-the-dow-are-up-but-what-about-american-well-being-87f90e6d?msockid=21e2177eb81168e92415036db99e698f. Accessed on 2 July 2025

Hadsell L, Jones AT (2020) The company you keep: satisfaction with life, economic freedom, and preference-policy mismatch. J Comp Econ 48(3):642–646

Hanauer N (2020) The top 1% of Americans have taken $50 trillion from the bottom 90%—and that's made the U.S. less secure. Time Magazine. Available at: https://time.com/5888024/50-trillion-income-inequality-america/. Accessed on 2 July 2025

Mineo L (2017) Good genes are nice, but joy is better. The Harvard Gazette. https://news.harvard.edu/gazette/story/2017/04/over-nearly-80-years-harvard-study-has-been-showing-how-to-live-a-healthy-and-happy-life/#:~:text=After%20following%20the%20surviving%20Crimson%20men%20for%20nearly%2080%20years

Mishel L, Kandra J (2020) Wages for the top 1% skyrocketed 160% since 1979 while the share of wages for the bottom 90% shrunk. Working Economics Blog. Available at: https://www.epi.org/blog/wages-for-the-top-1-skyrocketed-160-since-1979-while-the-share-of-wages-for-the-bottom-90-shrunk-time-to-remake-wage-pattern-with-economic-policies-that-generate-robust-wage-growth-for-vast-majority/. Accessed on 29 Aug 2025

Mondale WF (1970) Social advisers, social accounting, and the presidency. Law Contemp Probl 35(3):318–326. Available at: https://scholarship.law.duke.edu/cgi/viewcontent.cgi?article=3297&context=lcp. Accessed on 2 July 2025
Pew Research Center (2024) Views of the nation's economy: May 2024. Available at: https://www.pewresearch.org/politics/2024/05/23/views-of-the-nations-economy-may-2024/. Accessed on 2 July 2025
Toossi M, Morisi TL (2017) Women in the workforce before, during, and after the great recession. U.S. Bureau of Labor Statistics. Available at: https://www.bls.gov/spotlight/2017/women-in-the-workforce-before-during-and-after-the-great-recession/pdf/women-in-the-workforce-before-during-and-after-the-great-recession.pdf. Accessed on 29 Aug 2025
U.S. Social Security Administration (n.d.) Social security beneficiary statistics. https://www.ssa.gov/oact/STATS/OASDIbenies.html#:~:text=Table_title:%20Number%20of%20beneficiaries%20receiving%20benefits%20on,:%20|%20:%20|%20Disability%20Insurance:%20. Accessed on 29 Aug 2025
Waldinger R, Schulz M (2022) The good life: lessons from the world's longest scientific study of happiness. https://magazine.hms.harvard.edu/articles/good-life#:~:text=The%20Harvard%20Study%20of%20Adult%20Development%20began%20in,life%20marriage%20is%20linked%20with%20health%20and%20well-being

CHAPTER 9

For the Long-Haul: Sustainable Prosperity

If all mankind were to disappear, the world would regenerate back to the rich state of equilibrium that existed ten thousand years ago. If insects were to vanish, the environment would collapse into chaos.[1]

Now all that was left 'neath the bad smelling-sky
was my big empty factory...
the Lorax...
and I[2]

Big Mike was in trouble.[3] Big trouble. Under attack from a tropical fungal disease, he finally succumbed, wiped out. Fortunately, Big Mike's cousin, Cavendish, was ready to step in. Good news for banana lovers. You see, Big Mike, formally known as *Gros Michels*, was the world's best-selling banana at the time, and because it was sold so widely, its demise could have meant a potassium deficiency for many. Though the fungal disease eventually decimated Big Mike, scientists were able to breed another variety that grew just as well, Cavendish, even if it did taste a bit

[1] E. O. Wilson

[2] Dr. Seuss.

[3] Brown (2024).

L. Hadsell, *Social Economies*,
https://doi.org/10.1007/978-3-032-21916-9_9

different. Big Mike's demise, and Cavendish's ascendency, was 75 years ago, but history is repeating itself. Today, Cavendish is in trouble, also under attack from a fungus. This is particularly problematic because 99% of all bananas sold worldwide are Cavendish, and all Cavendish are clones, meaning that once one is infected it's only a matter of time before they all are. Worldwide production is threatened. Cavendish is expected to bite the dust by the end of this decade. But don't despair, a replacement is in the works, though this too will likely taste a bit different.

Meanwhile, prices for coffee, wine, and olive oil are rising, up 60% (2020 to 2024) for coffee, 80% for wine, and more than 500% for olive oil.[4] In each case, the primary culprit is monoculture combined with climate change, as crops concentrated in only one or two regions are particularly vulnerable to rising temperatures, unusually heavy rains and drought. The harm will fall on consumers, for sure, and growers and their communities, as production necessarily shifts to other areas. Southern England and Sweden already are becoming new homes for wine production that used to occur in France. Sacré bleu!

Monoculture—large-scale cultivation of a single crop—is the basis for much of modern agriculture, particularly in the U.S. You can see the result of monoculture in every aisle of the typical American grocery store—both in the abundance of food and low prices when times are good and the bare shelves and high prices when they are not, as, for example, during recalls, following severe weather, or during supply-chain interruptions such as during the 2020 pandemic and its aftermath.

That simple walk through the grocery store illustrates the risk-return trade-off spoken of so much in finance: in the long run, your investment grows faster the more risk you take—think tech stocks versus government bonds—but the more risk you take the greater the chances you'll go bust before ever reaching the long run. In terms of monoculture, greater yields and lower prices for consumers are the rewards that can be achieved by planting hundreds of acres of a single, identical crop or raising hundreds of thousands of a single, identical animal such as pigs or chickens in small spaces. But doing so comes with increased risk in the form of potential shortages due to weather, rapid transmission of disease, and trade wars.

That kind of trade-off is evident throughout the modern economy, including at the individual level. Nearly everyone engages in a similar

[4] Jon Emont (2024).

risk choice when choosing employment paths, for instance. We as individuals typically make the decision not to be a Jack-of-all-trades. We learn very specific skills in college or trade school, expecting improved chances of employment and higher pay in return. Specialization, touted since Adam Smith's time as the key to economic progress, is synonymous with increased returns—but also increased risk. For individuals, the risk is that your skill becomes obsolete, or that you lose employment possibilities when your employer moves production elsewhere.

Concentration, large-scale production (aka economies of scale), and specialization are key features of modern economies. And with them come tremendous benefits as well as potential harms extending well beyond shortages of bananas and rising prices for coffee and olive oil. It is these concerns—and the interconnection of the economic, ecological, and social environments—that is central to understanding the goal of sustainable prosperity.

9.1 Sustainable Prosperity

Sustainable prosperity looks to the long run, recognizing the capacity limitations of the ecological and social worlds in which economic activity takes place. Society places constraints on economic activity with norms and customs, family demands, and the like. The Environment has limited natural resources to offer as inputs into the production process and limited ability to absorb waste from that production, pollution ranging from agricultural run-off to carbon emissions. Rather than focusing on quarterly gross domestic product and ever-expanding production, sustainable prosperity pays attention to long-run economic, ecological, and social health, not for altruistic reasons but because a healthy society and a healthy environment are crucial to a healthy economy. As such, economic growth, and the resulting material well-being, without regard to how that growth is achieved, cannot be a goal. It is not sustainable. Sooner or later the ability of the environment to provide resources and absorb waste from economic activity, its carrying capacity, will be overwhelmed—and that support structure will be lost.

Accordingly, sustainable prosperity has three dimensions:

- Economic: measured by quality of material well-being rather than quantity. So the measure must be more than GDP. The economic focus is on development (creating better) rather than expansion or growth (creating more).

- Social: measured by social capital (participation in civic life: memberships, voting, etc.), health, distribution of income and wealth, opportunity, fairness, and the like.
- Ecological: measured by the amount of natural capital, which includes measures of diversity and amount of flora and fauna, including natural resources ranging from minerals used in the production of cell phones and electric vehicles, to marshes and estuaries that provide food and protection, to the filtering services provided by air, water, and soil.[5]

Each dimension can promote or subtract from the others. Rising incomes can lead to increased leisure time and less physically demanding lives. But economic activity can also come at the expense of social well-being, as we are currently seeing with the pervasive negative outcomes associated with "social media," whose effects on teen mental health and social discord are well-documented.[6] An economy benefits from strong social and political institutions, and a culture that is trusting, honest, and supportive of the rule of law. But markets can sometimes erode or crowd out the "non-market values" that support those institutions and culture (as described in Chapter 7). We also see environmental costs such as those imposed by intensive agriculture and expanding population. On the other hand, cover crops and trees provide valuable carbon sequestration, enhancing future environmental quality and human activity and supporting economic activity.

Concerns about GDP as the focus of attention extends beyond those enumerated in the previous chapter, as suggested in the above scenarios. Economist Herman Daly writes of the Treachery of Quantified Success Indicators, noting that what is being measured often changes behavior—a generalized Heisenberg principle. By paying so much attention to GDP we—voters, politicians, economists—become very good at increasing that

[5] Many natural resources provide more than one service: An oyster is not only delicious but also can filter up to 50 gallons of water daily, providing an example of a valuable eco-system service, important not only for environmental health but economic activity.

[6] The saddest part is that these negative effects are not unintended consequences but the result of intentional choice by social media companies. See, for example, whistleblower Frances Haugen's recent testimony before Congress, and Wynn-Williams (2025).

measure, often to the detriment of other important aspects of life. Too much emphasis on material well-being and too little regard for environmental and social well-being is detrimental not only to the environment and society, but the economy as well.[7]

A commitment to sustainable prosperity recognizes that economic growth over the past century-plus has greatly improved the lives of billions of people. It also recognizes that eight billion people and many of the economic processes they are engaged in are placing heavy strains on the ability of societies and earth to support it. The fishing industry provides a prime example. Fishing became a much larger-scale enterprise beginning in the 1950s, as large trawlers with refrigerated storage, towing miles-long nets replaced smaller boats. One consequence of the massive increase in scale was a 90% worldwide decline of predatory fish populations—such as tuna, marlin, swordfish, and sharks. Not that all fish declined by 90%, but that biomass of these top-level predators has fallen to 10% of 1950s levels.[8] The harm of overfishing is threatening world seafood supplies, and the loss of marine biodiversity is increasingly impairing the ocean's capacity to maintain water quality.

Overfishing is an example of "tragedy of the commons," which occurs when a natural resource (fish in the ocean, ground water, or clean air, for example) are freely available to anyone to use or take without cost. We are seeing similar outcomes in the southwestern U.S. states where overuse of water resources, especially groundwater for agricultural uses, is drying up those water deposits, leading to shortages and rising costs for farmers and others.

We also see massive declines in insect, bee, and bird populations—who are valuable not only in and of themselves but also for the ecological and economic value they provide, such as pollination essential for food production. Insects, for example, pollinate 85% of food and flowers, in addition to facilitating plant and animal decomposition and seed

[7] A Wall Street Journal editorial (January 7, 2025) provides a prime example of overreliance on GDP: it compares GDP per capita in the U.S. and Canada, concluding that Canadians are falling behind Americans because their growth rate was lower. No word on why it's lower, except to their "tax-and-spend policies" and "assault on oil and gas production." The former provides benefits to recipients ranging from national health care to defense. The latter, limits on production of oil and gas, address the urgent issues of climate change and air and water pollution.

[8] Worm et al. (2006, 2007).

dispersal.[9] Evolutionary biologist Jans Habel places a large part of the blame for these declines on agricultural intensification, that very same monoculture illustrated earlier, noting the accompanying habitat loss and use of fertilizers and harmful pesticides. Rapid climate change has exacerbated the problem.[10]

Interconnectedness of economy and environment can further be seen in how rapid climate change, substantially facilitated by human economic activity, is leading to large and sustained increases in home insurance rates across the U.S., where personal line insurers experienced losses of nearly $50 billion in 2022 and 2023.[11] More than 1 in 25 home insurance policies were not renewed in 2023 in counties along the southeastern and southern U.S. and in much of California.[12] (This was before the devastating fires in Los Angeles in January 2025, which will surely raise the rate of nonrenewal.) Rates for continuing coverage are rising drastically, by more than 40%, from 2018 to 2023, in many states, including California, Colorado, Texas, and Florida.[13] Note that at the most basic economic level, if consumers are paying more for insurance, then they have less money for other goods and services—and hence, a lower material well-being.

9.2 The Social Fabric

Among the take-aways from the 2024 election in the U.S. is that a strong economy measured by traditional metrics is not a substitute for strong social fabric. Though GDP growth was relatively robust (exceeding that of most other developed economies) and unemployment near all-time lows, the incumbent party lost the White House. Polls showed that many

[9] Zattara and Aizen (2021).

[10] Habel et al. (2019). The U.S. and Canada have seen a staggering decline in the number of birds over the last five decades: some 3 billion in all, including more than half of all grassland birds. A "net loss approaching 3 billion birds, or 29% of 1970 abundance.... declines are not restricted to rare and threatened species—those once considered common and wide-spread are also diminished... [with] implications for ecosystem integrity." Similar declines have been documented for butterflies, beetles, and bees in North America and Europe. Rosenberg et al. (2019).

[11] Libatique (2024).

[12] Rojanasakul and Flavelle (2024).

[13] Trapasso (2024).

voters felt something was wrong. The economy was not working for many people; both the economy and society were going in the wrong direction. Inflation had been high and so purchasing power was eroded, that was part of it. But inflation had greatly subsided by 2024, and average wages were again rising faster than prices. Part of the problem may well have been poor information and understanding, as some (including many economists) argued, but other factors surely played a part: many believed that economic opportunities were not being fairly distributed, largely because of international trade and immigration, leading to declining trust in each other and in economic and political institutions. In short, a decline of social cohesion.

Sociologist Robert Putnam has chronicled the decline of participation in civic life: memberships, voting, etc., since the 1980s, in academic journals and popular books such as *Bowling Alone*; *Our Kids*; and *The Upswing*. Economists Anne Case and Angus Deaton identify globalization and automation as a large part of the underlying causes of what is now referred to as "deaths of despair"—deaths from drug overdose, suicides, and alcohol abuse, which began taking nearly 100,000 American lives per year in the 2000s (extending through 2024, the time of this writing). They argue that the effects of globalization are worse in the U.S. than most other nations "because of America's unique history of race, its limited welfare provision, and its absurdly expensive health care system."[14]

Employment disruptions attributed to international trade are documented by economists such as David Autor, who estimates the U.S. job loss due to trade with China at around two million.[15] Trade may increase efficiency and national income—standard economic theory of comparative advantage strongly supports this claim—but job loss and the reduction in employment opportunities has costs as well, costs which reverberate throughout a community when jobs move elsewhere: diners and retailers also go out of business, school funding is reduced, employment opportunities dry up. In short, international trade is not without its own costs—to the economic and social fabric, which have value just as do the economic benefits of cheaper goods.

[14] Case and Deaton (2020, p. 214).

[15] See reference in Case and Deaton (2020, p. 219).

An important element of a healthy society and economy is a healthy political system. The recent populist movements seen in many developed countries reflect a tension between capitalism and democracy. While some, such as Milton Friedman, contend that democracy and capitalism go hand-in-hand and are mutually supportive, economic historian Trevor Jackson has argued that free-market capitalism and liberal democracy are contradictory, as they

> proceed from entirely different premises. Democracy is predicated on formal, substantive equality: one person, one vote. Capitalism is not, and is incompatible with substantive equality, because it is composed of workers and owners, success and failure, rich and poor. Capitalism is about self-interest and private gain; democracy is about public interest and civic responsibility.... Capitalism is predicated on atomized individuals, democracy on shared publics.[16]

There is no better example of the harm that pure self-interest can inflict on society than social media. Former Google and Facebook employee turned whistle blower Frances Haugen shared her first-hand knowledge of how tech companies encourage conflict as a way to increase click traffic, leading to higher profits. Comity is dull and dull doesn't sell. But does discord harm? Concurrent with the widespread adoption of these new technologies and the algorithms that guide them was a rise in teen suicides and depression. According to the CDC, the suicide rate among people aged 10–24 remained stable from 2001 through 2007 and then increased 62% from 2007 through 2021.[17] (The iPhone was introduced in 2007.) Overall suicide rates have increased 37% between 2000 and 2018.[18] The link between social media use and mental health problems is now clearly documented. The kicker is that it appears to be the direct result of decisions companies made in their drive for profit. Similar discord is being seen in our political system. It is ironic that companies that depend on stable economic and political systems are shaking the foundations of those institutions in their pursuit of profit.

[16] Jackson (2025, pp. 32–35).

[17] Curtin and Garnett (2023).

[18] Centers for Disease Control and Prevention (2025).

Society imposes limits just as the environment does. Sustainable economic systems require well-functioning institutions—family, community, political, and economic—and a supportive culture of trust, honesty, and cooperation to facilitate impersonal transactions. Corrosive practices that erode these institutions may increase economic growth in the short run but are not sustainable in the long run. The importance of various social institutions is detailed in Part 3 of this book.

9.3 Quality over Quantity

The catalog of how economic activity may negatively affect the environment and society is much longer than what is cited here. The good news is that positive effects are present as well. To reiterate, economic activity has many benefits—and so, we want a well-functioning economic system, one that provides material comfort. It is equally clear that economic activity occurs within natural and social constraints; natural resources are not unlimited, and society both affects and is affected by economic activity. The goal of sustainable prosperity is to enjoy the material benefits of economic activity without producing the widespread harm that reduces long-run viability of the economy—and environment and society.

Sustainable prosperity is development within the ability of natural resources and society to accommodate economic activity, where development may mean qualitative improvement, in contrast with the simple quantitative increase in GDP.[19] This view implies a maximum level of economic activity and a steady-state economy once that level is reached—that is, an economy with "growth" defined by increases in well-being without increases in GDP. The steady-state economy preserves a certain level of economic activity, and more importantly, quality of material well-being, while enhancing social capital and using no more than the long-term available natural resources.

An economy measured by qualitative development is much harder to define than one based on GDP. GDP is, after all, simply quantity produced times price per unit. Qualitative development means better goods and services, production and consumption that enriches lives and leads to a more equally distributed well-being. Excessive pesticide use

[19] Some economists refer to "sustainable development" (Daly 1997).

leading to mass extinction of bees would not qualify, even if those pesticides greatly increase crop yields. Neither would the growth of social media companies whose services foment social discord.

Though others will have their own list, sustainable prosperity has, to me, three key elements:

- Qualitative development;
- Diversification—business, ecological, social;
- Shorter supply chains.

All with the aim of maintaining economic, environmental, and social capital. The amount of available ecological and social capital will determine how much economic systems can grow, as these are the limits that contain the system. Thus, the scale of an economy must match the scale supported by ecological and social systems.

Key 1: Qualitative Development

Development rather than growth implies an optimal scale and preservation rather than expansion, as ever-increasing GDP assumes endless resources and unlimited capacity to absorb waste. Development is about respecting those limits in the short term so that economic well-being can be continued long term. Like everything else in life, economic growth has an opportunity cost. The maxim "there is no free lunch" applies as equally to production and consumption as it does to individual choice.

In such a no-growth, or steady-state, economy, technology is developed, resources are used more efficiently, ills of society such as poverty and homelessness are addressed, social capital is enhanced. Such a shift from our current growth-oriented mindset would require refocus of effort and skills and a change of thinking more than any redistribution through government action. Health care provides an example. The U.S. healthcare system is easily the most expensive among developed economies and yet provides well-below average health outcomes. Better health and an improved, more efficient health care system might very well mean a lower short-term GDP—less need for treatments, even as equity increases and people become healthier. Elsewhere, in agriculture, improvement without expansion can be achieved—and currently is—with practices that rely more on nature to control weeds and pests, reduce soil erosion, and increase yields. One method gaining renewed interest is no-till farming which replaces the common practice of tilling the top foot of soil before planting. No-till reduces soil erosion and pesticide use—and the accompanying run-off that is so detrimental to water systems, improving long-term productivity with no short-term harm to crop yields. Switching to no-till methods is a major reason for a substantial decline in soil erosion in recent decades.[20] Social media provides another prime example: with social media companies, economic value is created at the expense of social capital. The negative impacts in the long run—to social and political institutions—may far outweigh its illusionary short-term value measured by profits.

Even economic efficiency has opportunity costs. A concrete example comes from research on secondary education. Economic efficiency, defined as minimum cost per student (and consequent minimum taxes), suggests that high schools should be very large (say, 1000 students). Some studies by education researchers and economists suggest that learning is maximized in smaller schools (say, 500 students). Which goal is pursued? Either way, there's a cost to doing so, either in forgone learning or higher dollar expenditures. In other cases efficiency may mean faster production—perhaps coming at the expense of workers' health and safety. Efficiency may mean innovation, change which can come at a cost measured by negative psychological impacts as individuals adjust to new technology. The key is to pursue efficiency improvements that enhance social and environmental health.

Traditional economic growth relies on using more resources to produce more goods, a quantitative increase—an ever-expanding consumption of natural and social capital. Economic sustainability is less about expansion and more about improvement, increases in quality without increasing use of natural/social capital. A sustainable economy can persist forever within the ecological and social environment, as resource use is within nature's and society's regenerative capabilities. A traditional economy cannot.

Key 2: Diversification

Benefits of diversification are present in several areas. Diversified agricultural practices, such as planting multiple crops and raising genetically

[20] Huggins and Reganold (2008).

diverse animals, provide improved biodiversity and can help control pests and weeds and conserve water, without limiting crop yields or profitability.[21] Diversification can benefit individual businesses as it also benefits the environment. Its opposite, monoculture, has dangers illustrated by the examples opening the chapter.

Economists have long appreciated the value of diversification when building stable local and regional economies. Small local economies, where a large fraction of the population is employed by just one or a few large businesses, face increased dependence on the health of those businesses, and tilts bargaining power to the employer, away from employees and government. What this means in practice is that workers tend to be paid less, and municipalities tend to have more difficulty funding services such as schools. Research suggests that wages are lower and property tax rates are higher in rural areas with some large businesses (e.g., Amazon warehouses, Wal-Mart) than similar areas without those businesses. As the largest employer in town, they have "monopsony power"—the ability to set wages below levels that would occur in more competitive environments with more employers competing for workers. Workers also face the risk of disruption caused by a massive employer leaving town. When the main employer in my small town in rural upstate New York decided to move production in year 2000, 500 people were suddenly without jobs—in a town of 10,000 people. The economic fallout extended to other businesses, who relied on those employees' spending, and local government, including schools, that relied on the tax revenue generated not only directly from the large employer but from all the related businesses and the associated individuals, as declines in income, spending, and property values rippled through the economy.

When local economies are beholden to large businesses, government can become hostage in a "too big to tax" scenario. Consider Amazon and Seattle. In 2017, the Seattle city council proposed an employee-hours tax on businesses grossing at least $20 million per year, designed to fund programs to deal with homelessness, a burgeoning problem. Amazon's protests and threats to relocate led to the city council rescinding the planned tax. Although more than 500 companies would have been subject to the tax, Amazon was the largest employer in the city—with about

[21] Rosa-Schleich et al. (2019), Eder et al. (2024).

45,000 Seattle workers.[22] And although Amazon was and is highly profitable, it (unlike the hundreds of other, smaller companies) was able to exercise its clout and avoid the tax. In smaller towns and cities, businesses are similarly able to push for reduced tax burdens simply because of the leverage that comes from their size, threatening to leave or simply engage in expensive litigation. Research shows that regional economies that are diversified, with many employers in multiple industries have more stable employment, income, and tax revenues.[23]

Social interaction is another area in which diversity is important. Benefits range from a reduction in prejudice to increased innovation and greater social and economic mobility (explored in Chapter 19).

Rather than hinder economic development and social growth, diversity can enhance them. None of this can be surprising to anyone familiar with basic investment advice: portfolio diversification is a foundational idea in finance, as it allows for substantial long term returns while at the same time reducing risk. That is exactly the point here.

Key 3: Shorter Supply Chains

Sustainability advocates seek to meet social and environmental responsibility goals by shortening distance between supplier and customer, while also maintaining economic viability. While longer distance (think production of iPhones in Asia) often leads to lower cost of production, it also leads to less control over employment and environmental practices. Longer distance increases transportation costs, as well, contributing to environmental pollution. The magnitude of the problem increases dramatically when the societies involved operate under starkly different

[22] See Day and Beekman (2018).

[23] In a rare instance of such refusal to "go along," residents of Queens, New York, protested the proposed expansion of Amazon offices into their New York City borough in 2019, despite the 25,000 promised jobs and projected economic impact, because the government's $3 billion support for the project was seen as too generous (especially for a company that regularly earns tens of billions of profit each year) and because of fears that the expansion would mean rising cost of living. Amazon was seeking to expand outside of its homebase in Seattle, Washington, in large part because of recent public policies in that city (related to wages and cost of living). As reported in the New York Times, "when the Seattle City Council proposed taxing large employers to pay for homeless services and affordable housing, Amazon took a rare public stance and threatened to halt its expansion. In the end, the city retreated and got rid of even a pared back version of the tax it had adopted." The very definition of "too big to tax."

social and legal frameworks, such as with employment and environmental standards in many Asian countries compared to the U.S. The "race to the bottom" fear is that higher standards in the U.S., where we limit child labor, regulate workplace safety, limit daily and weekly work hours, and regulate pollutants will be weakened when competition is opened to places where similar restrictions do not apply.[24] As such, even if standards in the U.S. are not reduced directly, we benefit from the lower standards of our trading partners, even beyond lower prices: the U.S. has, for example, essentially offshored some of the carbon producing industries to China and elsewhere, reducing the U.S.' official carbon footprint through sleight of hand. Of course, carbon reduction in such a way is a pyrrhic victory as greenhouse gases are global.

Consumers care about price, quality, and, often, how those products are made. Producers care about costs of production and, ultimately, profit. In a sustainable economy, each also cares about social and environmental impacts of their choices. Many consumers want to know more about where and how their goods are produced, given increasing concern with lower labor and environmental standards outside the U.S. and Europe. Even production within the U.S. is a concern, as evidenced by the many consumers who are moving to locally sourced goods, especially food and drink. Many companies want to source their products in social and environmentally acceptable ways, if for no other reason than because not doing so can negatively affect profit when there's a public backlash resulting from the revelation of unacceptable practices by a supplier.[25] Companies do not have to be do-gooders to be concerned with social and environmental practices of their suppliers. While long-supply chains can be highly profitable in the short run, what is often neglected in this equation are the external costs, which may take years to appear.

An additional aspect that is hidden until it becomes a problem appeared during and after the 2020 pandemic. One of the lessons of that time is that reliance on far-off suppliers carries tremendous risks of shortages. Pandemic-related shortages from single-source overseas suppliers caused production delays and led to price increases for a wide range of products. These risks were not unknown and were not new: As one of

[24] The counter argument is that standards in the other country will be raised, as incomes rise. And we do see that in China, for example.

[25] Villena and Gioia (2020).

many examples, consider the shortages in 2011 of paint pigment used by major automakers, including Chrysler, Toyota, General Motors, and Ford, which resulted from the Fukushima nuclear accident in Japan. The paint factory near the nuclear power station was the only factory in the world producing that paint—and it was destroyed. Or consider Apple, which reported in 2021 that it lost $6 billion in sales due to a shortage of chips manufactured in Asia. On the horizon, we see potential shortages involving electric vehicles as China controls production of a vast majority of many metals and other parts for those systems. The 2021 CHIPS Act sought to secure for the U.S. supply of information, communication, and semiconductor technologies by promoting domestic production. Relying on other countries, especially adversaries, for key products puts the U.S. economy at serious risk.

Clearly, some products cannot be produced locally—growing tropical fruit in Michigan would be uneconomical and not environmentally friendly. Long-distance trade has its place. An emphasis on short supply lines, local production, is not all or nothing. Rather it's a recognition of the real potential costs of a long-distance producer consumer relationship.

9.4 Concluding Comments

We have discussed two conceptions of economic activity: one that is unbounded and another that has limits. How long can economic growth continue under the former? Clearly, in a world of finite environmental resources, unbounded growth is impossible. Economic Prosperity is so much more than growth. Dr. Seuss' story of The Lorax is a cautionary tale of the consequences of ecological destruction. As the story suggests, bigger is not always better and more is not always a gain. Rising social and political conflict represents a further danger. A shift to sustainable development requires awareness and buy-in, along with appropriate public policy. Just as proper economic goals might include full employment, price stability, and fair distribution of income and wealth, optimal scale deserves its place.[26]

Global warming gets the headlines, perhaps as it should, but the story of Big Mike and his cousin Cavendish is just as telling. Other limits to

[26] Daly (1997, p. 51).

unending growth are surfacing, from vast declines in pollinator population to plastics and forever chemicals in our water, air, and bodies. Pressing concerns, economic, ecological, and social, are with us today. An economy that works for everyone, today and tomorrow, within the limits imposed by nature and a just society must be the goal.

References

Brown HC (2024) Scientists see hope in race to breed banana of future. Wall Str J 11 October, p B1

Case A, Deaton A (2020) Deaths of despair and the future of capitalism. Princeton University Press, Princeton, NJ

Centers for Disease Control and Prevention (2025) Suicide data and statistics. Available at: https://www.cdc.gov/suicide/facts/data.html. Accessed on 30 Aug 2025

Curtin SC, Garnett MF (2023) Suicide and homicide death rates among youth and young adults aged 10–24: United States, 2001–2021. NCHS Data Brief No. 471, June. Available at: https://www.cdc.gov/nchs/data/databriefs/db471.pdf. Accessed on 30 Aug 2025

Daly HE (1997) Georgescu-Roegen versus Solow/Stiglitz. Ecol Econ 22(3):261–266. https://doi.org/10.1016/S0921-8009(97)00080-3

Day M, Beekman D (2018) Amazon issues threat over Seattle head-tax plan, halts tower construction planning. *The Seattle Times*. Available at: https://www.seattletimes.com/business/amazon/amazon-pauses-plans-for-seattle-office-towers-while-city-council-considers-business-tax/. Accessed on 30 Aug 2025

Eder A, Salhofer K, Quddoos A (2024) The impact of cereal crop diversification on farm labor productivity under changing climatic conditions. Ecol Econ. https://doi.org/10.1016/j.ecolecon.2024.108241

Emont J (2024) Climate change lands on your table. Wall Str J, 12 July, p A1

Habel JC, Samways MJ, Schmitt T (2019) Mitigating the precipitous decline of terrestrial European insects: requirements for a new strategy. Biodivers Conserv 28(6):1343–1360. https://doi.org/10.1007/s10531-019-01744-9

Huggins and Reganold (2008) No-till: the quiet revolution. Scientific American Magazine July: 70–77

Jackson T (2025) Never too much. The New York Review of Books, January 16:32–35

Libatique R (2024) US property-casualty insurers rocked by huge losses. Available at: https://www.insurancebusinessmag.com/us/news/property/us-propertycasualty-insurers-rocked-by-huge-losses-495480.aspx?itid=lk_inline_enhanced-template. Accessed on 29 Aug 2025

Rojanasakul M, Flavelle C (2024) See where home insurance policies were dropped in your state. December 21, 2024. Page A12. Available at: https://www.nytimes.com/interactive/2024/12/18/climate/insurance-nonrenewal-rates-policies-state-map.html. Accessed on 30 Aug 2025

Rosa-Schleich J, Loos J, Musshoff O, Tscharntke T (2019) Ecological-economic trade-offs of diversified farming systems—a review. Ecol Econ 160:251–263

Rosenberg KV, Dokter AM et al (2019) Decline of the North American avifauna. Science 366(6461):120–124. https://doi.org/10.1126/science.aaw1313

Trapasso C (2024) Here's how much home insurance rates have risen in every state. Available at: https://www.realtor.com/news/trends/the-states-where-home-insurance-rates-are-rising-the-most/?msockid=21e2177eb81168e92415036db99e698f. Accessed on 30 Aug 2025

Villena VH, Gioia DA (2020) A more sustainable supply chain. Harv Bus Rev. Available at: https://hbr.org/2020/03/a-more-sustainable-supply-chain Accessed on 2 July 2025

Worm B et al (2006) Impacts of biodiversity loss on ocean ecosystem services. Science 314(5800):787–790. https://doi.org/10.1126/science.1132294

Worm B et al (2007) Response to comments on "Impacts of biodiversity loss on ocean ecosystem services." Science 316(5829):1285. https://doi.org/10.1126/science.1139178

Wynn-Williams S (2025) Careless people: a cautionary tale of power, greed, and lost idealism. Flatiron Books

Zattara EE, Aizen MA (2021) Worldwide occurrence records suggest a global decline in bee species richness. One Earth 4(1):114–123. https://doi.org/10.1016/j.oneear.2020.12.005

CHAPTER 10

A Right Livelihood: Meaningful Employment

> If the nature of the work is properly appreciated and applied, it will stand in the same relation to the higher faculties as food is to the physical body. It nourishes and enlivens the higher man and urges him to produce the best he is capable of. It directs his free will along the proper course and disciplines the animal in him into progressive channels. It furnishes an excellent background for man to display his scale of values and develop his personality.[1]

> The need to work … will disappear within 25 years for those countries that adapt [AI] technologies.[2]

Short of death or dismemberment, what is the worst thing that could happen to you? The answer just might be, lose your job. Researchers have looked at the numbers and it seems the risk of death for unemployed persons is 63% higher than the risk for those who are employed, with the risk remaining elevated even after re-employment, suggesting that becoming unemployed induces a long-term change in the underlying mortality risk.[3] The news is worse for younger workers compared

[1] Indian philosopher and economist J. C. Kumarappa, as quoted in Schumacher (n.d.).

[2] Venture capitalist Vinod Kholsa, as quoted in De Avila (2024).

[3] McArdle (2014), Roelfs et al. (2011).

L. Hadsell, *Social Economies*,
https://doi.org/10.1007/978-3-032-21916-9_10

to workers nearing retirement (50–65 years of age) and for men: the risk of death associated with unemployment is 37% higher for men than for women. The unemployed are also more likely to suffer from poor health, suicide, and divorce.[4]

A mountain of research from economists, sociologists, psychologists, and health professionals supports the commonly held notion that the importance of employment extends beyond simple economic measures. In addition to generating income to buy essential things, work is an opportunity to realize human potential, to have purpose, to make a difference, and to achieve status. There are good reasons that full employment is a major macroeconomic goal. The cost of unemployment is not only lost income and lost economic production but also, potentially, loss of identity and harm to health.

Economists have many tools to examine labor markets and employment decisions, from both the employer and employee side. This is a well-developed area precisely because employment means so much, for fulfillment of both economic and social goals. Being employed is important, with the ultimate goal of meaningful employment: that is, employment that not only produces valuable goods and services but also fulfills a deep need for belonging and purpose. The ability to live a good, satisfying life has much to do with engagement in productive, meaningful work. When that work disappears, as it has in so many American communities in recent decades, mainly due to technological changes and international trade, the repercussions extend far beyond the strictly economic realm. The importance of work becomes even more salient with artificial intelligence looming on the horizon.

The most commonly cited measures of employment and unemployment focus on participation in formal labor markets. These measures are useful in guiding economic decisions, for individuals, firms, and government policy makers. Yet, the headline statistics are incomplete. Economists consider the impact that work, or its absence, has on individual, family, and community well-being. Building on work in organizational psychology, economists are also incorporating considerations of meaningfulness in their understanding of labor markets. This chapter is a

[4] Roelfs et al. (2011), Autor et al. (2016). Rather than being a result of unemployment, alcohol, and drug abuse may be a contributor to job loss: people with pre-existing health conditions are more likely to become and remain unemployed, suggesting that pre-existing health may be a common cause of both unemployment and mortality.

brief introduction to current thinking. Employment is important; meaningful employment even more so; unemployment can be devastating.

10.1 Employment and Meaning

A typical starting point for thinking about the economics of work begins with a focus on formal labor markets, leading to headline employment and unemployment statistics. Yet, much takes place beyond the official statistics. Changes in labor-force participation offers a prime example. Official labor-force participation (LFP) rose steadily after World War II, as more people of working age became employed in formal labor markets, peaking in the year 2000. One consequence was higher economic growth and greater measured economic well-being. But part of that growth was illusory, as much of the increase in LFP was simply a shifting of work from informal, unpaid tasks (housework, childcare) to paid markets. The same work previously not counted is now counted (Chapters 8 and 17 discuss this in more detail.)

Real wages also rose significantly for most of the period following World War II, as worker productivity increased dramatically, the result of trade and adoption of new technologies and methods (accompanied by a commensurate rise in human capital). At least in the initial years, wage increases were substantial and affected all income levels, as income inequality declined. Since the 1970s, the story has changed dramatically, as wages have stagnated for all but the highest income earners. Employment has become more tenuous and less economically rewarding for many.

People care a great deal about pay, and so stagnating incomes are a major source of concern for many, especially as housing, health care, and education become less affordable. Also of concern, though, is the nature of work itself. And yet, information about the quality of employment is often neglected in the monthly reporting. In a very basic sense, what matters for the official statistics is only whether or not one has a job (in the formal sector). Trying to fill this gap, many economists are focusing on quality of the employment and meaning of work as important components of compensation, alongside wages.

Evidence of concern with work's meaning shows up in ubiquitous lists of "best places to work" and in firm and industry pay differentials. Regarding the latter, Americans are, on average, willing to work for a lower wage for businesses they view as "good" (or conversely, require a higher wage for those they view less favorably). And employers, knowing this, are able to post job openings offering lower salaries.[5] Even the gender pay gap can be partially explained by self-reported differences between women and men in the importance they place on meaningful work: on average, women place greater weight on meaningful work, appearing to sacrifice income in the process.[6] Greater emphasis on meaningful work, and the subsequent movement into occupations that accommodate, may further help explain why women reported slightly increased happiness at work over the 1950–2015 period, a divergence from the experience of men, who report being somewhat less happy (especially the case for those with lower education levels).[7]

Entrepreneurs may represent an extreme expression of the value of meaning, choosing as they do the autonomy of self-employment over safety of being employed by others. Large surveys of entrepreneurs indicate that money is not the primary reason for starting their own business. Rather, non-monetary benefits such as the autonomy and independence that come with control over the work environment are at the top of the list.[8] In sum, just as compensating differentials are acknowledged for differences between jobs in terms of risk or physical pain, so too is compensation affected by the amount of meaning.[9]

What makes work meaningful? Meaningful work is:

> work and work accomplishments that are viewed as valuable, worthwhile, and aligning with one's values. [M]eaningful work tends to result from self-actualization or from working towards a higher purpose. More specifically, meaningful work may come from feeling a sense of unity with other people, serving others, from developing oneself, or from working towards realizing one's full potential.[10]

[5] Wilmers and Zhang (2022).

[6] Burbano et al. (2024).

[7] Though happiness among Black women declined substantially. Kaplan and Schulhofer-Wohl (2018).

[8] Astebro et al. (2014).

[9] Sorkin (2018), Burbano et al. (2024), and Cassar and Meier (2018).

[10] Stepanek et al. (2023).

More meaningful work, regardless of the type of work, is facilitated by greater job autonomy, skill variety, task significance, and feedback.[11]

Because meaning is subjective, to each his own, researchers ask people how much meaning they derive from various aspects of their work.[12] A typical measure poses statements such as the following and asks respondents how much they agree:

I understand how my work contributes to my life's meaning,
I view my work as contributing to my personal growth,
I know my work makes a positive difference in the world.

One does not have to be a high-level executive to respond positively to any of the statements though differences may exist in what brings meaning to work.[13] People who find more meaning in their work have higher job and life satisfaction, lower absenteeism, and are healthier and more productive—all better for the organization for which they work.[14] Not only is meaning valuable to workers, it has value to employers.

Meaning leads to greater satisfaction with work and life. Surveys report that most American workers are satisfied overall with their job.[15] In a recent poll, only one in eight reported that they were not satisfied and nearly half were "extremely or very satisfied," even though nearly 30 percent also said they were not satisfied with their pay. Among the strongest contributors to job satisfaction were relationships with coworkers and manager/supervisor and day-to-day tasks. Work relationships provide substantial social capital—these are people you see each workday, and often after-hours work and social events. A sense of belonging and meaning is enhanced by being part of a team, contributing with others to a greater good, whether it is as a member of a janitorial staff keeping a clean school or upper management planning the launch of a new product.

While satisfaction is not the same as meaning, it may be one component of meaningful work. The Buddhist perspective, discussed at length

[11] Stepanek et al. (2023), Cassar and Meier (2018).

[12] Steger et al. (2012).

[13] E.g., Bailey et al. (2019).

[14] Simon-Thomas (2018), Allan et al. (2018), and Gartenberg et al. (2019).

[15] Lin et al. (2024).

in Chapter 4, provides insight in this regard. For the Buddhist economist, meaning is brought about from work as purification of character. As one Buddhist economist noted,

> [work] nourishes and enlivens the higher man and urges him to produce the best he is capable of. It directs his free will along the proper course and disciplines the animal in him into progressive channels. It furnishes an excellent background for man to display his scale of values and develop his personality.[16]

In addition to providing valuable goods and services, meaningful work affords one an opportunity to build character, according to the Buddhist tradition. And in that way, satisfaction with work is enhanced.

While economists are concerned with ensuring that everyone who wants to work has a job and that pay reflects workers' contributions, we also keep in mind that the goal is not simply employment but employment with meaning. Though this additional requirement is more difficult to measure, it is just as important, perhaps more. Consideration of work's meaning also suggests a balance regarding related goals such as economic growth. Higher levels of GDP can be had by enhancing worker meaning but it can also be achieved, at least in the short term, at the expense of meaningful work through onerous work conditions, reduction in worker choices, diminished work relationships, and less flexibility.

10.2 Unemployment

As the opening paragraphs to this chapter indicate, consequences of loss of a job extend beyond one's checking account and the corresponding decrease in ability to pay rent, buy food, and get health care. Social ills related to loss of income and loss of purpose affect spouses, children, and personal health. In their study of the effects of unemployment on children of the unemployed, economists Milena Nikolova and Boris Nikolaev find that young children whose parents were unemployed report lower satisfaction with life when they themselves become young adults (18–31 years).[17] Other research suggests that preschool children have more social problems and less belief in self-determination when their mother

[16] Indian philosopher and economist J. C. Kumarappa, as quoted in Schumacher (n.d.)

[17] Nikolova and Nikolaev (2021).

losses her job.[18] Children whose parent experiences long-term unemployment are likelier to experience ill health (both physical and mental) when they become adults. Those children are more likely to be poor themselves as adults if a parent experienced unemployment and are less likely to complete a college education.[19]

Increased rates of divorce are not surprising given that money issues are a primary contention among couples. Rates of suicide increase among unemployed, as a loss of purpose and status combines with a reduced ability to provide materially for self and family, leading to despair. Other studies show that self-esteem declines as unemployment lengthens, with accompanying reductions in life satisfaction.[20] One conclusion is that we can expect a subset of the population to experience physical and mental health problems after particularly problematic episodes of unemployment such as occurred during the Great Recession of 2008–2010 or the pandemic shutdown in 2020, during which we witnessed extensive long-term unemployment and job dislocation. The studies mentioned above suggest we will see ill effects even ten, fifteen, twenty years after those events.

The largest causes of involuntary job loss, other than recessions, are international trade and technological change, both of which are normally viewed by economists as positive economic forces. Both lower costs of production, leading to lower prices for consumers, often increasing quality as well. Both lead to higher wages for some while others face significant adjustment costs, covering some combination of joblessness, retraining, and a permanent wage reduction. Given the importance of work, and meaningful, rewarding work in particular, the negative impacts should not be underestimated, especially since they tend to be concentrated (individuals lose a significant portion of their income; communities may lose a significant portion of their economic and social livelihood) while the benefits of trade are dispersed (we all save a few dollars on sweaters, for example). This is not to minimize the tremendous benefits of trade, from better autos to bananas and avocados for consumers in the U.S., nor the benefits of technological change, which has greatly improved availability and quality of many products. But neither should the

18 Frauke (2016).

19 Martínez-Jiménez (2023), Mooi-Reci and Wooden (2022).

20 Reitz et al. (2022).

costs be discounted. A group of economists led by David Autor, reflecting on the employment dislocation resulting from greatly increased trade with China beginning around year 2000, finds

> Adjustment in local labor markets is remarkably slow, with wages and labor-force participation rates remaining depressed and unemployment rates remaining elevated for at least a full decade after the China trade shock commences. Exposed workers experience greater job churning and reduced lifetime income. At the national level, employment has fallen in the US industries more exposed to import competition, as expected, but offsetting employment gains in other industries have yet to materialize.[21]

Similar anecdotal observations have been made by others, including Amy Goldstein in her reporting of economic, social, and personal disruptions resulting from closure of an auto production plant in Janesville, Wisconsin.[22] Goldstein uses personal narratives to tell the stories of those affected: declining wages, collapsing marriages and families, a tearing of the community fabric.[23] She provides a critique of job retraining programs, and the ability generally of many workers to adjust to sudden economic changes.

Lower income men are most negatively affected by job loss due to trade: income losses are proportionately much larger for men below the 40th percentile of the annual earnings distribution. We have witnessed accompanying declines in marriage rates among those with less formal education, and increases in disability claims, reflecting a decline in health and well-being among lob losers. Each of these effects have further increased economic, social, and health inequalities.[24]

Part of the problem many in the U.S. have with international trade is that some trading partners, such as China and similar countries, have labor and environmental standards and laws that are substantially laxer than in the U.S., creating an unequal playing field. Free trade works well only when parties involved share similar economic rules.[25]

[21] Autor et al. (2016).

[22] Goldstein (2017). See also Macy (2014).

[23] Senior (2017).

[24] Coile and Duggan (2019).

[25] See Financial Times columnist Rana Foroohar, as quoted in Kuttner (2024).

Technological change is responsible for at least as much job dislocation—loss—as international trade. New machines, including robots, and now AI, provide more efficient and lower cost methods of production that require less labor. Job losses in manufacturing are most often cited as examples of workers being displaced by trade and technology, but white-collar office workers, doing what Autor calls "middle-skill" work, are also subject to these changes. Such work, once performed by workers without a college degree, has largely disappeared.[26] Change started in the 1970s, with widespread adoption of computer technology. As middle-skill jobs disappeared, wages for non-college grads in urban areas declined. The result is that workers who once filled these jobs are much worse off, in terms of employment prospects, income, and everything that goes along with having stable employment.

Now that highly educated Indians and Chinese, and most recently (and ominously) artificial intelligence, are challenging high-skilled U.S. white-collar workers, those workers are beginning to pay more attention to issues such as displacement that have long-affected blue-collar workers. With regard to AI, the key for future employment will rest on the distinction between replacement and enhancement. If AI replaces work that is rewarding and fulfilling, that is quite different from AI that enhances already rewarding work. Nothing is known about which path AI will be allowed to take, as history serves as an incomplete guide given the nature of this new technology. We as a society are now able to influence the degree to which AI changes the amount and meaning of work, just as workers in France chose fewer hours of labor (and more leisure) rather than more pay between 1970 and 2020, and U.S. workers chose the opposite (as described in Chapter 2). The impact of AI on economic growth could be tremendous, but it may also lead to increasing dissatisfaction with work and life, adding to social distress and increasing inequality of income and wealth. Of course, it may just be possible that AI enhances human capability, increases job satisfaction, and leads to greater equality. Time will tell.

We should pause to consider multiple perspectives. For a neo-classical economist, the impact of AI on the nature of work, whether it adds to or subtracts from meaningful work, is of less importance than the increase in wages (for those for whom AI is a complement) or re-employment of

[26] Autor (2019).

workers (for whom AI is a substitute) to other productive work. Because work is a disutility, shorter work weeks and less onerous, though perhaps more mundane work, is an outcome to cheer. A universal basic income (UBI) or distribution of ownership of AI technology may be suggested by more liberal members of the mainstream, but technological advance generally meets with approval.

Buddhists and Marxists would see AI's replacement of human labor differently. For them technology that enhances the meaning of work and, for Buddhists in particular, work's power to purify the soul should be encouraged. Technology that replaces one's ability to achieve those means is to be discouraged; work is not simply a disutility, something to be avoided. Thus, a universal basic income or equity stake in AI would not address key needs of many and so are not an adequate response to AI. Marxists will point to the alienation that technology tends to reinforce, separating workers from meaning of work—and the value (production) they create. Marxists might accept the need for a UBI or equity stake but would also note the increased social problems resulting from potential worker dissatisfaction.

10.3 Policy Responses

What can be done to lessen the economic and social harms of unemployment and to encourage development of meaningful employment? For the former, standard public policy reactions of unemployment insurance and transition aid for education and training can help. Research suggests, not surprisingly, that more generous welfare and unemployment policies substantially reduce the negative economic and social effects of unemployment.[27] Policies vary widely across major economies, as seen in a sample of European countries and U.S. states.[28] The maximum duration of unemployment benefits in European countries, for example, range from six to 24 months, with adjustments in many countries depending on prior employment duration, age of worker, and prior income. In the U.S., U.K., and Ireland, the typical limit is six months. The monetary value of those benefits also varies greatly and is typically tied to prior earnings. Typical maximum monthly payouts are $4000 in Germany and Denmark

[27] Roelfs et al. (2011).

[28] European data from Unedic (2024).

to under $2000 per month in Italy and Spain. Finland has no explicit cap. In the U.S. benefit levels are determined at the state level, with maximum payouts ranging from $850 per week in Massachusetts and Washington State to under $300 in several southern states.

These differences do matter. Unemployment spells may last longer when benefits are more generous, as research shows, but those more generous benefits also support social, physical, and mental health. In their study of European unemployment policies, Clare Bambra and Terje Andreas Eikemo find that the more generous unemployment benefits of Scandinavian states (Denmark, Finland, Norway, Sweden) were associated with better health outcomes for the unemployed than were the less generous benefits of others, especially Anglo-Saxon states (Ireland, U.K.).[29] Programs with means-tested benefits, restricting benefits to only worthy candidates, were associated with worse health compared to non-means-tested regimes. In a study of U.S. unemployment insurance programs, Elira Kuka finds that more generous unemployment insurance increases health insurance coverage and utilization, leading to improved self-reported health, effects that are particularly strong when employment opportunities are scarcest.[30]

Other programs and policies aim to enhance work meaning. One approach encourages greater worker participation in decision-making, which can increase employees' sense of agency, a key factor in worker satisfaction.[31] German work councils and American worker cooperatives and Employee Stock-Ownership Plans (ESOPs) are examples. These structures give workers a say in decisions that affect their roles, boosting engagement and meaning. Even something as simple as input into determination of weekly work schedules can provide material benefit.

High on the agenda are policies to guide the coming changes from AI in a direction that will complement work and enhance meaning rather than replace them. Greater worker participation in decision governing technology adoption and international trade clearly would enhance

[29] Bambra and Eikemo (2009), who provide the following descriptions: Scandinavian countries are characterized by universal coverage, comparatively generous social transfers, and a commitment to full employment and income protection. In Anglo-Saxon countries, state provision of welfare is minimal, social protection levels are modest and often attract strict entitlement criteria, and recipients are usually means-tested and stigmatized.

[30] Kuka (2018).

[31] See OECD (2025) for a detailed discussion.

worker satisfaction. Government that moves beyond a free-trade, technology-forward stance, toward a new direction that considers more seriously the distribution of costs and well as the benefits, would enhance individual, family, and health.

10.4 Concluding Comments

Full employment is a laudable goal. It ensures that resources are being used to their fullest, creating goods and services and generating income. It averts the worst effects of unemployment, which extend far beyond loss of income. But it's not enough. Work must be meaningful; it must both add to economic activity and enhance individual and social well-being. Individuals and society can direct business and public policy toward the goal of meaningful employment, whether it's through trade or technology rules, or some other policy or influence. Full employment, in meaningful work, is a win for individuals, society, and for employers, as workers are happier, healthier, and more productive. Among the many lasting effects induced by the recent pandemic has had is a shift in thinking about place and purpose. Being kept away from work or school and the usual routines during that time no doubt led many to consider the deeper meaning of work.

Adam Smith recognized the potential downside of repetitive, specialized work in capitalist economies when he promoted capitalism as an alternative to the static economic systems of the eighteenth century. He recognized that as division of labor would bring higher incomes and economic growth, workers would become "as stupid and ignorant as it is possible for a human creature to become." Karl Marx likewise saw how division of labor created a knowledge wedge between owners/capitalists and workers, leading to alienation and exploitation. The key outcome of Marx's idea to replace capitalism with socialism is in the meaning that would be added to work, through participatory production and a lessening of the knowledge gap. Marxist ideology, like Buddhist economics, promotes work as an essential human activity. A key expectation of socialism, with its emphasis on democratization of work, is its ability to improve well-being through more meaningful work.[32] For Buddhists, work provides an opportunity to purify the soul.

[32] Spencer (2024).

Economists of all stripes are increasingly recognizing the importance not just of employment but also the nature of work. In a future surely to include widespread use of artificial intelligence, we need more than ever to consider not only the value of leisure but also the value of work.

References

Allan BA, Batz-Barbarich C, Sterling HM, Tay L (2018) Outcomes of meaningful work: a meta-analysis. J Manage Stud 56(3):500–528

Astebro T, Herz H, Nanda R, Weber RA (2014) Seeking the roots of entrepreneurship: insights from behavioral economics. J Econ Perspect 28(3):49–70

Autor D (2019) Work of the past, work of the future. Richard T. Ely Lecture, AA Annual Meeting, Atlanta, January 4. Available at: https://www.aeaweb.org/webcasts/2019/aea-distinguished-lecture-work-of-the-past-work-of-the-future. Accessed on 2 July 2025

Autor DH, Dorn D, Hanson GH (2016) The China shock: learning from labor market adjustment to large changes in trade. Annu Rev Econ 8:205–240

Bailey C, Yeoman R, Madden A, Thompson M, Kerridge G (2019) A review of the empirical literature on meaningful work: progress and research Agenda. Hum Resour Dev Rev 18(1):83–113

Bambra C, Eikemo T (2009) Welfare state regimes, unemployment and health: a comparative study of the relationship between unemployment and self-reported health in 23 European Countries. J Epidemiol Community Health 63(2):92–98

Burbano V, Padilla N, Meier S (2024) Gender differences in preferences for meaning at work. Am Econ J Econ Pol 16(3):61–94. https://doi.org/10.1257/pol.20220121

Cassar L, Meier S (2018) Nonmonetary incentives and the implications of work as a source of meaning. J Econ Perspect 32(3):215–238

Coile CC, Duggan MG (2019) When labor's lost: health, family life, incarceration, and education in a time of declining economic opportunity for low-skilled men. J Econ Perspect 33(2):191–210

De Avila J (2024) Musk, Dimon are hyped on AI, but not everyone is on board. Wall Street Journal, 11 April: B1.

Frauke P (2016) The effect of involuntary maternal job loss on children's behaviour and non-cognitive skills. Labour Econ 42:43–63

Gartenberg C, Prat A, Serafeim G (2019) Corporate purpose and financial performance. Organ Sci 30(1):1–18

Goldstein A (2017) Janesville. C-SPAN. Available at: https://www.c-span.org/video/?436317-4/amy-goldstein-discusses-janesville. Accessed on 2 July 2025

Kaplan K, Schulhofer-Wohl S (2018) The changing (dis-)utility of work. J Econ Perspect 32(3):239–258
Kuka E (2018) Quantifying the benefits of social insurance: unemployment insurance and health. NBER Working Paper 24766. http://www.nber.org/papers/w24766
Kuttner R (2024) The import of exports. New York Review of Books, 19 December: 71–73
Lin L, Horowitz JM, Fry R (2024) Most Americans feel good about their job security but not their pay. Pre Research Center. https://www.pewresearch.org/social-trends/2024/12/10/job-satisfaction/. Accessed on 30 Aug 2025
Macy B (2014) Factory man: how one furniture maker battled offshoring, stayed local—and helped save an American town. Little, Brown and Company, New York
Martínez-Jiménez M (2023) How parental unemployment impacts children's health in the long run. Imperial College Business School. Available at: https://www.imperial.ac.uk/business-school/ib-knowledge/health/how-parental-unemployment-impacts-childrens-health-the-long-run/. Accessed on 2 July 2025
McArdle M (2014) Unemployment: a fate worse than death. Time. Available at: https://time.com/9009/unemployment-is-worse-than-death/. Accessed on 2 July 2025
Mooi-Reci I, Wooden M (2022) Jobless parents, unhealthy children? How past exposure to parental joblessness influences children's future health. SSM Popul Health 19:101144. https://doi.org/10.1016/j.ssmph.2022.101144
Nikolova M, Nikolaev BN (2021) Family matters: the effects of parental unemployment in early childhood and adolescence on subjective well-being later in life. J Econ Behav Organ 181:312–331
OECD (2025) Exploring new frontiers in citizen participation in the policy cycle, OECD public governance reviews. OECD Publishing, Paris. https://doi.org/10.1787/77f5098c-en
Reitz AK, Luhmann M, Bleidorn W, Denissen JJA (2022) Unraveling the complex relationship between work transitions and self-esteem and life satisfaction. J Pers Soc Psychol 123(3):597–620. https://doi.org/10.1037/pspp0000423
Roelfs DJ, Shor E, Davidson KW, Schwartz JE (2011) Losing life and livelihood: a systematic review and meta analysis of unemployment and all-cause mortality. Soc Sci Med 72(6):840–854. https://doi.org/10.1016/j.socscimed.2011.01.005
Schumacher EF (no date) Buddhist economics. Available at: https://centerforneweconomics.org/publications/buddhist-economics/. Accessed on 2 April 2022

Senior J (2017) Book review: in 'Janesville,' when the G.M. plant closed, havoc followed. New York Times, 19 April. Available at: https://www.nytimes.com/2017/04/19/books/review-janesville-amy-goldstein.html. Accessed on 2 July 2025

Simon-Thomas ER (2018) The four keys to happiness at work. Available at: https://greatergood.berkeley.edu/article/item/the_four_keys_to_happiness_at_work

Sorkin I (2018) Ranking firms using revealed preference. Q J Econ. https://doi.org/10.1093/qje/qjy001

Spencer D (2024) Efficiency vs. meaningful work: a critical survey of historical and contemporary debates. Contrib Polit Econ 43:21–36

Steger MF, Dik BJ, Duffy RD (2012) Measuring meaningful work: the work as meaning inventory (WAMI). J Career Assess 20(3):322–337

Stepanek S, Paul M, Crawford D (2023) Umbrella summary: meaningful work. Quality Improvement Center for Workforce Development. Available at: https://www.qic-wd.org/umbrella-summary/meaningful-work. Accessed on 2 July 2025

Unedic (2024) Europ'Info 2024: unemployment insurance in Europe. https://www.unedic.org/storage/uploads/2024/10/07/Assurance-chomage-Europe_EN_240924_2_uid_6703f1b88e671.pdf

Wilmers N, Zhang L (2022) Values and inequality: prosocial jobs and the college wage premium. Am Sociol Rev 87(3):415–442. https://doi.org/10.1177/00031224221089335

CHAPTER 11

Economic Freedom

> Society is produced by our wants and government by our wickedness; the former promotes our happiness positively by uniting our affections, the latter negatively by restraining our vices.[1]

> True individual freedom cannot exist without economic security and independence.[2]

> Freedom is just another word for nothing left to lose.[3]

Many Americans will surely be surprised to learn that the U.S. economy is among the least regulated in the world, ranked 5th freest of government intervention among 165 countries, according to the Fraser Institute, a conservative economic think tank.[4] Labor markets are deemed particularly free, responsible in large part for the consistently lower unemployment rates in the U.S. compared to most European countries, where

[1] Thomas Paine.
[2] Franklin D. Roosevelt.
[3] Janis Joplin.
[4] Gwartney et al. (2023).

L. Hadsell, *Social Economies*,
https://doi.org/10.1007/978-3-032-21916-9_11

hiring and firing workers is much more onerous and unemployment benefits more generous. In short, U.S. labor markets are more dynamic, more flexible. There are clear benefits to freer, less regulated labor markets, for both employer and employee (for the latter, finding a willing employer is easier, as is changing jobs). There is also a downside to freer markets, namely less job security, which in the U.S. means more tenuous health care and retirement benefits. The U.S. has a long history emphasizing free labor markets. Early state and federal minimum wage laws and work hour restrictions, for instance, were consistently struck down by courts as unconstitutional infringements on right to contract. Only in 1938 did FDR's second attempt at a national minimum wage pass legal challenge. The proper role of government in individuals' economic decisions, or the right amount of "economic freedom," continues today to be hotly debated in labor markets and elsewhere.

The extent of economic freedom in all its forms—choice of where, when, and how much to work; what to buy or sell and for what price; what profession to pursue or business to operate as one sees fit—has strong social and political influences and implications.

11.1 The Meaning of Economic Freedom

Economist James Gwartney, lead developer of the Economic Freedom of the World (EFW) index referenced above (a measure commonly used by economists), defines economic freedom as "present when individuals are permitted to choose for themselves and engage in voluntary transactions as long as they do not harm the person or property of others." As such, the amount of government regulation, taxation, and spending is a large part of the EFW index. In this view, regulation limits choice, such as in labor markets (with minimum wage, licensing, work hours, and safety requirements) and product markets (with age, time, or place restrictions); taxation is tantamount to theft (as it is a forced taking); and government spending is assumed to be a wasteful misdirection of private resources.[5] This view is based on the historic rights tradition.

[5] The founding fathers were well aware of the dangers of government overreach. James Madison wrote in 1792, "That is not a just government, nor is property secure under it, where the property which a man has in his personal safety and personal liberty, is violated by arbitrary seizures of one class of citizens for the service of the rest." Madison (1792).

Such a view of freedom, though, is not universally shared among economists nor has it always been the primary meaning of such freedom. Historian Joyce Appleby, referring to the 1790s, a pivotal period in the formation of the U.S. conception of economic freedom, notes that "Probably the least familiar concept of liberty used then was that most common to us [today] – that is, liberty as personal freedom bounded only by such limits as are necessary if others are to enjoy the same extensive personal freedom."[6] The EFW conception of freedom is the result of liberalism emanating from Hobbes and Locke, and is one that has gradually gained dominance in American thought since the mid-twentieth century.[7] The prevailing conception in late eighteenth-century America was quite different, contending that -

> To be a free man … was to participate in the life of the polis or community. To have liberty was to share in the power of the state, to be actively involved in making and executing decisions. Thus liberty in this sense was associated with a republic – the rule of law …. Liberty in the classical republican tradition pertained to the public realm and not the private. Indeed, it was the capacity of men to rise above personal interest that made republics and therefore liberty possible.[8]

These two conceptions of freedom—one in the historic rights tradition and the other in the classical republican paradigm—are distinct and potentially contradictory concepts.[9] The former protects private, personal enjoyments whereas the latter "celebrates the public arena.“ "There is no suggestion of limiting the power of government in the classical tradition as long as that power serves the common good.“ Today's conception of freedom places primacy on the individual; the classical republican tradition of freedom stresses the commitments each of us have to others. The current conception of economic freedom makes no judgment about the proper goals for individuals; freedom to choose, regardless of the choice made, is paramount. The classical republican version, on the other hand,

[6] Appleby (1984).

[7] Also see Sandel (2022).

[8] Appleby, p. 16.

[9] Appleby, p. 18.

requires a conception of civic virtue, an idea of the kind of persons we all should be.[10]

The historic rights tradition of individual freedom that is so common in the U.S. today finds strong support among mainstream economists, as both conservatives and liberals generally agree with the primacy of individual choice. Their departure is mainly over whether opportunities exist for all to exercise those freedoms, and how to achieve that opportunity. Today's most frequently used conception of economic freedom bends toward the conservative side, asserting that less government intervention in the market economy creates more freedom as it respects property rights and individual choice. Proponents of greater economic freedom measured this way argue that economic freedom is valuable because it spurs a host of positive economic outcomes, and, in fact, considerable empirical evidence suggests that economic freedom by such measures has numerous benefits—in the form of higher economic growth, income, happiness, health, education, and disease prevention.[11]

Conservative economist Milton Friedman goes further, arguing that economic freedom has value even in the absence of economic benefits:

> ... freedom - economic, political, civil - is an end in itself not a means to other ends - it is what makes life worthwhile. We would prefer to live in a free country even if it did not provide us and our fellow citizens with a higher standard of life than an alternative regime.[12]

Even so, not everyone prefers more economic freedom to less. Regulations, for example, may be seen by some as infringements on individual choice while others may see them as needed protection from market forces. Minimum wage laws are a prime example. Some view them as an infringement on freedom of both employer and employee to make contracts as they see fit. Others view them as protection for workers in labor markets characterized by unequal bargaining power and potential coercion. Licensing requirements, food inspection, product quality, and banking regulation are other examples among many for which reasonable differences of support exist.

[10] Sandel (2022), pp. 5–6.

[11] Hall and Lawson (2014), Stroup (2007).

[12] Leeson and Palm (2020).

Consider licensing requirements, which Friedman and other libertarians have long railed against. While some requirements seem too onerous—hair braiders in Louisiana, for example, are required to complete 500 hours of training before they can receive a license—few of us would want to employ doctors, nurses, engineers, or any number of other professionals, without the winnowing of potential suppliers that results from licensing requirements.[13] Though buyers are cautioned to beware, and smart shoppers attempt to know what they are buying, few of us would want to have to verify every detail of everyone we employ or every product we buy, as it could quickly lead to decision fatigue, the phenomenon describing how decision quality can be impaired by the act of making previous decisions, often resulting from too many options and considerations. Abundant research suggests that verifying the credentials of every single seller/buyer with whom you interact each day leads to worse choices. A choice set can be too large, too complicated, just as it can be too restricted.

Decision fatigue is not about intelligence. In one study, judges were found to be less lenient in granting parole the more time that had passed since they took a break. In another, decisions by bank loan officers worsened as the day progressed, leading to substantial losses of potential revenue for the bank. In another study, surgeons were less likely to recommend surgery to patients seen at the end of the day compared to earlier.[14] Decision fatigue can be especially hard on the poor, who, with tight budgets, have to be aware of each dollar spent.[15] In one study, farmers' cognitive ability was measured before harvest, when finances were tight, and after, once farmers had received income for their crops. Cognitive ability was higher after harvest, suggesting that pre-harvest financial stress temporarily reduced farmers' decision-making ability. Similar research suggests that frequent use of self-control, as may be needed when spending tight budgets, also reduces decision-making ability, sometimes leading to poor spending decisions. These and other related studies suggest a kind of poverty cycle in which poverty leads to poor choices leading to more poverty. More generally, constant evaluation

[13] Though as of this writing, the law is being considered for repeal. Stennett (2024).

[14] Baer and Schnall (2021). Also, Shroff et al. (2022). For surgeons see Persson et al. (2019).

[15] Vohs (2013), Mani et al. (2013), Yglesias (2013).

and decision-making is exhaustive for anyone, so having some of those decisions evaluated ahead of time—by government-mandated professional licensing, food-safety requirements, and so on—may improve decisions.

A large part of the need for regulation is the prevalence of information asymmetry: when two parties in a market have vastly different levels of information or understanding. I am knowledgeable when making investment decisions but lost with medical decisions. I know a lot about gardening but not much about the internal workings of my car. I am reliant on the other party in some transaction—the physician or the mechanic—to not take advantage of me, as I have much less information, and understanding—than they do and am therefore at a disadvantage. Cultural norms and ethical boundaries provide one level of protection in such situations (as discussed in Chapters 6 and 15), as do government regulation and provision of information to consumers, seen by some as essential to functioning markets.

Protection from vagaries of markets, decision fatigue, information asymmetry, faulty decision-making, or just too many choices forms a solid base for government intervention. In the end, though, the amount of economic freedom preferred varies by person—some like more than others. It also varies widely by country around the world. The U.S. ranks quite high on the Economic Freedom of the World index, as do much smaller countries like Singapore and New Zealand, reflecting the preferences of citizens. It is no surprise that North Korea, Cuba, and Venezuela rank near the bottom. The ranking of the U.S. as among the freest economies in the world sharply contrasts with the political rhetoric of the past few decades in the U.S. Such a place in the rankings indicates that taxes, government spending, and regulation in the U.S. are lower relative to nearly every other country (and lower than any country with more than ten million inhabitants).

Variation in regulation and taxes is also seen when comparing U.S. states, where New York and California are bastions of government intervention (i.e., "liberal") and other states such as Florida and Texas are havens for a laissez-faire ("conservative") approach. Of course, despite their strong pro-government policies, New York and California have their share of individuals who put a premium on economic freedom, preferring less government intervention. Similarly, Florida and Texas have their share who prefer more government intervention. In fact, there is considerable overlap between California and Florida, in terms of where people fall in their support for government intervention, as shown in the nearby graph of responses to the survey measuring individual views on economic freedom described in Chapter 3. Recall that higher scores on the Capitalism Index indicate a more conservative, laissez-faire, free-market economic ideology, while lower scores represent a more liberal, government intervention approach. The graph shows that Florida has more freedom-loving conservatives, yes, but there's also an 80% overlap where residents of each state hold similar views; it's the remaining 20% of the population that is enough to lead to drastically different state policy (Fig. 11.1).

When we recognize that different people can have different preferences for freedom and that every state has a mix of preferences among its population, we realize that many people live with what they might consider to be either much more or much less economic freedom than they desire. Clearly California has conservative residents who prefer less government intervention just as Florida has liberals who prefer more government

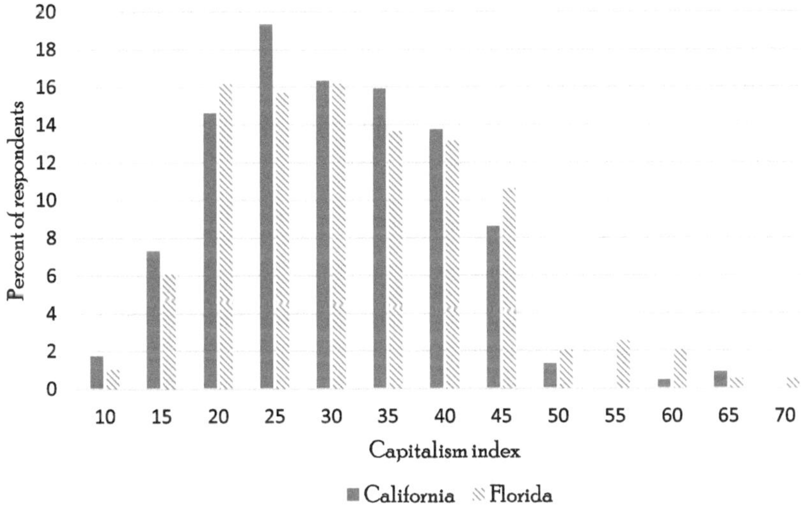

Fig. 11.1 Distribution of self reported economic ideology, CA and FL (Distribution of self-reported economic ideology (Capitalism Index) from "liberal" (left, lowest) to "conservative" for residents of two states. Note the large overlap of scores for individuals in these two states with very different public policies. (*Source* Author calculations based on responses to survey in Hadsell and Jones [2020])

intervention. Research I did with fellow economist Adam Jones suggests that differences between an individual's preference for economic freedom and the economic freedom they experience given their state policies have real consequences: it leads to lower satisfaction with life.[16] This is particularly true for individuals living in states with more economic freedom than they prefer (that is, for liberals living in a conservative state). The magnitude of the reduction in happiness for these individuals is of greater magnitude than the reduction from being divorced (rather than married) or unemployed (rather than employed). Which is to say, it's a big deal.

One option for individuals in a state that has too much or too little government for their liking is to move to a state with more suitable policies. Evidence suggests that this is happening, as states with higher levels of economic freedom generally have greater population inflows. Government regulation and taxes appear to be salient to many. But the evidence that this concern is driving migration is far from conclusive, as many factors are involved in decisions to move, and we have too little data on those decisions at the individual level to draw firm conclusions. Another option for dissatisfied residents is to vote for alternative policies, and our research indicates that individuals who are more dissatisfied with the amount of economic freedom in their state are more likely to vote. Such dissatisfaction appears to be a driving force in recent elections in the U.S. and Europe.

11.2 Other Conceptions of Economic Freedom

In contemporary discussion, some economists, most prominently Amartya Sen, accept that freedoms based on property rights and individual choice are important, but only if one is able to actualize them. The freedom to buy anything one wants, restricted only by one's income, is terrific for someone with a sufficient income but is not at all salient for someone with no means of earning the required income. Nor is income all that is required for one to have the ability to express freedom of choice in markets. Political freedom, freedom from discrimination, and so on are also required. Sen proposes a "capability" conception of freedom: freedoms are valuable only to the extent that people are capable of exercising those freedoms. Sen sees a set of linked freedoms:

[16] Hadsell and Jones (2020).

- political freedoms and transparency in relations between people;
- freedom of opportunity, including freedom to access credit; and
- economic protection from abject poverty, including through income supplements and unemployment relief.

Sen's conception sees a role for government to ensure rights and freedoms.

Many other conceptions of rights and freedoms arise from non-economists. President Franklin D. Roosevelt's *Four Freedoms*, enumerated in his 1941 State of the Union speech, suggests an emphasis on capabilities: Freedom of speech, Freedom of worship, Freedom from want, and Freedom from fear.[17] FDR's "Second Bill of Rights" lists the following rights upon which those freedoms are based:

- The right to a useful and remunerative job;
- The right to earn enough to provide adequate food and clothing and recreation;
- The right of every farmer to raise and sell his products at a return which will give him and his family a decent living;
- The right of every businessman, large and small, to trade in an atmosphere of freedom from unfair competition and domination by monopolies;
- The right of every family to a decent home;
- The right to adequate medical care and the opportunity to achieve and enjoy good health;
- The right to adequate protection from the economic fears of old age, sickness, accident, and unemployment;
- The right to a good education.

Clearly, FDR had what some consider to be a radical perspective—perhaps just as radical as that of the Founding Fathers, who, after all, advocated in the 1770s for a range of freedoms that were a significant break from the past: men are created equal (ok, so still limited in practice), "with certain unalienable Rights, that among these are Life, Liberty

[17] "The ideas enunciated in the Roosevelt's Four Freedoms were the foundational principles that evolved into … the Universal Declaration of Human Rights adopted by the United Nations in 1948 through the work of Eleanor Roosevelt." FDR Library (n.d.).

and the pursuit of Happiness." FDR's rights were meant to ensure the freedom necessary to fully participate in economic and political realms. The right to employment, a living wage, minimum income, housing, health care, food, and education are certainly as important today as ever. Without the security provided by these rights, there can be little freedom. Government intervention and oversight often is needed to ensure each of the above, although economists will differ on the strength of their agreement to such an assertion. Conservative economists will tend to insist, for example, that markets will ensure access to employment and decent income for all who are willing to work; that subsidized health care is an abridgement of freedom for those who are forced to pay taxes to fund it; and that social insurance (unemployment, social security) creates disincentives to work and save. Liberal economists would disagree with conservatives on many details (see Chapter 3 for a full discussion). Consider a right to education or health care, both particularly important today given the educational requirements of the U.S. economy and the high costs associated with health care. Each is required for full participation in a modern economy to say nothing of its importance to attaining a full life. Should distribution of essential goods and services such as these be left to markets unconstrained by government intervention (oversight, taxation, subsidies) when some people are clearly less able to obtain them?

11.3 Concluding Comments

Economic Freedom is a much larger concept than can be adequately covered in one short chapter, or even a single book, but hopefully this has been enough to get you thinking about the different perspectives of the role of government in markets—and more broadly, which freedoms are important to us.

Views about the meaning and the appropriate level of economic freedom differ among economists and the public and are a primary reason for various paradigms and ideologies, as discussed in earlier chapters. The crux of the liberal–conservative economic divide is the extent of government involvement in the economy.[18] Karl Marx, who, for example,

[18] Keep in mind that economic freedom is distinct from social freedom, such as related to gay rights, gun control, and abortion. You can see the conflict in American politics: conservative economic (liberal) policies promote freedom (government intervention) while conservative (liberal) social policies promote the opposite.

argued that workers in a capitalist society were free—free of the means of production, might well agree with 1960s folk/rock singer Janis Joplin that "freedom is just another word for nothing left to lose." Feminist economists will support the capabilities approach promoted by Amartya Sen: freedoms are of no use if one is at a distinct social or economic disadvantage. As these perspectives battle to be heard in the public realm, the implications for which prevails cannot be greater.

References

Appleby J (1984) Capitalism and a new social order: The republican vision of the 1790s. New York University Press, New York

Baer T, Schnall S (2021) Quantifying the cost of decision fatigue: suboptimal risk decisions in finance. Royal Society Open Science 8:201059. https://doi.org/10.1098/rsos.201059

FDR Library (n.d.). FDR and the four freedoms speech. https://www.fdrlibrary.org/four-freedoms. Accessed on 7 Jan 2022

Gwartney J, Lawson R, Murphy R (2023) EconomicfFreedom of the world: 2023 annual report. https://www.fraserinstitute.org/sites/default/files/economic-freedom-of-the-world-2023.pdf. Accessed on 30 Aug 2025

Hadsell L, Jones AT (2020) The company you keep: satisfaction with life, economic freedom, and preference-policy mismatch. J Comp Econ 48(3):642–657

Hall J, Lawson R (2014) Economic freedom of the world. Fraser Institute Annual Report.

Leeson P, Palm F (2020) Welfare. Public Choice 185(3–4):403–419

Madison J (1792). https://presspubs.uchicago.edu/founders/documents/v1ch16s23.html. Accessed on 30 Aug 2025

Mani A, Mullainathan S, Shafir E, Zhao J (2013) Poverty impedes cognitive function. Science 341:976–980

Persson E, Barrafrem K, Meunier A, Tinghög G (2019) The effect of poverty on risk preferences and rationality. Health Econ 28(10):1194–1203

Sandell MJ (2022) Democracy's discontent: A new edition for our perilous times. Harvard University Press, Cambridge, MA

Shroff R, Vamvourellis K (2022) The influence of resource scarcity on decision making. Judgm Decis Mak 17(6):1176–1207

Stennett D (2024) Louisiana hair braiders, florists, could see looser rules under House bills. The Advocate. https://www.theadvocate.com/baton_rouge/news/business/louisiana-hair-braiders-florists-could-see-looser-rules/article_a251db45-7120-5bb3-975a-444288f8c7eb.html. Accessed on 30 Aug 2025

Stroup MD (2007) Economic freedom, democracy, and the quality of life. World Dev 35(1):52–66

Vohs KD (2013) The poor's poor mental power. Science 341:969. https://doi.org/10.1126/science.1244172

Yglesias M (2013) Bad decisions don't make you poor. Being poor makes for bad decisions. Slate. Available at: https://slate.com/business/2013/09/poverty-and-cognitive-impairment-study-shows-money-troubles-make-decision-making-difficult.html. Accessed on 2 July 2025

CHAPTER 12

Profits: The Purpose of Business?

> There is one and only one social responsibility of business–to use its resources and engage in activities designed to increase its profits so long as it stays within the rules of the game, which is to say, engages in open and free competition without deception or fraud.[1]

More than three million people in the U.S. who are at risk for anaphylactic shock—serious allergic reaction—rely on the drug epinephrine delivered by the patented EpiPen. In 2007, the drug company Mylan acquired the rights to sell EpiPen. Within a couple of years, Mylan began drastically raising the EpiPen's price, from roughly $100 to, by 2016, more than $600. With effective marketing and few options for consumers, the number of EpiPens sold increased at the same time that the price was rising and EpiPen maintained market share of more than 90%.[2] Costs of manufacturing the drug seem to be unrelated to the price rise. Mylan paid about $34 for the manufacture of each EpiPen and the drug (epinephrine) itself costs about $1 per dose; manufacturing and packaging are estimated to be an additional $5 per dose. The disconnect between cost of production and price to consumers becomes even clearer when we note that the

[1] Milton Friedman

[2] Miyashiro (2017).

L. Hadsell, *Social Economics*,
https://doi.org/10.1007/978-3-032-21916-9_12

price in some other countries is far lower: about $50 per two-pack in the U.K. and about $100 in Canada.

As a result of the drastic price rises, Mylan endured public and Congressional scrutiny. Its primary defense was that it was only doing what for-profit companies do: maximizing profits, and there is nothing wrong with that.[3] But is the sole purpose of business to maximize profit? Or are there broader social reasons for their existence? That is to say, whose interests should businesses serve?

As legal creations, corporations and some other forms of business are given protections that elude people, including limited liability and, in the case of corporations, perpetual life. Do they consequently then have an obligation to the givers of said protection, i.e., society? In other words, should the business serve more than just its stockholders/owners? Should its goal, its purpose, extend beyond profit maximization? Do they also have an obligation to customers, workers, suppliers, and the community?

12.1 Constellation of Interests

Many economists on the conservative end of the ideological spectrum assert that maximizing profit—and therefore owner/shareholder wealth—is the only valid purpose of business. The argument is that profit maximization is achieved in a competitive environment by firms that efficiently provide the goods and services that consumers demand. By seeking profits, businesses must provide what consumers want, at the lowest price possible, satisfying their moral obligation to society and owners to use resources prudently. Archetypal conservative Milton Friedman famously pronounced in the early 1970s, "the sole purpose of a business is to generate profits for its shareholders," suggesting that seeking anything other than profit maximization is wrong, unethical. This has largely been the mantra of American business since.

The primary argument of economists like Friedman is that business success, measured by profits, represents a clear and objective measure of the good done for society, as consumers freely choose which products and firms to patronize—and unprofitable firms, those not efficiently satisfying

[3] A similar story can be told for Turing Pharmaceuticals, which raised the price of Daraprim, the sole approved treatment for a parasitic disease, from $13.50 to $750 per pill (Reich, 2018).

consumer demand, wither. Surely there is a great deal of logic to this.[4] And yet, that is not the end of the discussion. Consider monopolies such as Mylan's with its EpiPen. As holder of a patent protecting the design of the EpiPen (enforced by the legal system), Mylan seeks to maximize its return on the investment used to create it, much as other companies do in countless similar situations. The company will note that many millions of dollars were spent developing the product, with no guarantee of eventual success. Many development projects do, in fact, fail, returning nothing to their investors. They argue the high profits from successful products are fair compensation for the high risks taken. Still, some are asking if a profit-centric purpose of business is too narrow, even in situations less extreme than this. What about other stakeholders: customers, employees, suppliers, the community? Should customers' inability to pay the asking price for a much-needed product be of concern to the business? Is employee health a valid concern? Should impacts on social structure of the community influence business decisions? In short, should we expect business to serve a larger social purpose beyond profit maximizing? And if we do, what are the consequences? Such questions seem particularly relevant in an age of social media, whose purveyors have been accused of sacrificing individual and social well-being for profits, and artificial intelligence, the widespread adoption of which will upend society in unknowable ways.

At least two main concerns arise from the contention that the sole purpose of business is to maximize profit. First, the claim that profit maximization is an objective goal, whereas other goals represent subjective preferences, is simply incorrect. Choice of any goal is subjective, as one goal has to be valued above the possible alternatives. Justifying profit maximization because it requires that resources be used efficiently doesn't negate the fact that such a goal is one of many possible. The choice to place profits above other considerations is a value judgment. Providing a logical rationale makes it no less so. In short, the argument that the sole

[4] Observation of firm behavior reveals motivations sometimes more complex than simple profit maximization. Some firms appear to want to maximize market share or sales revenue. Within the organization, managers and workers often have goals that conflict with each other, and with owners of the firm. Managers may want to maximize the number of employees they manage—thereby increasing their compensation. Workers may want to maximize their own well-being, working less when they are not closely monitored.

purpose of business is to maximize profit is normative. Only after we have acknowledged this can we then discuss the alternatives on equal footing.

A second concern follows: focusing solely on profits and shareholder wealth to the exclusion of other perhaps equally or even more important aspects of life leads to potential individual, social, and ecological harm—even as the economic system upon which it is based is efficient in some narrow sense. It is not clear that profit maximization is in fact the best choice from society's perspective (nor even from the much narrower perspective of consumers, whom businesses say they ultimately serve). Mylan's price increases for the EpiPen represent one way consumers can be harmed. These price increases were based on Mylan's market power (i.e., status as a monopoly) rather than cost increases for supplying the product or changes in consumer demand. Consumers who could afford the higher prices transferred some of their wealth to Mylan; consumers who could not afford the higher prices went without, suffering consequences such as poorer health.

In other cases, we might consider environmental damage, such as climate change or acid rain, or the harm that excessive focus on efficiency has on workers enduring the repetition and monotony that often is associated with specialization. Specialization—focus on increasingly narrow, specific tasks—boosts efficiency and profits. But the increasingly narrow focus of repetitive work may lead to physical harm (such as carpal tunnel syndrome, the degeneration of tendons at the base of the wrist; or eyestrain from prolonged viewing of computer screens) and worker discontent.[5]

Or we might point to workers who have little or no say in determining their work schedules. According to the Bureau of Labor Statistics, one in five *salaried* workers were told their work schedule less than one week in advance. Among wage and salary workers aged 25 and over, the most constrained group was those with less than a high school diploma, in which one in three workers learned of their work schedule less than one week in advance. For workers with a bachelor's degree or higher the share was one in seven. More than a third of wage and salary workers did

[5] From a Marxist perspective, alienated labor refers (in one sense) to "labour in which the worker finds no purpose, no pleasure or contentment, no needs fulfilment, no independence or power, no mental growth or physical development." Mukhopadhyay (2020). One can also think of the goal of work associated with Buddhist economics in this context—purification of soul—as being greatly diminished by excessive specialization.

not have a flexible work schedule and had employers who decided their schedule without their input.[6] The problems created by such practices are particularly acute for households with children when childcare must be found on short notice—uncertain schedules do not facilitate stable childcare (similarly for eldercare). Uneven schedules limit opportunities to engage in planned non-work activities, ranging from recreation to formal education and even other employment, which is perhaps the main reason employers impose such schedules.

One might even consider another form of harm to be the adjustment costs associated with job loss unrelated to employee performance. Trade and technological innovation, hallmarks of an efficient for-profit system, require workers, suppliers, and the surrounding community to adjust, often abruptly, to new circumstances—reasonable when the changes are small or infrequent, or when those affected have invested little in the business, less so beyond that.

Substantial employment changes lead to community-level impacts, cascading via a multiplier effect, affecting workers, suppliers, and the local government. Amy Goldstein provides a vivid portrait of such changes in her chronicle of economic, social, and personal disruptions resulting from closure of an auto production plant, once the city's largest employer, in Janesville, Wisconsin.[7] Goldstein uses personal narratives to tell the stories of those affected: declines in wages, collapses in marriages and families, a tearing of the community fabric.[8] She provides a critique of job retraining programs, and the ability generally of many workers to adjust to sudden economic changes. Similar reverberations occurred in my hometown, a small town of 10,000 people in upstate New York when the major employer closed a textile mill employing 500 people. Secondary businesses closed, property values declined, homeowners decreased investment in their biggest asset, and local tax revenues fell. The high school opened a charity shop offering notebooks, coats, and personal care products such as soap and shampoo. The mill moved to lower cost production in non-union, lower tax North Carolina, and eventually, a decade later, to China, inflicting the similar pain on its North Carolina community.

[6] U.S. Bureau of Labor Statistics (2019).

[7] Goldstein (2017). See also Macy (2014).

[8] Senior (2017).

We might even consider how production itself can cause problems—most often in the form of air, water, and noise pollution. A gravel company with heavy trucks rumbling nearby, causing mountains of dust and noise, or a hog farm with large waste pools with the accompanying foul odor and polluted water are not uncommon examples. Do businesses have a responsibility to neighbors to mitigate harmful effects, even if doing so adds extensive costs for the firm? Perhaps the biggest example of ecological harm is global warming, though plenty of other examples abound, from "forever chemicals" (PFAS) to plastics. Similar questions concerning responsibility businesses have to consumers apply widely—most notably with social media. Do companies have an obligation to protect vulnerable consumers? Is it ethical to earn profits while exploiting individuals and harming social cohesion?

What obligation do companies (and their customers) have to others? What legal, social, and ethical constraints bind the decision of business to maximize profit? Surely, profit at-all-cost is not a desirable goal. The question is not should legal, social, and ethical constraints bind business decisions but which ones and how much.[9]

12.2 Shared Value

If we accept that profit is a necessary goal of business but that it is too narrow then we must ask how can customers, employees, suppliers, and the community be considered?[10] Many business leaders, academics, and politicians have been talking recently about alternatives to profit maximization, principles most often based on a concept called "Shared Value."[11] The Business Roundtable, for instance, representing interests of many of the largest companies in the U.S., has advocated alternatives to profit maximization as the sole purpose of business, focusing on the long-term impacts of business practices on the welfare of interested parties, arguing that the change of focus reflects "the business community's unwavering commitment to continue to push for an economy

[9] Another even more controversial example is gun shops.

[10] I understand that not all will. An editorial in the Wall Street Journal as I first wrote this paragraph praises the pull-back of environmentally and socially focused (ESG) initiatives. In short, a denunciation of anything but profit maximization as the goal of business. Wall Street Journal (2024).

[11] Porter and Kramer (2011)

that serves all Americans."[12] Business Roundtable members are no left-wingers: JPMorgan Chase & Co. chairman and CEO Jamie Dimon was the Roundtable's chairman in 2019, when the organization publicly proclaimed profit-centric purpose inappropriate. In fact, that public statement had a strong mainstream ideology foundation:

> Americans deserve an economy that allows each person to succeed through hard work and creativity and to lead a life of meaning and dignity. We believe the free-market system is the best means of generating good jobs, a strong and sustainable economy, innovation, a healthy environment and economic opportunity for all.

So, certainly not a radical organization. But is the Roundtable serious about stakeholders other than shareholders? The pledge provides weak and vague commitments to various stakeholders:

- Customers: "meeting or exceeding customer expectations."
- Employees: "fair" compensation, providing "important" benefits, training, and education. A commitment to "foster diversity and inclusion, dignity and respect."
- Suppliers: "Dealing fairly and ethically with."
- Community and environment: "Supporting the communities in which we work. We respect the people in our communities and protect the environment by embracing sustainable practices across our businesses."
- Shareholders: generating long-term value.

No concrete measures. In fact, two years after the Roundtable proclamation, a study from researchers at the University of Pennsylvania observed that "companies that had signed the Business Roundtable statement were more likely than other big companies to announce layoffs in the early months of the coronavirus pandemic of 2020—even as they paid out more money to shareholders."[13]

"B corporation" certifications may be an alternative in the direction of operationalizing the concepts central to shared value. Certified B

[12] Business Roundtable (2019). Gelles and Yaffe-Bellany (2019).

[13] Useem (2020).

corporations are verified by the non-profit organization B Lab. B corporation charters integrate interests of all stakeholders into the fiduciary duties of directors and officers.[14] As of early 2022, more than 4,600 businesses worldwide were designated B-corps. Because B-corp status is privately awarded, it has no legal backing. A similar organizational form, the "benefit corporation," is government designated and comes with legal standing. Currently certified by around three dozen U.S. states, these businesses include society, workers, the community, and the environment, alongside shareholders/owners, in their legally binding list of stakeholders. Also known as "public-benefit corporations" or PBCs, these businesses are required by law to consider the effect of corporate actions on multiple stakeholders. PBCs can fulfill their social and environmental responsibilities by, for example, donating a portion of their profits to charitable causes, reducing their carbon footprint, or hiring hard-to-employ people.

Benefit corporations and B-corps are not non-profits. They still seek profit but do so within constraints enumerated in their corporate purpose. Reasons for seeking either B-corp or Benefit Corporation status are twofold.[15] One is its lofty goal: a desire to make a positive impact by "creating a new economy with a new set of rules."[16] The second is practical: the hope that the designation will garner support from potential customers, creating goodwill and, potentially, more business.

An alternative approach is the steward ownership model.[17] In this formulation, businesses create perpetual-purpose trusts as an alternative to profit maximizing. Initiated by the organization Purpose Foundation in Germany in 2015, it came to the U.S. shortly afterward. As a perpetual-purpose trust, a business is bound to serve a particular, stated purpose rather than the interests of owners. Thus, the trust has a legal responsibility to a purpose rather than the more traditional maximization of shareholder wealth. The use of a perpetual-purpose trust works especially well for retiring business owners who want to preserve their focus on social value and for newer, younger entrepreneurs who seek an alternative to the typical profit-minded sources of capital.

[14] Kim and Schifeling (2016).

[15] Kim and Schifeling (2016).

[16] Kim and Schifeling (2016), p. 4.

[17] Romeo (2022).

ESOPs—employee stock-ownership plans—represent an additional option. In ESOPs, workers are the owners, and the fiduciary responsibility is to maximize worker wealth. One criticism of ESOPs is that meeting its stated purpose may mean selling the business to for-profit buyers, leading to a change in corporate goals (as happened to craft-brewer Fat Tire Beer Company). Such a designation also neglects other non-employee aspects (such as community and environment). Publix Super Markets and W. L. Gore (maker of waterproof Gore-Tex fabrics) are among the largest ESOPs.

A very different view is that shortcomings associated with a profit-centric focus can best be addressed with government oversight without changing the profit-maximizing framework.[18] This view touts the benefits of efficiency and competition associated with the goal of profit maximization, noting that market economies based on profit maximization have lifted billions out of poverty in the last century. Proponents argue that rather than distracting for-profit businesses with other less well-defined goals, it is best to allow the system to work as is, with government oversight of relationships between business and workers (e.g., health and safety laws), customers (truth in advertising laws), community (requiring prior notification when a large business closes down), and environment (pollution regulation).

Which approach is best? While the ultimate goal of any business is to be profitable, is profit, as Milton Friedman asserts, the "one and only one social responsibility of business"? While staunch free-market advocates would have it no other way, many, even some owners, disagree. A majority of shareholders have, for example, in recent years supported corporate policies consistent with shared value, including requirements to disclose: effectiveness of pollution policies (DuPont, with 81% shareholder approval); political contributions (Duke Energy, 52% approval); lobbying activities related to global warming (ExxonMobil, 64% approval); effectiveness of protecting the human rights of workers suppliers (Wendy's, 95% approval).[19]

[18] Clyde et al. (nd).

[19] Hart and Zingales (2022).

12.3 Goals vs. Purpose

One key to understanding the proper role for and organization of business is to differentiate between goals and purpose. As business professor Paul Clyde explains,

> A goal is something we strive for that should be aligned with our purpose. Reaching our goal will help us accomplish our purpose. Goals usually emerge from a visioning process, or at the very least a "plan" that keeps us headed in the right direction, serving our purpose. Goals are meant to … serve our purpose. Our purpose does not serve our goals — it helps us create them.[20]

Colin Mayer of Oxford University defines purpose as a "fundamental reason for being." Thus,

> purpose is not the sole pursuit of profits, but the animating force for achieving them.... The purpose of business is not to produce profits. The purpose of business is to produce profitable solutions to the problems of people and planet. And in the process it produces profits. But profits are not per se the purpose·[21]

Mayer provides the example of Novo Nordisk, a maker of insulin. In the early 2000s, the company realized that because of pervasive poverty in areas with high type 2 diabetes, their insulin product provided little relief. Clarifying the difference between goals and purpose, Novo Nordisk decided that its.

> purpose was not to produce insulin, it was to help to treat people who got type 2 diabetes of which insulin might be one approach but there were many others. So they started thinking about what was the most appropriate form in which to provide treatment for diabetes in different locations when it realized, well, actually, its purpose was not just to treat people who've got diabetes, its purpose was to try and prevent people from getting type 2 diabetes in the first place, which was often a matter of lifestyle changes. So it worked with local communities [and] NGOs to try and find ways of influencing the lifestyles of people in different parts of the world. Now

[20] Hewertson (2014).

[21] The Future of the Corporation, Economy and Society (2019), beginning at 30:00.

> you might say that's all very noble but isn't it rather unfortunate for Novo Nordisk's business model, because it meant that it was going to sell less insulin? The answer was exactly the opposite because what emerged from that was that Novo Nordisk was deemed to be a trustworthy supplier not just of insulin but of health products much more generally and for advice and assistance in finding real solutions. It demonstrated a real interest in the benefits it was conferring on its customers, its patients and the various parties it was working with. And as a result of that its business bloomed and flourished on the back of the trust that it created with the various parties with which it was working.[22]

For Meyer, the key is bilateral commitment: business commits to its core purpose and those who help to create it, "and those people in turn commit to creating that corporate purpose, and that gives rise to reciprocal relations of trust and reciprocity."

12.4 Ownership and Property Rights

Movement away from the single-minded focus on profit maximization will require a change to the common conception of ownership and property rights—claims to the benefits derived from owning property. We might start by thinking of ownership as either active or passive.[23] Day-to-day involvement in the use of assets is indicative for the former. In contrast, stockholders (investors) are representative of passive ownership, as they transfer to others (managers) day-to-day decisions regarding their property.[24] Because of this dual nature of ownership, property rights are thus differentiated. One view of this duality is described as the principal-agent problem in Agency Theory. In this view, the conflict between owners, who presumably want to maximize profits, and agents (managers and their subordinates), who have a range of other goals, all pointing to maximizing their own welfare, is resolved by providing the right set of incentives to align the agents' goals with those of the owners. Owners are seen as having primacy in this relationship, as they own the assets and are risking their capital. That is, workers' interests are aligned to those of owners, not the other way around.

[22] Ibid.

[23] Blair (1995).

[24] Bearle and Means (1932).

A second view holds that because stockholders surrender direct control of their assets—take a passive role—they therefore relinquish some of their ownership/property rights and the benefits thereto. Managers, responsible for day-to-day decisions, are entitled to a share of the benefits derived from that property. This recognition of the ownership rights of managers, and by extension, workers and other stakeholders, opens the door for goals other than profit maximization.

In explaining this second perspective, Margaret Blair describes how property rights can be separated into five categories, as depicted in Fig. 12.1: right to possess, right to use, right to dispose of, right to exclude others, and right to manage and control. In a typical corporate set up, managers possess the owners' property—i.e., productive assets such as buildings, machinery, and so on. These are under the managers' care. Managers' day-to-day decisions also determine how those assets are used. Those assets are under the managers' management and control. As such, under this view a portion of the property rights associated with the asset are directed to the manager. Owners/shareholders share in decisions regarding the use and management/control of a firm's assets; they also have the right to dispose of those assets, either directly by selling the asset or indirectly by selling their ownership interest. Under this perspective, contributions of effort and sacrifice determine what is a just distribution of benefits from those assets.[25] How one views these interests will inform one's view of property rights and hence, compensation for managers and owners.

12.5 Risky Business

We also hear the contention that owners/shareholders have the right to be compensated for taking risks associated with investing in business ventures, as described in the bedrock economics of the risk-return relationship: riskier investments must promise greater returns if those investments are to be appealing to investors. Pharmaceutical development offers a prime example. Hundreds of millions of dollars are typically spent researching and developing each new drug, with no promise of a positive future return. Such large expenditures will only be undertaken by the private sector if investors are provided appropriate compensation for

[25] Blair, p. 225.

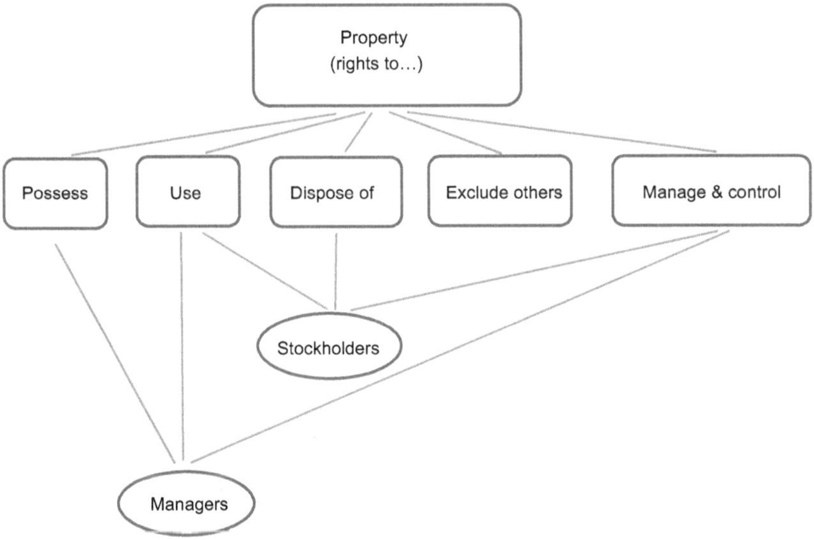

Fig. 12.1 Separation of Ownership and Control. Property Rights as a Bundle of Rights (The relationship between property ownership and rights. Based on Blair (1995), p. 224)

the risk taken—i.e., only if large profits can be expected for successful drugs. Extended to businesses generally, the idea is the same: opening a new coffee shop, gas station, or software company, or developing a new product is risky, given the small chance of success. Only the promise of a large return on investment elicits interest from potential investors or entrepreneurs. While quite logical and reasonable, there are at least three replies questioning the primacy of owner/investor claims to profits[26]:

1. Investors can easily diversify their investments such that extraordinary risk in ventures such as pharmaceutical development can be eliminated. This is a foundational concept of finance: creation of portfolios of varied investments can eliminate or, at least, greatly reduce, any firm-specific (or even product-specific) risk and so those risks should not be rewarded. Only systematic risk, risk which cannot

[26] Blair, p. 229.

be eliminated, should be rewarded. Bottom line: the ability to diversify risk, whether or not actually done, greatly reduces the claim the investor has to the profits (or losses) of one particular business. Note that employees, suppliers, and communities are often much less able than investors to diversify their risks related to the business.

2. Limited liability shifts some risk to others—customers, suppliers, workers, lenders. Corporations (and certain other business forms) enjoy limited liability: legal protection from having to make good on financial losses that exceed their initial investments in the firm. This greatly limits downside risk for investors—and should therefore limit claims to profits based on risk.
3. Investors typically can easily sever their involvement in a firm—by selling stock, for example. Employees, suppliers, and the community find it much more difficult to do so. Employees can find new jobs, but high costs often are involved, including costs associated with loss of human capital (knowledge, expertise) that is specific to that employer or product: moving to another job means loss of the earnings premium associated with that know-how. Suppliers and communities often build long-term relationships with businesses, with corresponding long-term investment (e.g., in infrastructure and personnel), creating risk for them if those relationships disappear or diminish. Investors' ability to easily change their investment exposure by selling ownership rights greatly reduces their risk associated with ownership, just as not having this ability increases risk for other parties.

Taken as a whole, these three arguments provide a serious counterweight to the notion of shareholders as the only claimants on the profits of the firm, and on the primacy of profit maximization itself. If stakeholders other than shareholders are to be duly compensated for the risks they take then a business purpose that encompasses more than shareholder profit maximization should be considered.

Criticisms of Shared Value, B-corp status, and similar approaches to revamping business goals and purpose highlight the "difficult to quantify" aspect of alternatives to profit. We may appreciate that value to workers is measured by more than wages and at the same time reasonably argue that that value is too difficult to quantify: How much is dignified and meaningful work worth? How is that measured? Value to the community of a good corporate neighbor may be more than the number of people employed, or tax revenue generated, but how is it measured? If it can't be measured, how do we know we are satisfying the business' purpose? Profit is a simpler alternative.

A further criticism is that having managers pursue more-difficult-to-measure goals just exacerbates the principal-agent problem: the long-standing issue of managers pursuing their own goals (or in the case of shared value conceptions: preferences of workers, suppliers, or community) rather than owners'. This concern was partially addressed earlier when we separated property rights into five components, which says, in part, that managers (and others) have more at stake than is typically recognized and therefore should have more say in the use of a firm's assets, and the benefits derived from them. Nonetheless, expanding goals also expands the potential for abuse by those who are entrusted with meeting those goals. The primary issue here is accountability: if profits are the focus, shareholders react to poor profits by selling their shares or voting for a change in management; if a range of goals in addition to profit are the focus, who holds the business accountable if those goals are not achieved? As important, how are the goals decided upon? And if ownership rights are to be distributed, how do we decide what are the appropriate shares of ownership?

These are all important criticisms—but they should not be seen as unsurmountable. After all, just because something is easily quantifiable does not mean that it is worth having. And similarly, just because something is difficult to quantify does not mean it is not worth pursuing.

12.6 Concluding Comments

Whose interests should businesses serve? Focusing on profit alone has its shortcomings, as do alternatives. The main idea with Shared Value and similar alternatives discussed in this chapter is that businesses' responsibilities extend beyond shareholders/owners to a much wider group of stakeholders that includes customers, employees, suppliers, and the community, in addition to the shareholders.[27] Refocusing on a wider array of constituents leads to wealth creation in a broader sense, enriching all stakeholders, including owners.

[27] Corporate stakeholders are "groups and individuals who benefit from or are harmed by, and whose rights are violated or respected by, corporate actions." Freeman (1997).

Society already recognizes stakeholders as important partners. Employee interests are protected by a multitude of labor and safety regulations, from overtime pay and rest requirements to limitations on handling hazardous chemicals. Community interests are recognized in laws that limit corporate activities: some types of businesses are not allowed to operate outside certain hours of the day or on certain days of the week, and many states and localities require large firms to provide the government and other interested parties (e.g., labor unions) notice upon planned cessation of operations. Some argue that corporations, as creations of the state, with special protections and rights (such as limited liability and perpetual life), and a legally declared equivalence to people in terms of political participation, are not simply a "nexus of contracts," agreements between individuals, as some see it, but rather are social creations, with responsibilities that extend beyond any individual obligations created in contracts for services.

Perhaps the biggest question of all is, can socially responsible firms, following the goals outlined above: (1) provide greater wealth for society and (2) survive in a competitive market-based environment? One possible outcome for an individual firm of widening the focus to more stakeholders is that revenues will decline, or costs will increase—looking after the interests of employers, suppliers, and community can have costs, after all. But another possibility is that a different focus for the business may lead to increased worker productivity (reducing costs), greater cooperation between business and local government (with lower regulatory compliance costs), and preference from suppliers (reducing inventory costs). Perhaps there'll even be appreciation from customers, leading to increased sales revenue. Thus, viability of shared value businesses is ultimately an empirical one.

References

Bearle A, Means G (1932) The modern corporation and private property.

Blair M (1995) Whose interests should corporations serve. The corporation and its stakeholders. Brookings Institution, Washington, DC

Business Roundtable (2019) Business Roundtable redefines the purpose of a corporation to promote 'an economy that serves all Americans'. 19 August. Available at: https://www.businessroundtable.org/business-roundtable-redefines-the-purpose-of-a-corporation-to-promote-an-economy-that-serves-all-americans. Accessed on 20 Jan 2022

Clyde P, Haynes K, Xu T (nd) The social impact of profit-maximizing firms. Social Science Research Network. Available at: https://ssrn.com/abstract=3284113. Accessed on 2 July 2025

Freeman RE (1997) A stakeholder theory of the modern corporation. In: Beauchamp TL, Bowie NE (eds) Ethical theory and business. Prentice Hall, Upper Saddle River, NJ, pp 66–76

Gelles D, Yaffe-Bellany D (2019) Shareholder value is no longer everything, top C.E.O.s say. New York Times, 19 August. Available at: https://www.nytimes.com/2019/08/19/business/business-roundtable-ceos-corporations.html Accessed on 11 Jan 2022

Goldstein A (2017) Janesville. C-SPAN. Available at: https://www.c-span.org/video/?436317-4/amy-goldstein-discusses-janesville Accessed on 2 July 2025

Hart OD, Zingales L (2022) The new corporate governance. NBER Working Paper 29975

Hewertson R (2014) Knowing the difference between a purpose and a goal. The Business Journals. Available at: https://www.bizjournals.com/bizjournals/how-to/growth-strategies/2014/03/knowing-difference-between-purpose-and-goal.html Accessed on 2 July 2025

Kim S, Schifeling T (2016) Varied incumbent behaviors and mobilization for new organizational forms: The rise of triple-bottom line business amid both corporate social responsibility and irresponsibility. SSRN. Available at: https://ssrn.com/abstract=2794335 or https://doi.org/10.2139/ssrn.2794335

Macy B (2014) Factory Man: How one furniture maker battled offshoring, stayed local—And helped save an American Town. Little, Brown and Company, New York

Miyashiro AK (2017) Mylan's EpiPen Pricing Scandal. https://sevenpillarsinstitute.org/mylans-epipen-pricing-scandal/. Accessed on 30 Aug 2025

Mukhopadhyay R (2020) Karl Marx's theory of alienation. https://www.researchgate.net/publication/351458559_Karl_Marx's_Theory_of_Alienation. https://doi.org/10.13140/RG.2.2.20186.47044.

Porter ME, Kramer MR (2011) Creating shared value. Harvard Business Review.

Reich R (2018) America has a Shkreli problem. Wilmington Star News, 14 March, p. A19.

Romeo N (2022) Can companies force themselves to do good. New Yorker Magazine. Available at: https://www.newyorker.com. Accessed on 2 July 2025

Senior J (2017) Book review: In 'Janesville,' when the G.M. plant closed, havoc followed. New York Times, 19 April. Available at: https://www.nytimes.com/2017/04/19/books/review-janesville-amy-goldstein.html. Accessed on 2 July 2025

The Future of the Corporation, Economy and Society (2019) [video] with Prof Colin Mayer and Sir Paul Collier. Available at: https://www.youtube.com/watch?v=_3uv4iP1c5U. Accessed on 2 July 2025

U.S. Bureau of Labor Statistics. "Job Flexibilities and Work Schedules Summary". Economic News Release. September 24, 2019. https://www.bls.gov/news.release/flex2.nr0.htm.

Useem J (2020) Beware of corporate promises. The Atlantic. Accessed on August 30, 2025 at https://www.theatlantic.com/ideas/archive/2020/08/companies-stand-solidarity-are-licensing-themselves-discriminate/614947/

Wall Street Journal (2024) The retreat from ESG proxy voting. Wall Street Journal, 16 May, p. A14.

CHAPTER 13

Incentives and Rewards

> A society that puts equality before freedom will get neither. A society that puts freedom before equality will get a high degree of both.[1]

Imagine dividing the country into five groups, from the poorest on the left to the richest on the right, each with 20% of the population. Focus on wealth (or "net worth"), not income; so, consider assets minus liabilities, or what you own minus what you owe. Now think about these two questions: (1) How do you suppose all wealth in the U.S. is distributed among those five groups? That is, what percentage of total wealth do you estimate each group has? and (2) What do you consider the ideal distribution of wealth?

Responses from a survey of Americans indicate a wide discrepancy between actual and perceived distribution (as shown in Fig. 13.1). The consensus perception was that the wealthiest 20% have slightly more than 50% of all wealth in the U.S. But the actual distribution shows that the top 20% of households have more than 80% of wealth. Perhaps more striking is the difference between respondents' perceived distribution and their ideal distribution. In the respondents' ideal distribution, the wealthiest would have half of what respondents think they have, and only a third of

[1] Milton Friedman

L. Hadsell, *Social Economics*,
https://doi.org/10.1007/978-3-032-21916-9_13

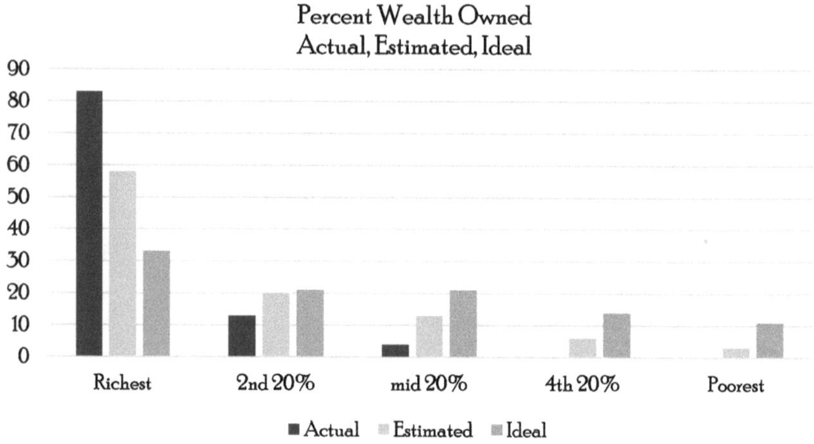

Fig. 13.1 Wealth distribution (U.S. wealth distribution. Estimated and Ideal distributions are based on responses to surveys by Norton and Ariely [2011]. Actual distribution is at the time the survey was administered [2005]. Wealth distribution is substantially the same in 2025)

what they actually have. The wealthiest in the U.S. are far wealthier than typically perceived and far wealthier than ideal. In other words, the actual distribution is both more unequal than they think it is and much more unequal than they would prefer. The story is similar for the distribution of income, though income is not quite as unequally distributed as wealth.

Inequality of both wealth and income in the U.S. has risen dramatically since about 1980 and is greater than in most other economically developed countries, though even with large and growing inequality, and notwithstanding the aforementioned survey results, Americans are least likely among economically developed countries to believe that their inequality is "too large."[2] This chapter explores the reasons for large economic inequality and why we tolerate it.

The freedom to succeed or fail on one's own, free from government constraint or assistance has been central to this country's ethos since its beginning and may help explain why Americans generally tolerate such large inequality. We see fierce push back in political discourse against taxes and spending directly aimed at redistribution, and as a result the U.S.

[2] Sawhill and Morton (2007).

economic system, despite the common perception among Americans of being heavily taxed and regulated, is among the freest in the world, with lower taxes and spending than most other countries. There's a strong conviction among many in the U.S. that economic success is generally the result of hard work and a willingness to take risks, and that economic failure results from sloth and bad choices. The implication is that while many in the U.S. may think inequality is larger than ideal, the emphasis placed on freedom and the belief in the *American Dream* means that inequality is not seen by many as a problem, especially when one can climb the economic ladder through grit and hard work. Here we encounter another common misperception among Americans: we will see shortly that actual economic mobility is also less than ideal in America and less than it is in many other countries.

13.1 Why Unequal?

As detailed by others, the primary drivers of increasing wage inequality over the past half century include increased demand for knowledge-based labor (i.e., college-educated workers), technology changes, and globalization. Also playing a role are winner-take-all markets (where star performers have much higher incomes than next-tier talent), lower rates on top incomes, and cost of employer provided health care—which can add more than five dollars per hour to labor costs, making employment of lower-wage workers much less appealing. Still, there's more to the story.

Consider the widening education gap. The wage premium that college graduates earn above that of non-grads peaked around 2000.[3] Before 2000, the differential reflected increasingly higher wages for college grads, as demand for them increased faster than their supply, and declining demand for high school grads. Since about 2000, wages for recent college graduates have declined (once adjusted for inflation), as the increasing domestic supply of such workers has outpaced the demand for them. For those without a college degree the outcome is little better; China's admittance to the World Trade Organization (WTO) in 2001 accelerated the decline in blue-collar work in the U.S. The gap between the two persists but is declining because both are losing ground, with college grads faring a bit worse. Part of the reason for declining college-educated income is

[3] Cleveland Federal Reserve (2012)

computer and communications technology, connecting U.S.-based work to a dramatically larger pool of skilled workers overseas, especially in India. Expect the decline in white-collar wages to continue with widespread adoption AI. What began fifty years ago as a threat only to blue-collar workers is now knocking on the office door.

We have also witnessed a hollowing out of so-called "middle-skill" work—white-collar office, administrative, and clerical jobs, particularly notable in urban areas where workers without a college degree once often held such jobs.[4] Change started in the 1970s, with widespread adoption of computer technology and increased international trade. Middle-skill jobs disappeared and as a result wages for non-college grads in urban areas declined. Labor economist David Autor notes, "While workers are vastly more educated and jobs are vastly more skill-intensive in today's cities compared to five decades ago, non-college workers in these places perform substantially less skilled work than they did decades earlier"—with the related decline in wages. In short, fewer opportunities for non-college workers in urban areas is a main driver of the inequality seen in the education gap.

Changing marriage patterns also play a role. Individuals tend to marry someone with a similar education level—called assortative mating.[5] College grads marry other college grads, while lower income high school-only grads do likewise, with much less economic success, widening inequality between households.[6] Further, compared with college graduates, women without college degrees "are more likely to enter into cohabiting partnerships early and bear children while cohabiting, are less likely to transition quickly into marriage, and have much higher divorce rates" when they do marry, all of which are associated with lower income.[7]

An additional consequence of assortative mating is the widening gap between households in their ability to provide their children not only the right education, but also the connections and financial support so-often helpful in getting first jobs and homes. Children in high-income/wealth

[4] Autor (2019).

[5] Lundberg et al. (2016).

[6] We have also seen increased geographic segregation by income, which further exacerbates inequality through peer effects and social networks.

[7] Lundberg et al. (2016), p. 80.

households score higher on SATs, are more likely to attend and complete college, and earn higher incomes as adults. I will return to this discussion with additional details later.

13.2 A Problem? Or a Benefit?

Now, though, let's ask the question that is central to the discussion: is inequality, even vast inequality, a problem, or should inequality be tolerated or even encouraged because it provides benefits that exceed any negatives? To properly address these questions, we need to recognize first that there are both benefits and costs associated with economic inequality, and that those benefits and costs extend beyond typical economic measures—impacting society in a wide range of ways.

One argument for why inequality, perhaps even large inequality, is necessary and beneficial is that the potential for a much higher income serves as a motivator—for everyone along the distribution. The American Dream assumes that those who want to succeed can through good choices and hard work, suggesting that inequality is not necessarily undesirable: One person may desire to earn a high income by earning a college degree, working additional hours, taking on more responsibility, and climbing the corporate ladder while another person with similar potential declines to exert the same effort and thus chooses to forgo the additional income. One might reasonably argue that the unequal outcomes that result from free choice regarding work effort, educational attainment, desire for advancement, and so on, are fair return to the individuals.

Later, we will address several problems with this perspective. For now, let's accept the merit of the argument and consider first whether inequality serves as a motivator. Do pay differentials incentivize people to work harder and make different choices? How individuals react to differential pay between managers and those they manage provides insight here.[8] Economist Zoe Cullen finds that salary differences between an employee and their boss (one or two levels up), what we can call vertical inequality, is motivating: it elicits more effort and better performance from subordinates, consistent with career concerns and hope for advancement. But she found that salary differences between individuals with similar job titles—horizontal inequality—is demotivating, associated with

[8] Cullen and Perez-Truglia (2022). Cullen et al. (2024).

lower effort and performance. This latter inequality was seen as unfair, as we might expect, stifling effort and reducing cooperation among coworkers.[9]

Psychologist Nicolas Sommet and colleagues also examine how inequality is perceived and whether it is motivating or demotivating.[10] They suggest that perception is based on comparison which elicits "social status competition"—reaction to inequalities by differential status.[11] In essence, many people have a desire to be perceived as high-status (higher in the income distribution) and a fear of being perceived as low-status. Among these people, the striving for high status (an "appetitive" or approach motivation), results in an increase of workhours, more economic risk-taking, and more conspicuous consumption. Similarly, a desire to avoid low status (an "aversive" or avoidance motivation), reflects a "fear of failure" and can result in withdrawal from competition (for a promotion or employment), seen as a reduction in effort.[12] The former might be seen as a "will to win" and the latter a "will not to lose"—in this case, losing is avoided by withdrawing from the competition.

One's view of the motivational aspects of inequality (and its fairness) may hinge on the level of economic mobility—the ability to move up or down the income/wealth distributions. After all, the thinking goes, if the opportunity to rise or fall on the income ladder is available to all then poor kids can succeed through grit and hard work, just as rich kids can fail through timidity and sloth. The American Dream is based on the notion that all have a good shot at economic success. Our lives may begin with the luck of the draw but what we do with that luck goes a long way to determining where we end up later on.

So what do the data say about relative economic mobility? By now, the conclusion that economic mobility is not quite as good as portrayed in the typical American Dream story is well-known among social scientists and is illustrated in Fig. 13.2, representative for the U.S. It shows how individuals starting in either the lowest or highest 20% (quintile) of the income distribution move over a 17-year period. The blue bars (left in

[9] See Tokumaru (2016).

[10] Sommet et al. (2019).

[11] Reflecting a slew of research that suggests social status is a key contributor/factor. See also Wilkinson and Pickett (2010).

[12] See Wilkinson and Pickett (2010), p. 226.

each pair) indicate that people who began in the lowest earning households mostly remained there nearly two decades later: 42% of the poorest remained in the lowest quintile and 23% moved up to the next to lowest quintile. Only 8% made it all the way to the top. Of course, if they had an even chance of moving up, then the bars would be all the same height—those who started in the lowest group would be evenly distributed across all groups 17 years later (and the same would be true for the top 20% group). We don't see anything close to that—and it's hard to imagine this lack of movement is by choice. The story for those starting in the highest 20% is a mirror image. More than half (54%) remained where they started, and another quarter stayed in the next to top group. Few fell from the top to the bottom over the two-decade period.[13]

That was intragenerational mobility, movement of individuals over time. Another common measure looks at individuals compared to their

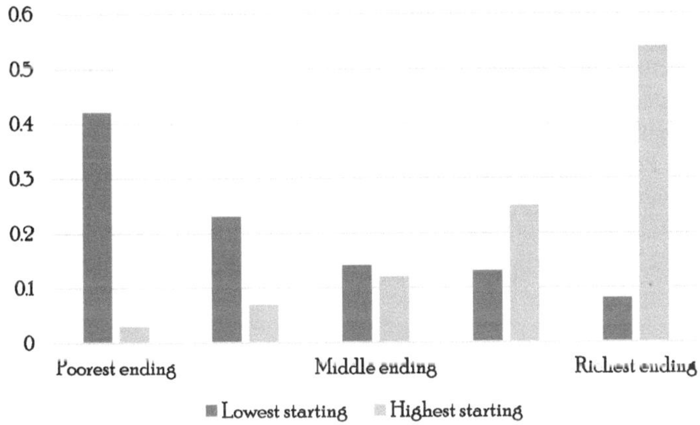

Fig. 13.2 Relative Intragenerational economic mobility in the U.S (For individuals starting in the lowest income (poorest) and the highest income (richest) quintiles: share of each group in each quintile at end of 17-year period, 1974–1991. Author graphic based on data in Gottschalk (1997), p. 37)

[13] The data depicted show mobility from 1970–1987. A similar tale is told using more recent data. See Bengali and Daly (2013).

parents—intergenerational mobility.[14] Intergenerational mobility presents a similar pattern, as shown in Fig. 13.3, which is a little more comprehensive (and messy) than the previous. The five groups of bars are ordered from poorest to richest at birth and show where individuals within each group end up as adults. That is, the height of each bar shows the percentage of people in each adult income quintile grouped by their birth income quintile. For instance, the first group of bars shows where people who started in the poorest quintile end up as adults: nearly 45% who started in the bottom stayed in the bottom (first) quintile (bar #1); just over 20% of that beginning group moved to the second quintile (bar #2), and so on. Just over 5% moved all the way from the bottom to the top (bar #5).

What one notices immediately is the "pull" from the ends: Individuals starting in the lowest two groups have a much higher chance of staying in that end of the distribution than they have of moving up; and individuals starting in the highest two groups have a much higher chance of staying in that end of the distribution than falling. In short, if you are born to poor parents, you are very likely to be poor as an adult; and if you are born to rich parents, you are very likely to be rich as an adult. This tendency to stay "close to home" reflects what economist Mary Daley calls either the "Parental Penalty" or the "Parental Advantage."[15] The parental advantage is similar in the U.S. relative to other developed countries, while the parental penalty is larger, reflecting the relatively small social safety net in the U.S.: less support for pre-k education; less generous maternity

[14] The four types of economic mobility ask similar questions:

a. Absolute, Intergenerational: Do offspring have higher income than parents did?
b. Absolute, Intragenerational: Does an individual's income increase over her/his lifetime?
c. Relative, Intergenerational: Are offspring higher/lower on the income ladder compared to their parents?
d. Relative, Intragenerational: Is an individual higher/lower on the income ladder compared to their own position years earlier?

Relative mobility, unlike absolute mobility, accounts for shifting goal posts in terms of rising incomes associated with growing economies.

[15] Daley (2012). Note that Daley contends that only at the ends—the bottom and top 20%—do parents appear to have a major influence on offspring economic mobility; that in the middle 60%, the distribution is evenly split across the groupings. I disagree with that assessment, as explained more in Chapter 18.

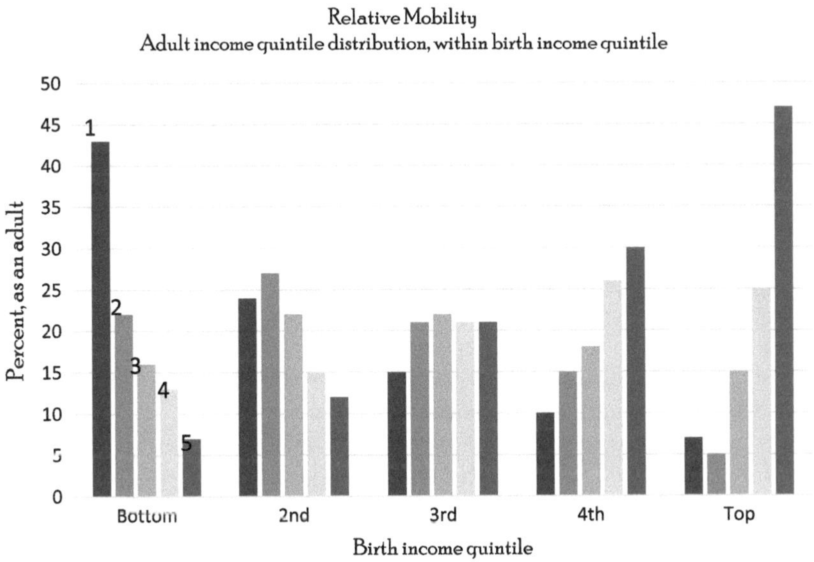

Fig. 13.3 Relative intergenerational mobility (*Source* PSID data and Daley [2012])

leave; substandard health care for the poor; and the like. In other words, a "freer" economy—one with much less government intervention.

What are some explanations of the "Parental Advantage"? Why do individuals in the top quintile rarely fall from that position? Abigail McKnight of the London School of Economics says richer parents create a "glass floor"—financial and emotional support for their children during rough patches, forestalling eviction, bankruptcy, and so on that might otherwise befall the adult child. Even assisting with a downpayment for a home or auto provides a tremendous boost not available to children of parents with lesser means. Richer parents also help their children develop soft skills (communication and social skills), self-esteem, and confidence, all valued by the market. Differences between families in support for children can be summed up in terms of three kinds of "capital":

- Economic (savings, home equity, and so on);
- Social network; and

- Cultural (interest in art galleries, museums, and the like).[16]

The highest segments of society, the "elite," are high in all three, with social networks providing a vital difference, according to Sociologist Michael Savage. Children of well-off parents are provided with a leg-up that remains throughout the child's life. The same life-long effects, pulling in the opposite direction, can also be said of children of less well-off parents, reflecting the parental penalty.

For children of poorer parents, barriers persist even if one is successful in getting a foot in the door. What happens afterward, promotion and advancement, appears to be as much of a stumbling block. Studying British data, Sociologist Sam Friedman finds that even after controlling for education, training, experience, and other factors that one expects to affect promotion into high-level positions, individuals from working-class backgrounds were 17% less likely to be in a high-level position and were paid less compared to individuals from "elite" backgrounds. It was worse for women and in certain professions (e.g., finance, medicine, IT) as well as certain geographic areas (in this case, cities such as London). Cultural capital is likely one influence: "getting along," networking, "fitting in" can tip the scale. We are social creatures, after all.

Economic mobility in many other developed economies—Denmark, France, Sweden—exceeds that seen in the U.S., with the greatest difference appearing at the bottom of the distribution.[17] The pithy expression "If you want to live the American Dream, you should move to Denmark," appears to be supported by the data. This is true even though the U.S. has much freer—i.e., less regulated and taxed—labor markets than almost all other industrialized countries, and so, presumably, more opportunity.

13.3 Just Get an Education

College is often put forth as the great equalizer. Is it? Yes and no. Figure 13.4 shows four groups of individuals: the left two groups are people born into the poorest households; the right two groups are those born into the richest. Each set of groups is further divided into those who did not earn a college degree and those that did. For each of the four

[16] McKnight (2015).

[17] New York Times (2012).

possibilities, the graph depicts in which quintile of the income distribution individuals within each particular starting group ended up as adults.

The middle two sets of bars are most interesting, showing similar outcomes for individuals from very different starting points. The difference is that one group had to earn a college degree to get there while the other did not. For those born into the poorest families, earning a college degree helps you move away from the low end of the distribution while a similar individual who does not get a college degree (that left-most group of the four) is likely to remain near the bottom. In that sense, getting that degree is a great equalizer. Looking at the two outside groups, we see that for those born into the richest families, earning a college degree helps you remain at the highest end of the distribution. And for the poorest, not getting a college degree leads nowhere. Simply put, reaching the top of the distribution, or even the middle, is easier for people born into high-income households. College appears to be a great equalizer for those in the bottom, in the sense that if you get a college education, you

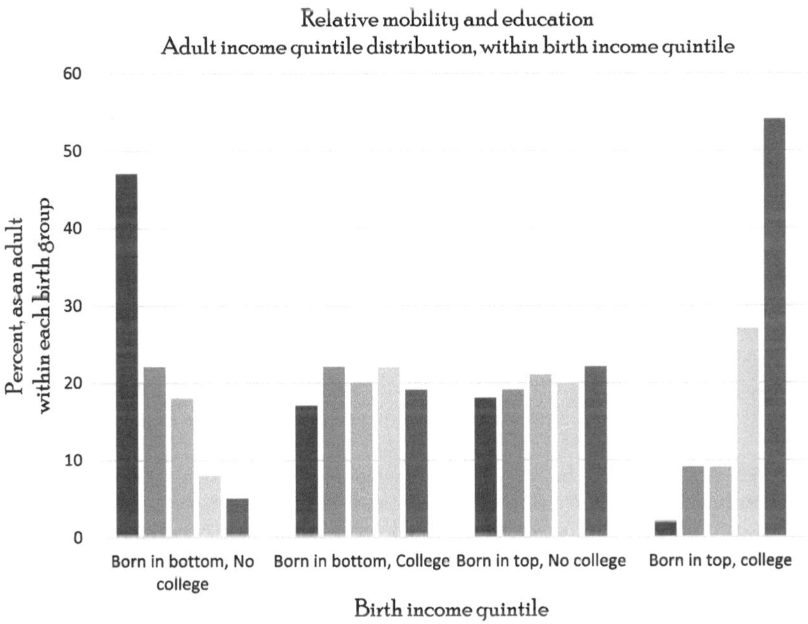

Fig. 13.4 Education and mobility (Based on Daley [2012])

have a roughly even chance of getting anywhere in the income distribution. But how much of a "great equalizer" depends on one's perspective. Even opening access to college for the poorest members of our society, through state-supported colleges, financial aid, and so on, does not level the playing field, does not provide the same opportunities that appear to be available to kids in the richest households. If the opportunities were similar then the first and third groups of bars (no college) would look much similar, as would the second and fourth groups (college).[18]

Despite the benefits of graduating from college, children in the lowest income group are less likely to attend college, due in part to a combination of economic and social reasons, including financial constraints, lack of encouragement, lack of academic and social support, and poor K-12 preparation. Particularly tragic is that even highly qualified poor students often do not attend college. Sociologist Robert Putnam has noted that kids from poor families with high SAT scores are less likely to attend college than the low scoring students from rich families.[19] The economic impact? Less-able richer kids are 35% more likely to become high earners than bright poor kids.[20]

Thus, in sum, the U.S. has among the most unequal income distributions and among the least mobile. If you still believe in the superior ability and ease of economic mobility in the U.S., then I ask, into which American family would you rather be borne, a low-income one or a high-income one? Any answer other than indifference suggests skepticism in equality of opportunity.[21]

13.4 Concluding Comments

The share of income going to the top 1% has doubled since 1980, from roughly 10% to 20. Since 2000, the college education premium has stagnated, as communication technology has dramatically widened the pool

[18] This observation is based on analysis without taking into account genetic and environmental factors. These are discussed in detail in Chapter 18.

[19] Putnam (2016). Also Putnam (2015).

[20] McKnight (2015), based on U.K. data. Children of low-cognitive ability from rich backgrounds overtake high-cognitive-ability children from poor backgrounds even before arriving at (k-12) school.

[21] Comedian George Carlin joked, "It's called the American dream because you have to be asleep to believe it."

of educated workers, driving down wages for recent college graduates. AI promises to accelerate this process in the coming decade, likely leading to even greater inequality (i.e., declining education premium, and higher income at the top 1%).

At the same time, we see limited economic mobility. The "parental pull" is particularly strong: adults tend to be in a similar place on the economic spectrum as their parents. Even college is not the leveler it is often thought to be. But is inequality harmful, or is concern driven more by envy than lack of opportunity? Is the current level of inequality too much? Or is it simply a reflection of market forces and individual choices? These questions are explored in the next chapter.

References

Autor D (2019) Work of the past, work of the future. Richard T. Ely Lecture, AA Annual Meeting, Atlanta, January 4. Available at: https://www.aeaweb.org/webcasts/2019/aea-distinguished-lecture-work-of-the past-work-of-the-future. Accessed on 2 July 2025

Bengali L, Daly M (2013) U.S. economic mobility: The dream and the data. FRBSF Economic Letter 2013–06, 4 March.

Cleveland Federal Reserve (2012) The college wage premium. Available at: https://www.clevelandfed.org/newsroom-and-events/publications/economic-commentary/economic-commentary-archives/2012-economic-commentaries/ec-201210-the-college-wage-premium.aspx. Accessed on 2 July 2025

Cullen Z, Perez-Truglia R (2022) How much does your boss make? The effects of salary comparisons. J Polit Econ 130(3):766–822

Cullen Z, Perez-Truglia R et al (2024) Is pay transparency good? Journal of Economic Perspectives 38(1):153–180

Daley M (2012) U.S. income inequality in perspective. Federal Reserve Bank of San Francisco, April.

Lundberg S, Pollak RA, Stearns J (2016) Family inequality: Diverging patterns in marriage, cohabitation, and childbearing. Journal of Economic Perspectives 30(2):79–102

McCain R (1992) A framework for cognitive economics. Praeger, Westport, CT

McKnight A (2015) Downward mobility, opportunity hoarding and the 'glass floor'. Centre for Analysis of Social Exclusion (CASE), London School of Economics.

New York Times (2012) Comparing economic mobility. http://www.nytimes.com/interactive/2012/01/04/us/comparing-economic-mobility.html?_r=0Accessed on 30 Aug 2025

Norton MI, Ariely D (2011) Building a better America—one wealth quintile at a time. Perspect Psychol Sci 6(1):9–12

Putnam R (2015) Our kids: The American dream in crisis. C-SPAN Discussion. Available at: https://www.c-span.org/video/?325084-1/robert-putnam-our-kids. Accessed on 31 Jan 2022

Putnam R (2016) Our kids: The American dream in crisis. Simon & Schuster.

Sawhill I, Morton J (2007) Economic mobility: Is the American dream alive and well? The Economic Mobility Project. The Brookings Institution, Washington, D.C.

Sommet N, Elliott AJ, Jamieson JP, Butera F (2019) Income inequality, perceived competitiveness, and approach–avoidance motivation. J Pers 87(4):767–784. https://doi.org/10.1111/jopy.12432

Tokumaru N (2016) Fairness ideals, hidden selfishness, and opportunistic behavior: An experimental approach. Social Preference, Institution, and Distribution 3:21–46

Wilkinson R, Pickett K (2010) The spirit level: Why equality is better for everyone. Penguin Books, London

CHAPTER 14

Optimal Inequality

> A little over three years ago, a utility worker in Maryland won $2 million from a scratch-off lottery game that he bought for $30. Turns out his luck hasn't run out yet. Last week, the Maryland Lottery announced that the now retired utility worker had won another $2 million in a scratch-off game.[1]

In this chapter, I turn to the question of how much inequality is justified. This is not a straightforward question, for economists or anyone else. There is no single, correct answer, as a significant portion of one's response relies on how much we think we deserve what we have.

Figure 14.1 is a rough depiction of the primary factors identified by economists and others as important to economic success. Few will deny the major role played by the qualities in the center circle of the diagram: education, work experience, work ethic, etc., are important factors in one's economic success. Likewise, few would deny the primary role that parents play in developing those qualities. Put the two together and a more complete picture of the reasons for income inequality begins to appear. Parents are key to understanding the persistence of inequality—clearly seen in the intergenerational mobility figures described in the previous chapter. Parents in households with higher incomes tend to pass

[1] This is not the first double-winner. National Public Radio (2021).

L. Hadsell, *Social Economics*,
https://doi.org/10.1007/978-3-032-21916-9_14

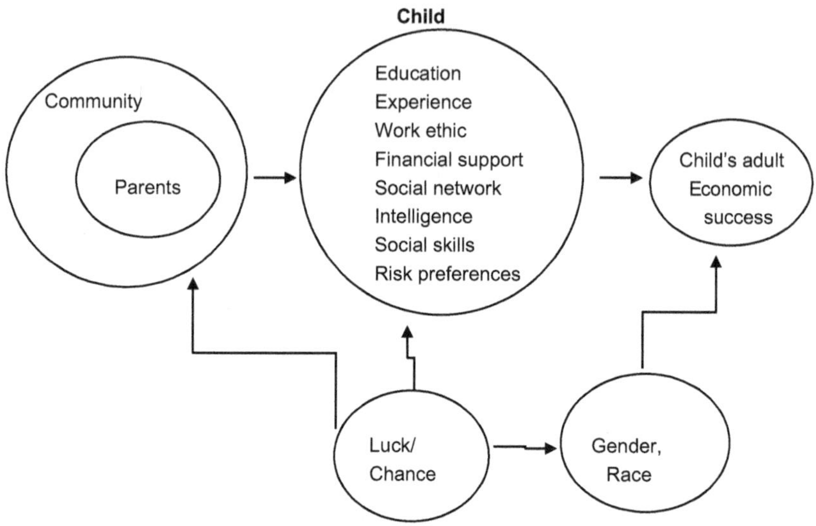

Fig. 14.1 Factors affecting economic success

on to their offspring the very attributes that made the parents successful while lower income parents tend to do the same, just in the opposite direction. Environmental factors add a bit of randomness but as data on economic mobility seem to indicate, in the current environment where you start has a lot to say about where you end up.[2]

What has not been made explicit so far in our discussion of the determinants of individual economic success is the role played by luck. Recent research suggests that chance plays a major role in qualities listed in the center circle. A large part of it is explained by a mundane yet powerful observation: No one gets to choose their parents. Parents' choices largely determine the quality of their children's K-12 school, financial resources available to pay for college, quality of peers, social networks, and connections. Additionally, as detailed in Chapter 18, DNA passed from parents to offspring also plays a significant role in shaping a wide range of economic outcomes.

[2] Bowles et al. (2001).

As we saw in the previous chapter, being lucky enough to be born into a high-income household drastically increases the child's chances of getting more and better education, gaining early and significant work experience, being protected from financial stumbles, and so on. And all of that drastically increases your chances of being a high-income adult yourself. Parents also play an enormous role in shaping children's work ethic, social skills, risk preferences, and a host of other qualities that impact economic success, as discussed in detail in Chapter 18.

None of this is to argue that poor kids can't make it big. In fact, the data presented earlier show that some do. Sometimes, though not often, someone born to parents in the lowest income group will rise to be in the highest as an adult. I fall into this category. But people like me are not typical, nor even likely. It happens—but not often enough. And even though I have worked hard and made some good decisions to get me where I am today, and even though I've overcome some adversity, I recognize the large amounts of luck, mostly good, that I've had. Many decisions appear to be excellent only in hindsight; life could easily have gone the other way.

I am also not arguing that talent and hard work should not be rewarded with higher incomes. Incentives matter, and higher rewards generally elicit greater effort, although even here, behavioral economists and psychologists warn us to be careful how we structure incentives. Still, I highly doubt that Elon Musk, Bill Gates, or Jeff Bezos would curtail their effort if returns for that effort were markedly lower (due, for instance, to significantly higher tax rates).[3] And I doubt they would, or could, expend more effort or be more creative if returns to their effort were higher (due to lower taxes). These individuals have brought great

[3] In a 2014 study of high-income countries, economists found that "those countries that reduced top marginal income tax rates the most between the 1960s and the 2000s saw the largest increases in pre-tax incomes reported on individual income tax returns in the top 1% of the income distribution. This suggests that high-income people did exhibit some kind of behavioral response to the reduced marginal tax rates.... On the other hand, the authors find no correlation between which countries had the largest cuts in top marginal income tax rates and which countries had the highest rates of growth in real GDP per capita over the same period." Bakija (2024, p. 53). Another reason for the increased income of the top 1% is that a lower tax makes tax avoidance and tax evasion less attractive.

value to society and are highly capable—they are also incredibly lucky to live at this time (computer and Internet age), live where they do (a democratic and capitalist society), and with the support they have received over the years (from family, friends, and government).[4] It is not that successful people do not work for that success, nor that effort and marketable skills should not be rewarded, it is that the qualities being rewarded by the market are distributed arbitrarily, depending on the time, place, and household one is born into.

Further, beyond education and work effort we also know from research that being taller, attractive, and with a deeper voice are all rewarded with higher income (on average, of course). Each is largely the result of luck (height, for example, is 80% heritable and otherwise generally outside of one's control). Is the additional income associated with being taller justifiable? A man in the 75th percentile of the height distribution compared to the 25th—a difference of four inches—earns about 9% higher income, on average—roughly $4500 per year in 2024.[5] Studying CEOs of 800 large companies, Duke University researchers found that leaders with lower pitch voices are paid significantly more: "A decrease of 25% in voice pitch is associated with an increase of $187,000 in annual [CEO] salary," according to the researchers.[6] Markets may provide those returns because those attributes are valued, but are individuals who are taller or have deeper voices morally deserving of the economic gains associated with those qualities?

Note how many of the market-valued qualities, from education and intelligence to risk preferences and height, are the result of providence, as they are directly connected to one's parents, both genetically and through the environment that parents shape. To what extent, then, are the market rewards for these qualities in any sense deserved? Ethicist Michael Sandel, who has engaged with economists on this question, argues,

[4] Note that Elon Musk was born and raised in South Africa. He moved to the U.S. in his early 20s, after a short stint in Canada. Of course, Gates and Bezos also choose to stay in the U.S., though they are certainly free to ply their skills elsewhere. Being in the U.S. does have certain advantages. They know it as well as anyone.

[5] Case and Paxson (2008).

[6] See Van Vugt (2013).

> Morally, it is unclear why the talented deserve the outsize rewards that market-driven societies lavish on the successful. Central to the case for the meritocratic ethic is the idea that we do not deserve to be rewarded, or held back, based on factors beyond our control. But is having (or lacking) certain talents really our own doing? If not, it is hard to see why those who rise thanks to their talents deserve greater rewards than those who may be equally hardworking but less endowed with the gifts a market society happens to prize.[7]

14.1 An Additional Consideration: Discrimination

Race and gender, and the associated discrimination, are also factors outside the control of individuals. How pervasive is market-based discrimination? In a paper titled "Are Emily and Greg more employable than Lakisha and Jamal?" economists at the University of Chicago and MIT sent fictitious resumes in response to actual help-wanted ads in Chicago and Boston.[8] To manipulate perceived race, resumes were randomly assigned black- or white-sounding names (taken from lists of most common names, by race) but otherwise the resumes were equivalent, and there was no explicit indication of race. Resumes with white-sounding names received 50% more callbacks for interviews. Callbacks were also more responsive to resume quality for white-sounding names than for black ones. Brad and Kristin (at 15.9 and 13.1%, respectively) got the most callbacks for white-sounding names while Jermaine and Ebony (each at 9.6%) topped the list of black-sounding names. At the other end, with the lowest callback rates were Todd and Emily (at 5.9 and 7.9%) and Rasheed and Aisha (at 3.0 and 2.2%). The researchers' conclusion: "Differential treatment by race appears to still be prominent in the U.S. labor market." While particularly interesting, this research reports nothing new in the sense that racial discrimination in markets has been well-documented in labor, housing, and consumer markets.

[7] Sandel (2020), p. 4.

[8] Bertrand and Mullainathan (2004).

Click on the nearby QR code to see the graphic from the New York Times that shows how white and black boys who were raised in high-income household fared as adults.[9] The most interesting aspect is that although the white boys ended up clumped near the top of the distribution as adults, black boys were essentially randomly distributed across the income ladder—about 20% in each quintile. Starting point provided a boost to chances for economic success for white boys. No such boost existed for black boys.

Just as evidence of racial discrimination in many settings is well-documented, evidence is clear that gender discrimination persists, even after decades of progress. The Economist magazine's "Glass-ceiling Index," comprised of measures of higher education, labor-force participation, pay, childcare costs, maternity and paternity rights, business-school applications, and representation in senior jobs, shows how women fare economically in major industrialized countries.[10] The index suggests that, though declining, gender discrimination continues and cuts across race, though it varies significantly by society, even among western industrialized countries. Nordic countries—Iceland, Sweden, Norway, Finland—for example, consistently are in the top five of The Economist's rankings as best for women. The U.S. is in the bottom half (20th of 29). South

[9] Badger et al. (2018). For 10,000 boys the results show, for black boys, 21% fell to the bottom quintile as adults, 22% to the middle, and 17% remained in the top. For white boys, the corresponding percentages were 10, 16, and 39. For black boys, 36% stayed in the top two quintiles; for whites, 63% stayed.

[10] Economist Magazine (2016). The U.S. Department of Labor defines the glass ceiling as "the unseen, yet unbreachable barrier that keeps minorities and women from rising to the upper rungs of the corporate ladder, regardless of their qualifications or achievements." Federal Glass Ceiling Commission (1995).

Korea, Japan, Turkey, and Switzerland are at the bottom.[11] (Gender discrimination is elaborated on elsewhere in Chapters 4 and 17).

Social class also appears to form a basis for discrimination. As sociologist Richard Wilkinson observes, "[W]e judge people by their accent, clothing, language, and choice of reading matter, the television programs they watch, the food they eat, the sports they play, the music they prefer, and their appreciation – or lack thereof – of art."[12] These judgments affect market opportunities, income, and economic mobility. In his study of British data, sociologist Sam Friedman found that even after controlling for education, training, experience, and other factors that one expects to affect promotion into high-level positions, individuals from working-class backgrounds were 17% less likely to be in high-level positions and earned less compared to individuals from "elite" backgrounds. It was worse for women and in certain professions. One explanation is that class/cultural similarity is important to being identified as a candidate for promotion. Attributes of social class act as markers, passed from generation to generation. As a result, Friedman argues that social class should be a protected category, much as gender, race, and physical disability.[13]

Economists talk about two forms of discrimination: either "taste"/ preference-based (by an employer, seller, or buyer) or statistical-based. Taste-based discrimination acknowledges individual preferences for dealing with someone of a certain race, gender, attractiveness, social class, or what have you. Preference can be the result of a conscious choice, or it can be subconscious, but either way it is the result of individual inclination. Statistical discrimination is based on group averages. For example, basing a hiring decision on the candidate's group affiliation if data reflect (or are believed to reflect) differential characteristics (such as productivity or expected job tenure) for that applicant's relevant association (race, gender, and so on). Women of childbearing age face statistical discrimination because they are more likely than men to take time off work due to childcare (though this is changing in the U.S. and varies significantly across economies, as much of it is culturally based). Another example of the practical implication of statistical discrimination, and of unintended consequences of trying to address it, flows from passage of a law in

[11] Economist Magazine (2022).

[12] Wilkinson and Pickett (2010).

[13] LSE iQ Podcast (2024).

Oregon in 2015 prohibiting employers from asking job applicants questions regarding arrests and incarceration. This was designed to decrease discrimination against individuals with criminal records. Because potential employers could no longer tell if someone had been arrested or served time, they went with the averages: subsequent studies indicate that blacks, who have higher rates of arrest and incarceration than whites, were less likely to receive job offers after the new law.[14] In the absence of individual data, employers used group averages to form their expectations.

Some economists, particularly conservatives in the neo-classical paradigm, argue that discrimination is at most minor and transitory in competitive markets, as the profit motive will drive discriminatory firms out of business: if one firm will not hire productive minorities, another firm will; if one business will not sell to certain groups then another business will, taking profits away from the discriminatory business. Critics of the conservative view contend that evidence of widespread gender and racial discrimination has persisted forever, even if the gaps appear to be lessening. Markets may even preserve discrimination if customers and coworkers value such discriminatory practices. A further criticism, emanating from sociology, is that economists tend to neglect significant institutional discrimination:

> A substantial body of evidence suggests that limiting the study of discrimination to the actions of potentially prejudiced individuals dramatically understates the extent to which people experience discrimination; understates the extent to which discrimination may account for social inequality; and understates the extent to which discrimination may play a role in markets.[15]

An example of institutional discrimination (albeit unintended) is the seemingly innocuous practice of referral-based hiring, in which current employees recommend potential employees to hiring managers. Given that social networks tend to be fairly homogeneous, a business with employees who are mostly of one race or social class will have referrals—and eventual hires—that are likely to be of the same group. So even though referral-based hiring is a financially sound practice from the employer's perspective—as referred employees tend to be more

[14] Schick and Wilson (2024).

[15] Small and Prager (2020).

productive than non-referred employees and stay with the organization longer—it may also perpetuate exclusion of a segment of the population from employment with that firm. As subconscious and unintended as it may be, discrimination still occurs.

If multiple forms of discrimination are as prevalent as the research clearly indicates, we must again wonder how economic inequality based on those prejudices can be justified. Or, in other words, how a system that perpetuates those bases for inequality can be permitted.

14.2 The Macro View

At the macroeconomic level, economists have documented the negative effect of too much inequality on economic growth though, recently, findings suggest that the negative effect appears to be concentrated among countries with high poverty.[16] Why should higher inequality be associated with lower economic growth? Perhaps inequality is working as a demotivator rather than a motivator, as gaps that are too large inhibit effort. It is also likely that inequality leads to misdirected resources, lessening expansion of productive capabilities. For example, in the U.S., concentration of wealth improves the educational opportunities for students in schools in wealthy areas while other, much poorer areas lack resources to provide a sound education. At the margin, the forgone potential gains in the poor districts far outweigh the realized gains in the wealthier areas, a net loss for society and for the individual—of human capital, but also of hope and locus of control. Shifting funding from wealthy districts to poorer ones would benefit students in the latter more than it would harm students in the former. Reallocation of resources for education is one public policy that would increase equity, well-being, and economic growth at the individual and national levels.

Beyond strictly economic outcomes, economic inequality is correlated with numerous health and social indicators ranging from life expectancy to crime and drug addiction. Public health officials call the nexus of economic and social conditions that affect health the social determinants of health (SDOH). Beyond income, economic factors that affect health in the SDOH framework include education, unemployment and

[16] Breunig and Majeed (2020).

job insecurity, working conditions, food insecurity, housing and environmental surroundings, social inclusion and non-discrimination, and access to affordable health services of decent quality.[17] According to the World Health Organization, SDOH.

> can be more important than health care or lifestyle choices in influencing health. For example, numerous studies suggest that SDOH account for between 30-55% of health outcomes. In addition, estimates show that the contribution of sectors outside health to population health outcomes exceeds the contribution from the health sector.

Analyzing data from multiple countries, sociologists Richard Wilkinson and Kate Pickett show that within a country, life expectancy is closely related to income (see Fig. 14.2): simply put, richer people live longer.[18] More and better health care, better diet, and time to exercise are reasons, as are improved social position and status for higher income individuals—which, again, has been shown in research to affect health and longevity. The positive relationship between socioeconomic status and health is well established and can have long-lasting effects. Poverty is particularly problematic: As one health economist writes, the "negative effects of low family incomes on children's health become larger as a child ages, with the harmful effects of low income on a child's health likely to accumulate over the child's lifetime."[19] We also see that more unequal societies have lower average life expectancy, higher rates of infant mortality and mental illness, and less trust.

The harm of inequality can be seen in aggregate by relating income inequality to an index of social problems, comprised of a dozen metrics ranging from infant mortality to homicides, mental illness, and trust in a cross-section of developed countries. The correlation is striking: higher inequality strongly associated with higher levels of social problems.[20]

Economic inequality also has potentially profound implications for social and political institutions. Results of recent U.S. presidential elections, the 2016 Brexit vote in the U.K., and the rise of far-right political

[17] World Health Organization (n.d.).

[18] Wilkinson and Pickett (2010).

[19] Condliffe and Link (2008).

[20] Wilkinson (2012).

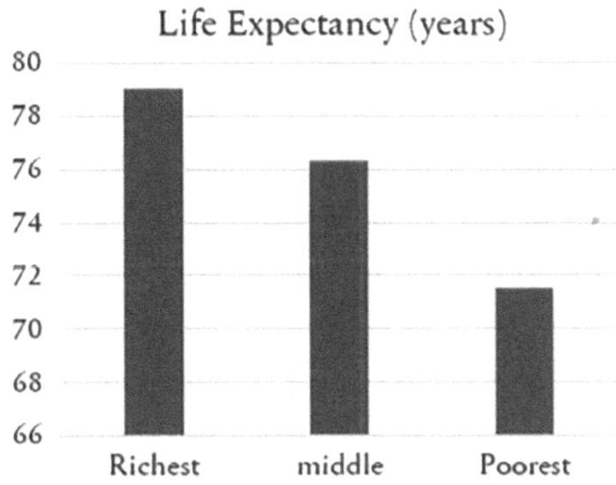

Fig. 14.2 Life expectancy and wealth

parties across Europe are suggestive. Indirect evidence is seen in the rural–urban split in voting behavior (in the U.S., majority vote in urban areas is Democratic while in non-urban areas it is Republican, no matter the state)—part of which reflects differences in cultural values but part of which also reflects differential economic fortunes.

14.3 Tyranny of Merit?

Michael Sandel argues that one result of ignoring the significant level of arbitrariness in economic success -

> is the morally unattractive attitudes it promotes: hubris among the winners and humiliation and resentment among the losers.... These moral sentiments are at the heart of the populist uprising against elites. More than a protest against immigrants and outsourcing, the populist complaint is about the tyranny of merit. And the complaint is justified.[21]

William McDonough, at the time president of the New York Federal Reserve, so not a left-wing radical, warned in a 2003 commencement speech at the Johns Hopkins School of Public Affairs that excessive inequality "was unsustainable in a democracy."[22] This of course only echoes history—in recent episodes as enumerated above and less recent ones such as during the 1930s Great Depression, when the Socialist Party

[21] Sandel (2020).

[22] Bowles et al. (2005), p. 343.

received its largest vote shares in U.S. presidential elections and Adolf Hitler rose to power in Germany.

More could be written (and has been elsewhere) about the corrosive effects of economic inequality but to summarize this and the previous chapter so far:

1. Data show that inequality of income and of wealth are larger in the U.S. than most Americans realize or want; inequality is higher in the U.S. than in most other developed economies; economic mobility is limited and less than in many other developed economies.
2. Economic theory suggests that when inequality is too small, not enough incentive is provided to use market-valued talents nor to exert effort to acquire them; when inequality is too large or of the wrong kind (horizontal rather than vertical, for example) motivation is stifled.
3. Evidence (more of which is provided in Chapter 18) shows a significant portion of the reasons for economic success are beyond the individual's control. Perhaps best summarized: Choosing the right parents is the best choice anyone can make to ensure their own economic success.
4. Economic inequality can have significant detrimental impacts on individuals' economic, social, and health outcomes.

With all this in mind, the task then is to achieve an optimal level of inequality, one that both motivates and is fair and just. The question is, how much inequality is the right amount?

14.4 Optimal Inequality

Even with the economic and social negatives associated with economic inequality, some inequality is necessary. The right level of inequality provides positive motivation and reward for pursuing one's talents and sharing them with others via the marketplace while limiting harm to those on the lower end of the distribution. The question is, how much inequality do we want? Let me suggest two ways of thinking about it.

One approach is to choose the level of inequality that provides incentives so as to achieve maximum economic gain. We might measure economic gain by GDP, though of course, GDP is not all that matters and sometimes other important measures are at odds with GDP. But this approach provides a conceptual starting point for talking about optimal inequality. At low levels of inequality, when everyone earns more or less the same, more inequality improves motivation, as it provides more incentive for effort—to gain knowledge and skills, to simply work more hours, or to take entrepreneurial risks (to start a business, for example). After a point, though, when inequality is too much, additional inequality serves as a demotivator, leading to less effort. This reduction in effort will be at both ends of the income distribution. At the lower end, the system seems stacked against you. At the higher end, after some income level, individuals tend to prefer additional time off rather than additional pay. The point separating the two areas of not enough inequality and too much, is the optimal level of inequality.

Following this line of thought, we have several ways of achieving the optimal level of inequality. Obvious possibilities are taxes, redistribution via a social safety net, reform of labor laws, and support for economic opportunity (more equal funding of K-12 schools; affordable quality pre-K; safe neighborhoods; support for parents).[23] Spending that focuses on early-life opportunity, beginning with prenatal care and early childhood support are key. Of course, the U.S. has some degree of all of these. The trick is to get the right amount of each. And as you may guess that's no easy task. With regard to taxes, a 2014 report estimates that the optimal ("social welfare maximizing") top marginal individual income tax rate in the U.S. is "somewhere between 62 and 83%," rates not likely achievable given the current political climate and an actual top rate in 2024 of 37%, a rate that has been declining for decades. On the other hand, the rate was generally above 90% in the twenty years following WWII, referred to by some as the "Golden Age of Capitalism"—an era with high economic growth and increasing equality.[24] So it's not clear that a much higher tax rate would be an economic killer, as some may suppose.

[23] Income and wealth taxes can be thought of as alternatives to inheritance tax. After all, most individuals do not inherit the bulk of what they get from their parents when their parents die. Rather, inheritance occurs over the lifetime of the child, as discussed earlier and in the later chapter on the economic role of parents. So tax that inheritance as it occurs, from current income, and fund the opportunities that will make a difference to children when they become adults.

[24] Bakija (2024). See Tax Policy Center (2023).

A second approach to thinking about optimal inequality continues with the recognition that economic systems result from myriad choices society makes. But rather than take the current system as a starting point, and tweak it by changing taxes and spending, we instead will redesign it from the ground up. How exactly could society do this? Philosopher John Rawls provides a thought exercise that may help. This exercise seeks the ideal society in terms of a set of rules and policies that we can all agree are fair. A major problem seen by Rawls—and what we see in survey responses and experimental research—is that, quite naturally and expectedly, one's current position in society, based on income, wealth, gender, race, age, skill set, and so on, influences one's perception of what an ideal society looks like.[25] In other words, my current socioeconomic status will be correlated with what I think is fair. I do not want to think that my success is based mostly on good fortune just as others do not want to think their lack of success is based largely on their lack of effort and poor choices. Someone who is successful will likely view the current set of rules as fair, even in a widely unequal society. Even casual observation of the wealthiest in our society generally supports this claim. Someone who is not quite so successful in that system will be less likely to view the system as fair—and often, as the evidence shows, there is ample reason to believe this is the case.

Consequently, Rawls suggests we shed knowledge of our current position in society, our own abilities, traits, and so on, so that we enter his thought experiment behind a "veil of ignorance." That is, we imagine that we do not know our current standing—and so cannot project an expected standing in whatever society we deem optimal. Without knowing our current or future abilities and attributes (education, gender, race, place of birth) we are more likely to create a fairer society for all, one we can all agree on. We will not want to risk creating a world in which we may be at a great disadvantage. Beyond an agreement on basic liberties, Rawls' "difference principle" states that the agreement reached will conclude that inequality can be justified only if such inequality raises the well-being of the least advantaged in society. Thus, exorbitant wealth for Bill Gates, Elon Musk, or Jeff Bezos is justified if that high wealth leads to increased

[25] Bowles et al. (2005). Tokumaru (2016).

living standard for those on the other end of the distribution.[26] Most of us would like to possess the riches of these individuals but because each of us, behind a veil of ignorance, has an equal chance of being in that least-advantaged group we would want to ensure, as a form of insurance, that our own potential position is not too disadvantaged.[27] And we would be willing to accept large wealth differences as long as it benefited us. As such, this approach would not foreclose the possibility of very wealthy individuals and large inequality, as long as it ensures an acceptable minimum.

The system agreed upon by following Rawls' difference principle would likely ensure that market-valued skills would be compensated, even if those skills are obtained purely by chance.[28] That is, it would likely not prohibit incentives for individuals to use their productive resources. Nor would the system necessarily prohibit poverty. Whatever level of inequality chosen would be deemed fair, as it was decided upon behind the veil of ignorance.

14.5 One More Approach

One additional approach rejects the notion of optimal inequality that is anything other than what is observed in an unfettered market—that is, a market with minimal government interference. This approach values economic freedom above all else and considers alterations to the current distribution an abrogation of that freedom, and therefore unacceptable: today's distribution is wrong only to the extent that government interferes with markets—so limiting government intervention in markets is the key to achieving optimal inequality. This is the Libertarian view, which

[26] The same may be argued for trade policy: good only to the extent that the least well-off benefit.

[27] We would also want to ensure that economic mobility is real and attainable.

[28] Even if economic success is ultimately based mostly on luck (as I believe the research strongly indicates), society may still find it helpful to have some inequality as a motivator, because the fact is that some people are more talented than others, work harder than others, and take more risks than others, and in doing so create benefits for the rest of us, in the products and services they provide. Even if market-valued endowments are obtained via chance individuals will react to incentives in deciding if and how to use those endowments. Too little return for that additional effort may mean the effort isn't provided. (We certainly saw that happen in the former U.S.S.R. and eastern European countries under communism.)

contends the best way to help the poor is with increased opportunity combined with free markets.[29] Main tenets of this view may be summed up as:

1. If it is earned and justly acquired then there is no obligation to give back.
2. The gap is not what matters, but rather whether incomes are growing ("a rising tide lifts all boats").
3. Wealth is created; it is not a fixed pie. If you create your wealth, you deserve it, as you are enlarging the economic pie, which is enjoyed by others.
4. As long as nothing impedes economic mobility, inequality is permissible.

A criticism of (1) is based on the findings that luck plays a large role in economic success. If this is so, is economic success fully earned? Many also contend that unequal bargaining positions mean that many trades are not totally free (coercion exists). Argument (2) was prevalent in the U.S. from 1945 to 1980, as incomes rose from one generation to the next and inequality declined. With the slowdown in economic growth and rising inequality in recent decades, absolute mobility has become a less convincing argument. Argument (3) supposes that markets create wealth through cooperative behavior—and most economists will wholeheartedly agree.[30] Yet markets also have imperfections (monopolies; externalities; discrimination) that limit this argument. Argument (4) seems to be accepted by a large segment of the U.S. population. Americans tolerate (generally approve of) inequality more so than Europeans do, in the belief, false in my view, that economic mobility in the U.S. is alive and well, though I concede this is a matter of interpretation and perception.

[29] Epstein (2011).

[30] But Sandel (2020), p. 116, insists, "Rather than assuming one's market value is the proper measure of one's contribution to society, we should deliberate about what counts as a contribution to the common good. The COVID-19 pandemic has made vivid the value of the work performed not only by doctors and nurses but also agricultural workers, grocery store clerks, delivery workers, and others who perform essential but modestly paid work."

14.6 Concluding Comments

Inequality is endemic to capitalism. The right amount and type of inequality motivates individuals to strive and create, reaping the rewards of their efforts. At the same time, evidence suggests that excessive inequality is harmful to individuals and society. We also know that inequality is largely passed from generation to generation and that many market-rewarded attributes are obtained essentially by chance, primarily the result of being born into the right households, with the accompanying financial and social support. I continue the discussion of the role of parents and society in shaping economic success in Part 3 of this book.

References

Bakija J (2024) The US individual income tax: Recent evolution and evidence. Journal of Economic Perspectives 38(3):33–60

Badger E, Miller CC, Pearce A, Quealy K (2018) Extensive data shows punishing reach of racism for black boys. New York Times, 19 March. Available at: https://www.nytimes.com/interactive/2018/03/19/upshot/race-class-white-and-black-men.html. Accessed on 2 July 2025

Bertrand M, Mullainathan S (2004) Are Emily and Greg more employable than Lakisha and Jamal? A field experiment on labor market discrimination. American Economic Review 94(4):991–1013

Bowles S, Edwards R, Roosevelt F (2005) Understanding capitalism. Oxford University Press

Bowles S, Gintis H, Osborne M (2001) The determinants of earnings: A behavioral approach. Journal of Economic Literature 35(3):1347–1373

Breunig R, Majeed O (2020) Inequality, poverty and economic growth. International Economics 161:83–99

Case A, Paxson C (2008) Stature and status: Height, ability, and labor market outcomes. J Polit Econ 116(3):499–532

Condliffe S, Link CR (2008) The relationship between economic status and child health: evidence from the United States. American Economic Review 98(4):1605–1618

Economist Magazine (2016) The best and worst places to be a working woman. Available at: https://www.economist.com/graphic-detail/2016/03/03/the-best-and-worst-places-to-be-a-working-woman. Accessed on 2 July 2025

Economist Magazine (2022) Glass ceiling index, 7 March. Available at: https://www.economist.com/graphic-detail/glass-ceiling-index. Accessed on 2 July 2025

Epstein R (2011) PBS Newshour interview. Available at: https://www.pbs.org/newshour/show/does-u-s-economic-inequality-have-a-good-side. Accessed on 2 July 2025

Federal Glass Ceiling Commission (1995) Solid investments: Making full use of the nation's human capital. Washington, DC: U.S. Department of Labor, pp. 13–15. Archived 2014–11–08 at the Wayback Machine.

LSE iQ Podcast (2024) Why do so many people mistakenly think they are working class? https://www.bing.com/videos/riverview/relatedvideo?q=lse+iq+podcast+Sam+Friedman+++working-class&mid=A7455E4CA78A2EC1DE6AA7455E4CA78A2EC1DE6A&FORM=VIRE. Accessed on 30 Aug 2025

National Public Radio (2021) Maryland lottery man wins $2 million dollar prize twice. Available at: https://www.npr.org/2021/11/01/1051113368/maryland-lottery-man-wins-2-million-dollar-prize-twice. Accessed on 8 Feb 2022

Sandel M (2020) The Tyranny of Merit: What's become of the common good? Farrar, Straus and Giroux

Schick T and Wilson C (2024) Oregon's Drug Decriminalization Aimed to Make Cops a Gateway to Rehab, Not Jail. State Leaders Failed to Make It Work. Pro Publica. https://www.propublica.org/article/oregon-leaders-hampered-drug-decriminalization-effort. Accessed on 30 Aug 2025

Small ML, Prager D (2020) Sociological perspectives on racial discrimination. Journal of Economic Perspectives 34(2):49–67

Tax Policy Center (2023) Historical highest marginal income tax rates. https://taxpolicycenter.org/statistics/historical-highest-marginal-income-tax-ratesAccessed on 30 Aug 2025

Tokumaru N (2016) Fairness ideals, hidden selfishness, and opportunistic behavior: An experimental approach. Social Preference, Institution, and Distribution 3:21–46

Van Vugt M (2013) The sound of a leader: CEOs with deep voices do better. Psychology Today. Available at: https://www.psychologytoday.com/us/blog/naturally-selected/201306/the-sound-leader-ceos-deep-voices-do-better. Accessed on 2 July 2025

Wilkinson R, Pickett K (2010) The spirit level: Why greater equality makes societies stronger.

World Health Organization (n.d.) Social determinants of health.

Wilkinson R (2012) How economic inequality harms societies. TED Talks. https://www.youtube.com/watch?v=cZ7LzE3u7Bw. Accessed on 30 Aug 2025

PART III

Social Influences

CHAPTER 15

Unwritten Rules: Social Norms and Customs

> Unless the number of individuals in a group is quite small, or unless there is coercion or some other special device to make individuals act in their common interest, rational, self-interested individuals will not act to achieve their common or group interests.[1]

> Kin selection and reciprocal altruism are the foundation of the kinds of cooperative behavior observed in many animals. Humans also bias cooperation in favor of kin and reciprocating partners, but the scope, scale, and variability of human cooperation greatly exceed that of other animals.[2]

First, answer the following -

1. Suppose that while on a weeklong vacation you are asked to conserve water—the town you are visiting is experiencing a drought. Among other things, you are being asked to shorten your showers by between 1/3 and 1/2 of their normal duration: a written request to keep your showers short is posted near the shower. No one will know if you comply with the town's request. Do you?

[1] Economist Mancur Olsen, as quoted in Ostrom (2000).

[2] Psychologist Coren Apicella and Anthropologist Joan Silk (2019).

L. Hadsell, *Social Economies*,
https://doi.org/10.1007/978-3-032-21916-9_15

2. You and someone else not known to you are invited to play a game. You will be provisionally given $100 and are asked to make an offer to share a portion of the $100 with the other player. The other player can accept or reject the offer. If they accept, they keep what was offered and you keep the rest. If they reject the offer, you both get $0 (you have to return the $100). How much do you offer?

15.1 Self-Interest and Its Limits

Markets rely on the overriding influence of self-interest. Adam Smith famously noted that it is not by the goodness in the hearts of butchers and bakers that meat and bread are on our dinner table. Yet, pursuit of self-interest without regard for social norms and customs can be detrimental to individuals and markets, increasing uncertainty and mistrust and leading to loss of economic value.[3] Even with his advocation of an economic system reliant on pursuit of individual gain, Smith recognized the importance of limiting that self-interest.

Sometimes the limits to self-interest in economic settings based on social norms and customs (more broadly, culture) are compatible with one's immediate personal advantage, other times they are not.[4] Examples of the latter include contributing to public goods which will be provided regardless of your contribution; working hard when no one is watching; being fair (e.g., not charging too high a price) in situations when you have an information or power advantage that could prove profitable; and honesty in exchange when dealing with strangers. Agreeing to limit water use while on vacation, as in the above scenario, is another example—conservation of a common resource.[5]

Consider a prime area of interest to economists: public goods. Public goods, such as national defense, public TV and radio, or knowledge resulting from basic research, are things for which benefits flow to everyone, regardless of their individual contribution to paying for its

[3] McKenzie (1987).

[4] See Ostrom (2000), McKenzie (1987). Culture influences a wide range of economically relevant choices, including female labor participation and fertility choices, job effort, and family structure. See Guiso et al. (2006), pp. 23, 37.

[5] Not working too hard can also result from custom—as enforced by coworkers who do not want to be made to "look bad."

provision. These are commonly undersupplied by the private market precisely because people cannot easily be excluded from enjoying them (that is, they cannot be required to pay, so the effective price is zero), creating a self-interest to "free ride," which can be too tempting for many individuals to resist. Similarly, common resources, such as fish in the ocean, are also non-excludable but are rivalrous, meaning the fish are there for anyone to catch and once it's caught, it's gone. We cannot each catch the same fish; and if we all catch fish without limit, they will soon be gone. Individuals sometimes do act against their pure self-interest—as we see when people voluntarily contribute to Public TV or when they honestly report all taxable income even when they are likely to get away with not doing so, providing evidence of cooperation and honesty that extends beyond one's pure self-interest.

Yet, self-interest is hard to resist. Tax evasion is real (in some countries more than others). Many people listen to public radio without contributing. Sometimes the effects can be dire. Overfishing has caused a massive decline in fish population since the 1950s, nearing 90% of ocean stock by one count.[6] The financial and housing sectors leading up to the Great Recession of 2008, or Wall Street in the late 1990s and the subsequent economic collapses provide examples of the negative fallout from excessive self-interest.[7] Another is provided by psychologist Eleanor Maccoby:

> In a theater in a small city in the English Midlands, attached to the backs of many of the seats is a small rack that once contained opera glasses. The racks were coin operated: the insertion of a shilling released the opera glasses from their holder. At the end of a performance, the user would return the glasses to the rack, which locked automatically. The glasses would then be ready for a member of the next audience. The glasses were small, and in the darkness a user could easily slip them under a coat or into a pocket and carry them out of the theater without being seen. But for many years almost no one took them. The rate of theft was so low that the

[6] Worm et al. (2006).

[7] Cohn et al. (2014) provide experimental evidence that a significant number of bank employees are more dishonest than the general public.

> intake of shillings covered the losses and yielded a profit to the management. In the 1960s the rate of theft began to rise and reached a point where the management could no longer afford to replace stolen glasses. So the system fell to disuse; only empty racks remained to remind the theater-goer of a convenience made possible by the honesty of an earlier generation.[8]

Adam Smith recognized that too much self-interest could undermine society. His *Theory of Moral Sentiments* begins, "How selfish so-ever man may be supposed, there are evidently some principles in his nature, which interest him in the fortune of others…." Smith discusses "the moral forces that restrain selfishness and bind people together in a workable society." He argues that conscience and principle lead us to care for others, that conduct within the social structure is grounded in our morality, and that this will restrain our selfish tendency, "enforced by inward shame and self-condemnation." Similarly, Alfred Marshall's (1920) *Principles of Economics* textbook, the leading introduction to economics in its time, discussed custom, cooperation, fairness, friendship, and dishonesty in trade—all in the first chapter. Other leading economists at the early stages in the development of economic science felt "comfortable using cultural explanations for economic phenomena. John Stuart Mill regarded cultural constraints as sometimes more important than even the pursuits of personal interest."[9] But by the mid-1960s, mainstream economics had arrived at a new understanding, as exemplified by the contention of economist Mancur Olsen quoted at the beginning of the chapter: self-interest was assumed to be the only logical, rational motivator and markets work because there is an overwhelming reliance on it. Today, after reams of research demonstrating the real effects of norms and customs, and culture more generally, on economic choices, the discipline is moving back toward its roots.

Research makes clear that norms and customs affect attitudes regarding cooperation, honesty, trust, and fairness.[10] Origins of norms and customs

[8] Maccoby (1980), p. 296.

[9] Evensky (2005), p. 26.

[10] Guiso et al. (2006), p. 29: "The appealing feature of trust is that it can be thought of as 'the subjective probability with which an agent assesses that another agent or group of agents will perform a particular action'…, and as such can be easily incorporated into standard economic models."

include religion, family, and neighbors—all discussed in further detail in subsequent chapters. For now, let's briefly look at some of what we know about various cultural influences on economic actions, focusing in turn on cooperation, trust and honesty, and fairness.

15.2 Cooperation

People tend to show a level of cooperation that may at first seem at odds with pure self-interest.[11] Economists once viewed cooperation as a challenge to the primacy of self-interest in the same way Charles Darwin, whose theory of natural selection influenced development of similar ideas in economics, "viewed cooperation as a perplexing challenge to his theory.... Natural selection generally favors the evolution of behaviors that enhance the fitness of individuals" whereas cooperative behavior benefits the recipient at the expense of the giver.[12] That view is changing.

We observe cooperation in myriad ways. The first scenario at the beginning of this chapter illustrates. It is based on the author's personal experience in the early 2000s while visiting Block Island, R.I. (a small island 13 miles off the mainland). Due to an extended drought, public officials of the island popular with tourists asked restaurants and hotels to conserve water and to ask their guests to do the same. For visitors, compliance was voluntary, without strict enforcement. No one would know if we took long or short showers, for example, yet the island presumably would not have enough water if too many people ignored the plea to conserve. Although not stated, the voluntary restrictions could turn into mandates if the voluntary approach was unsuccessful. So even though I return year after year the overriding self-interest for me and most others was to ignore the pleas—being clean is a much more immediate concern than a possible water shortage after I leave. This is a classic common resource/public goods problem because individuals have great incentive to rely on others to conserve water while using as much water themselves as they wish. After all, each individual alone has no meaningful impact on the water supply.

When I asked nearly two hundred undergraduates about this in an anonymous survey, a surprisingly high percentage (67%) indicated they

[11] See, for example, Thaler (1992).

[12] Apicella and Silk (2019).

would comply with the request to use less water, in effect sacrificing personal gain for the greater good. Surprising if we believe that self-interest is paramount. Sixty-seven percent seems especially high because the level of anonymity is high (you do not know the locals and they do not know you) and the risk of discovery is low (no one will know if you comply, and the penalty for non-compliance is low). Agreeing to conserve water implies a strong commitment to relatively weak relationships and cooperation, even when the risk of discovery (and penalty) is low. (Of course, it is also easier to answer this way in a hypothetical situation.) In fact, experimental studies generally show that the strength of the relationship between parties and the risk of penalty for breaking the rules or customs appear to be prominent in explaining many similar situations where one is asked to limit self-interest.

Public radio and television are testament to the fact that cooperation is alive and well, if not universal, so are the hundreds of experiments examining cooperation done by economists, sociologists, and psychologists. In a typical experiment, four people are told the following: each will be given an initial sum of $10 by the experimenter; each person can then decide, in secret, how much of that $10 to contribute to the community pot; the money in the community pot will then be doubled; the pot is then divided among all players, regardless of whether they contributed to the pot. If all four contribute $10 each the pot will grow to $80 (after the $40 is doubled by the experimenter) and each person will get $20. But notice that if only three contribute, the pot grows to $60 and each person, including the one who did not contribute, will get $15 when the pot is divided. The player who did not contribute his $10 to the pot has $25 at the end while the others have just $15. When everyone contributes players walk away from the game with $80 total; if one free rides while the others contribute, the total declines to $70. The self-interest for the individual is to free ride even though the group is better off if everyone contributes. The typical cooperation rate in experiments such as this ranges from 40 to 60%.

This holds for large sums of money as well. Economist Richard Thaler and colleagues, for example, examined choices of contestants on a popular British game show (*Golden Balls*) that involved stakes averaging over $20,000, in which contestants had to decide to cooperate and share the pot of money ("split" in parlance of the game) or not ("steal"). If both players split, then each receives half the pot. If one player chooses to steal and the other chooses to split, the former gets the entire pot and the latter gets nothing. If both players choose steal, then each gets nothing. The temptation for the self-interested individual is to steal and take the entire pot, but because steal is the dominant strategy for both players, it works only if the other player splits. Split is a fool's choice if you think the other person will follow their self-interest and steal. The expected move is for both to steal.[13] But this is not the overwhelming outcome. Players chose split 53% of the time. Thaler and colleagues also found, consistent with prior research, that men were less likely than women to cooperate—with a twist: this was true only for younger contestants and reversed after age 40.[14] Based on the consistent findings across many similar studies, Thaler concludes, "Humans are nicer and more mannerly than" the rational, self-interested individual imagined by economists of the 1970s; their "first instinct is to cooperate as long as they expect others to do likewise."[15]

Cooperation is essential not only for the provision of public goods and sharing of game show money but for the workings of society itself, including multiple facets of the economy. People, individually and as members of teams and organizations, have numerous opportunities for personal gain at the expense of others, from cheating on taxes to dumping waste into the environment. Some do these things. The vast majority do not. And that is the only way the economy—and society—survives. Cooperation and compromise allow legislation and policies to be enacted, deals to be made. Of course, numerous cultural factors facilitate cooperation, some of these are discussed in later chapters. Biology also plays a role – as discussed at the end of this chapter.

[13] You may recognize this as the prisoners' dilemma game, in which the expected (self-interested) outcome is for each to "steal." The strategies/payoffs (payoff matrix) would look like this:

player1-player 2 actions: respective payoffs.
split-split: 50,50.
split-steal: 0,100.
steal-split: 100,0.
steal-steal: 0,0.

[14] Van den Assem et al. (2012).

[15] Thaler (2016). For results showing conditional contributions see Fischbacher et al. (2001).

15.3 Trust and Honesty

Trust: firm belief in the reliability, truth, ability, or strength of someone or something; to place confidence in.

How important is trust in economic settings? Consider the nature of most transactions in modern developed economies: impersonal and often with a long-distance separating buyer and seller. As the distance (geographic, time, knowledge) increases between consumer and producer the cost of verification of product quality, acceptable production methods, etc., increases, and the value of honesty rises. Consumers need to trust that sellers are honest in their representation of the product or service. The increasing preference for locally produced goods, food especially, is evidence of the value consumers place on trust, among other things, as local firms can be more easily monitored and therefore are more trusted. Likewise, firms invest a great deal in reputation and brand building as key elements of forming trust—because consumers value it. Online rating systems such as Google Reviews, Yelp, and Angie's List, and more traditional sources such as Consumer Reports, are examples of private market provision of information aimed at increasing trust between buyer and seller and thereby facilitating market interactions. Consumer testimonials and money-back guarantees are examples of producer efforts. Government also often plays a role in trust building, such as with food inspection, licensing, and enforcement of truth in advertising laws. Such efforts at building trust reduce the individual's cost of acquiring information about the other party's honesty, facilitating market transactions. And just as trust based on a good reputation can grease the wheels of commerce, lack of trust can slow it. Tarnished reputations can ruin an organization. The consequences can be just as dire for consumers. A bad credit history, for example, can drastically increase costs of borrowing, and reduce other market possibilities, as employment and rental applications are sometimes accompanied by credit checks.

Trust is paramount when not every facet of an agreement between buyer and seller can be spelled out and monitored. In other words, in just about every case. Someone employing a roofer to replace a roof, trusts that s/he will honor the details of the contract, using materials and workmanship as stated in their agreement. Most contracts cannot address all contingencies. And in many relationships an asymmetrical information advantage arises—one party knows more about the product or service than the other. After a quick inspection, the mechanic likely knows more than you about the condition of your vehicle (and whether you really need that expensive repair). Same for the used car salesperson. And the physician, financial advisor, lawyer, dentist, grocer, and on and on—you name it, one party in just about any exchange is likely to have an information advantage. Information asymmetry carries an obligation for the more-informed party to be honest, or provides an opportunity to be dishonest, and thus requires trust by the less-informed person that the other party is honest. Unrestrained self-interest may lead the more-informed party to take advantage of the other—especially if they are strangers and the transaction will not be repeated and if the less-informed party is unlikely to discover their disadvantage. As such, unrestrained self-interest would also lead to a substantial decline in commerce. When economist Kenneth Arrow said that "virtually every commercial transaction has within itself an element of trust" he was underscoring the prevalence of asymmetric information and highlighting the importance of trust to well-functioning markets.

Reliable, trustworthy firms gain "loyal" (i.e., repeat) customers and benefit from customer recommendations. Reliable, trustworthy customers—who pay bills on-time—receive better sale terms (e.g., discounts; credit sales). Reliable, trustworthy employees are paid more and enjoy other perks, and more reliable, trustworthy employers have lower hiring costs and have happier, more loyal, and more productive employees.[16]

An economist might formalize the concept of trust as "the subjective probability with which an agent assesses that another agent or group of agents will perform a particular action"[17]—but of course this is a mouthful and so only serves as a guide to how we think about the responses to the simpler survey questions asking about trust. Results of surveys by Pew (see Fig. 15.1) show Americans' average level of trust is in the middle of the pack of a small sample of advanced economies. Some European countries, particularly the northern countries of Denmark, Netherlands, and Sweden have comparatively high levels of trust while southern European countries of Italy, Spain, and France have lower levels. Trust and Protestant religion are empirically related, a connection explored in more detail in a later chapter.

[16] Zak (2017).

[17] Gambetta (2000).

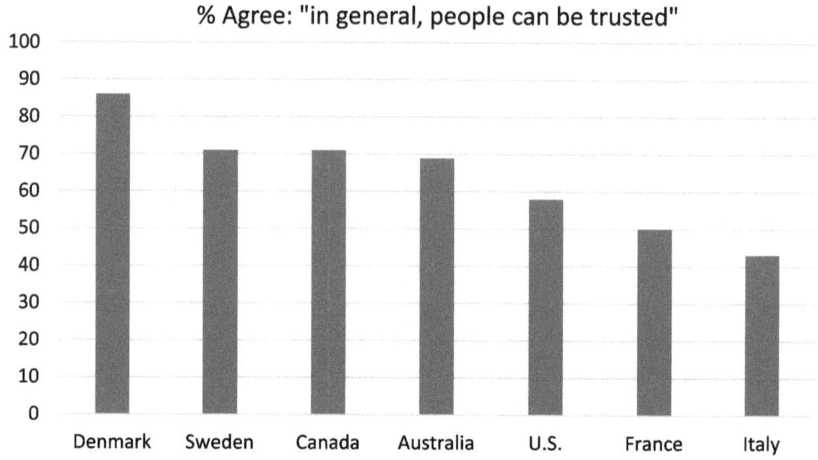

Fig. 15.1 Trust (Based on data from Pew [2020])

Research clearly supports the view that the level of trust in society affects economic growth. Some economists go so far as to argue that "trust and trustworthiness appear as the keystone for successful economic development."[18] Why? Economic development typically involves a transition from personal transactions between entities known to each other to anonymous ones (in decentralized markets). A great deal of trust is involved when dealing with strangers. With more trust comes more trade, more economic activity. The importance we place on trust can be gleaned from the nearby sidebar, which illustrates how trust is sometimes broken.

Department of Justice

U.S. Attorney's Office
Northern District of Iowa

FOR IMMEDIATE RELEASE Monday, August 19, 2019

Field of Schemes Fraud Results in Over a Decade in Federal Prison for Leader of Largest Organic Fraud Case in U.S. History

[18] Algan and Cahuc (2010).

A Missouri man who fraudulently sold millions of dollars' worth of non-organic grain as though it was organic was sentenced on August 16, 2019, to more than ten years in prison in federal court in Cedar Rapids. Three farmers from Nebraska who supplied him with non-organic grain were also sentenced to federal prison for their roles in a scheme to defraud customers across the United States.

Randy Constant, age 61, from Chillicothe, Missouri, received the prison term after a December 20, 2018, guilty plea to one count of wire fraud. Constant admitted the fraudulent scheme involved at least $142,433,475 in grain sales, and the vast majority of those sales were fraudulent. At his plea hearing, he admitted that, from 2010 to 2017, he misled customers into thinking they were buying certified organic grain when the grain he was selling was not organic. Constant admitted falsely telling customers the grain he sold was grown on his certified organic fields in Nebraska and Missouri when the grain was not organic either because he purchased the grain from other growers, the certified organic fields were sprayed with unauthorized chemicals, or organic grain was mixed with non-organic grain. Constant made many of the sales through a brokerage he owned that operated in Ossian, Iowa, known as Jericho Solutions. As part of the plea, Constant also agreed to forfeit $128,190,128 in proceeds from the fraudulent scheme.

Evidence at Constant's sentencing showed that, for 2016, his sales equaled approximately 7% of all comparable organic corn grown and 8% of all organic soybeans grown in the United States. Overall, from 2010 to 2017, Constant sold more than 11,500,000 bushels of grain, over 90% of which was falsely marketed as organic. That amount of grain would fill approximately 3600 rail cars or 14,375 semi-trailers.

Constant's grain was mostly used as animal feed, primarily for chickens and cattle. That livestock was then sold as organic meat or products from the livestock were sold as organic products. Because of Constant's fraud, most of the livestock that was fed his grain was not organic, causing thousands of consumers to purchase what they thought was organic meat for a premium price across the country.

Source: Department of Justice (2019).

At the individual level, more trusting people tend to participate more in economic activity—with higher incomes as a result.[19] But can people have too much trust, or too little? In other words, is there an optimal level of trust for the individual, in terms of income maximization? Apparently, yes. A trio of economists finds that people with either low or very high levels of trust have significantly lower income than those with intermediate levels of trust. Their finding is "consistent with the idea that some people make trust mistakes.“[20] In a world of knaves as well as knights, being too trusting has a cost, as does not being trusting enough.

Corruption

Honesty is a key in doing business and in governing. The Corruption Perception Index (CPI) "ranks 180 countries and territories around the world by their perceived levels of public sector corruption. The results are given on a scale of 0 (highly corrupt) to 100 (very clean"." Use the following QR code or URL to read more.

Source: Transparency Internation (n.d.).

[19] The level of trust affects degree of participation in markets: see Tu and Bulte (2010), who study of Chinese households and formal vs informal labor markets.

[20] Butler et al. (2016).

15.4 Fairness

People expect from others a certain amount of fairness in economic settings—and often this expectation constrains self-interest. Hostile reactions to being charged too high a price, for example, are well-documented. Price gouging laws, which prohibit "exorbitant" price increases, usually defined as some percentage over normal price after a natural disaster, are codified examples of this sentiment. Wage reductions are likewise often perceived as unfair and can lead not only to negative feelings among workers but also lower productivity.

Evidence that self-interest is commonly tempered by concerns of fairness come from, among other sources, experiments based on the ultimatum game, as partially depicted in the second scenario at the beginning of this chapter. In this game, individuals are given a small sum of money by the experimenter and are told to offer a portion to a second player. The portion shared can be as little as nothing and as much as the whole endowment provided by the experimenter. The second player can accept or reject the offer. If she accepts then she keeps what was offered and the first player keeps the rest. If she rejects the offer, they both leave with nothing (the original endowment is taken back). So if player 1 is provided $10 and offers $1 and player 2 accepts, player 2 gets $1 and player 1 gets $9. If player two rejects, the $10 is taken back and both end up with $0. One may see the parallel between the game and real-life situations such as wage negotiations (especially in the context of high profits).

The overwhelming incentive for perfectly rational, self-interested players with no regard for fairness is for player 1 to offer nothing and for player 2 to accept whatever is offered—because, after all, even receiving nothing is no worse than what they started with. Yet when this game is played the typical offer by player 1 is one-quarter to one-half of the initial allocation, and player 2 tends to accept.[21] Low offers are often rejected; player 2 apparently feels insulted by low offers and would rather walk away with nothing (also making player 1 earn nothing) than accept. It is unclear whether positive offers by player 1 reflect player 1's concern for fairness or recognition by player 1 that an offer perceived by player 2 as

[21] The vast majority of offers are between 40 and 50%. Offers of less than 25% are often rejected. Further, offers vary substantially from group to group in their studies of multiple societies. See Bowles et al. (2005). See also Croson and Buchan (1999); Abdulkadiroğlu and Bagwell (2013).

unfair will likely be rejected. (The primary question for player 1 is what offers player 2 will think are fair.) It is in player 1's self-interest for player 2 to accept the offer—so player 1 must make a fair offer (again, if they think player 2 is concerned with fairness). For player 2, there's no such ambiguity, at least in one-shot games: rejecting any offer is not in their best interest, if their goal is to maximize winnings. The dynamics may change if the game is played multiple times: then player 2 may want to build a reputation of concern with fairness (whether they actually have one or not), sending a signal that only "fair" offers will be accepted. An alternative game addresses this ambiguity: in the dictator game player 1 does not need to be concerned with whether player 2 will accept or reject, as player 2 must take whatever is offered. Player 1 gets to dictate the amount. Offers still exceed zero, though they generally are somewhat lower than in the ultimatum game.

The fact that we see substantial offers in both games and rejection of low offers in the ultimatum game provides evidence of concerns with fairness.[22] Economist Richard Thaler offers the following real-life scenario:

> You are lying on the beach on a hot day. All you have to drink is ice water. For the last hour you have been thinking about how much you would enjoy a nice cold bottle of your favorite brand of beer. A companion gets up to go make a phone call and offers to bring back a beer from the only nearby place where beer is sold, a fancy resort hotel. He says that the beer might be expensive and so asks how much you are willing to pay for the beer. He says that he will buy the beer if it costs as much or less than the price you state. But if it costs more than the price you state he will not buy it. You trust your friend, and there is no possibility of bargaining with the bartender. What price do you tell him?

The median response from a group of participants in an executive education program was $7.75.[23] When the underlined passages are replaced with "a small run-down grocery store" and "store owner" the median response becomes $4.50. Thaler attributes the different responses to differences in perceived cost to the seller and the notion that a higher

[22] Richard Thaler provides additional discussion, examples, and extensions of this game and others in his wonderful book "The Winner's Curse."

[23] The values shown are inflation adjusted. The original values were $2.65 and $1.50, in 1985.

price "seems fair for a resort hotel, but a "rip-off" in a run-down grocery store."

Though the $1000 concert ticket prices may suggest otherwise, Taylor Swift recognizes the importance of fair pricing, especially in relationships that one wants to cultivate. Ticket distribution for her 2023 Eras Tour raised the ire of many fans, as they had difficulty getting tickets by a method, and at a price, that seemed fair. Ticket distributor Ticketmaster was accused of monopolizing the ticket distribution—and bungling the process, as its website crashed under heavy demand. Scalpers purchased tickets with no intention of attending the concerts and then resold them at much higher prices. Swift condemned the sources of her fans' ire, Congress investigated, and government regulators filed suit against Ticketmaster "alleging unlawful business practices that have been detrimental to the live music industry." Forty years prior, another mega performer expressed similar concern with fairness—even more effectively (as was possible in a time before Ticketmaster and StubHub). The Rolling Stones, touring the U.S. in 1979, limited ticket prices (to less than $30 in today's money) and quantity (to four tickets per person), using various methods to allocate tickets, including first-come, first-served and lotteries.[24] Many economists will argue that such pricing policies are inefficient, pointing to time wasted waiting in long lines as obvious evidence. Efficient allocation is achieved when tickets go to the highest bidders, as those who are willing and able to pay the most are the ones who value the tickets the most. Others argue that concerns with fairness outweigh efficiency concerns. The former view appears dominant today, at least among economists and industry price setters, as tickets to entertainment and sporting events have become much pricier in recent years, with resale websites offering tickets to the highest bidder—replacing the price models ostensibly preferred by many performers.

Similar concerns appear in wage bargaining. The recent agreement between the U.S. Women's National soccer team and the U.S. soccer governing body settled a long-running dispute over equal pay and benefits between the men's and women's teams, including lawsuits by some women players alleging discrimination.[25] While law courts disagreed with the illegality of pay differentials, dismissing the lawsuits, the U.S. soccer

[24] Thomas (1981).

[25] Das (2022). Also, Hernandez (2022).

governing body clearly saw advantages to leveling compensation. It was the "right" thing to do, in the words of Alex Morgan, a star player on the women's team. It was also the economic thing to do: though players on the U.S. men's team were paid substantially more and enjoyed perks such as chartered flights not available to players on the women's team, the women's team reportedly generated more revenue (and was more successful on the field). What is "fair" is open to interpretation and is contentious. In this case, fairness, gender equity, and pay based on economic value created (i.e., revenues generated) aligned.[26]

15.5 Evolutionary and Biological Foundations

Concerns with cooperation, trust, fairness, and other pro-social behaviors have biological bases. Biologists argue that cooperation, for example, is an evolutionary consequence. Selective cooperation with other cooperators, e.g., close relatives, enhances survival, and is observed in other animals as well as in humans. Examples of cooperation in nature include small group hunting by wolves, flocking behavior by birds, penguins who huddle as a way to reduce heat loss, and V-formation flight by migrating birds—though "the scope, scale, and variability of human cooperation greatly exceed that of other animals."[27] In other words, cooperation is not an aberration, an irrational behavior; it is, rather, essential to survival for many.

Neuroeconomists, who combine neuroscience and economics to study brain mechanisms underlying decision-making in economic interactions, find that individuals appear to derive pleasure from cooperation and from punishing behavior perceived as unfair.[28] A primary source of that pleasure is oxytocin, a neuropeptide hormone secreted by the hypothalamus at the base of the brain.[29] Experimental results show that additional oxytocin in the bloodstream is associated with increased cooperation in

[26] See also Goldin (2025).

[27] See references in Kasper et al. (2017), Apicella and Silk (2019).

[28] Zak et al. (2005), Tzieropoulos (2013).

[29] Oxytocin widely used to induce labor (by administering the synthetic version, Pitocin). The word oxytocin is derived from the Ancient Greek word meaning swift childbirth. Oxytocin is popularly referred to as the "love drug" for its association with trust, empathy, and relationship building.

the provision of public goods.[30] The natural variation of oxytocin levels from person to person and variation in oxytocin receptor genes appear to be partly responsible for differences in levels of cooperation. Oxytocin is associated with a host of pro-social behaviors including increased reciprocity and ingroup trust, concern for fairness, and the enforcement of cooperative norms through peer punishment.[31]

Testosterone and estrogen have also received attention from researchers. Higher levels of testosterone are associated with increased risk-taking (as might occur, for example, in games such as Golden Balls). One study recruited 98 males, aged 18–23 years and measured testosterone levels in their saliva. Risk preference was measured by the amount bet in a game of chance, with $250 provided by the researchers. If the bet paid off (as determined in the game by a coin toss) the participant won an additional amount equal to their wager. Otherwise, the wagered amount was lost. So, a $100 bet would pay either $350 or $150, depending on the coin toss. They found that men with higher testosterone levels made larger wagers—that is, they were more risk-taking. The researchers speculate that increased risk-taking is the result of an evolutionary process related to mating that initially placed greater emphasis on male fitness and then subsequently on wealth.[32]

Concern with fairness, or perhaps positional status, also seems to be subject to testosterone levels. Men with higher testosterone levels are more likely to reject low offers in an ultimatum game. They are also more likely to make low offers.[33] The much higher levels of testosterone in men vs women (at about 15 to 1) are thought to explain men's generally greater competitiveness and risk-taking.[34] Because testosterone's influence begins in utero, as the brain develops, individuals have different levels of testosterone. So higher levels have been measured in pro football players versus ministers, and in trial versus non-trial lawyers.

[30] Fehr et al. (2005).

[31] Han and Ma (2024).

[32] Apicella et al. (2008).

[33] Burnham (2003). Testosterone is associated with numerous other economically relevant variables and choices, including investment decisions and asset prices.

[34] Testosterone and estrogen are correlated in some studies with consumer purchases, particularly of the positional variety meant to provide signals to others of the purchaser's wealth and status. Such behavior can be explained as an outcome of evolutionary forces, as wealth and status are associated with improved mating chances.

While some studies find little or no correlation between testosterone (or estrogen) with economically relevant variables, and much remains unanswered, "mounting evidence suggests that hormones causally contribute to a wide range of behavioral propensities." As economist Coren Apicella notes, such findings are consistent with several observations including lower levels of risk-taking in women and older-aged individuals and increases in risk-taking in men following monetary wins (e.g., the house money effect) and when in the presence of attractive women.[35]

15.6 Concluding Comments

Cooperation, honesty, trust, and fairness represent a very short list of the influences of social norms and customs on markets. Evidence is clear, rational individuals sometimes forgo short-term gains in exchange for mutual benefits. Rather than being hindered by such behavior, economies are enhanced. Without them, markets would likely slow considerably.

Individuals and groups, such as parents, neighbors, peers, and institutions, including religion, all shape individual attitudes toward these and a host of other economic-relevant attitudes.[36] Research exploring these sources is examined in more detail in the following chapters. Adam Smith was right: we cannot rely on the goodness in people's hearts to supply the goods and services we want but neither can we have a workable society without constraints on self-interest.

References

Abdulkadiroğlu A, Bagwell K (2013) Trust, reciprocity, and favors in cooperative relationships. American Economic Journal: Microeconomics 5(2):213–259

Algan Y, Cahuc P (2010) Inherited trust and growth. American Economic Review 100(5):2060–2092

Apicella CL, Carré JM, Dreber A (2015) Testosterone and economic risk taking: A review. Adapt Hum Behav Physiol 1:358–385

Apicella CL, Silk JB (2019) The evolution of human cooperation. Curr Biol 29(11):R447–R450

[35] Apicella et al. (2015). For a study that finds no correlation see Zethraeus et al. (2009).

[36] E.g., Dohmen et al. (2012).

Apicella CL, Dreber A, Campbell B, Gray PB, Hoffman M, Little AC (2008) Testosterone and financial risk preferences. Evol Hum Behav 29(6):384–390
den Assem MJV, van Dolder D, Thaler RH (2012) Split or steal? Cooperative behavior when the stakes are large. Manage Sci 58(1):2–20
Bowles S, Edwards R, Roosevelt F (2005) Understanding capitalism. Oxford University Press
Burnham T (2003) Caveman economics: Proximate and ultimate causes of nonmaterially maximizing behavior. Working paper, Harvard University.
Butler JV, Giuliano P, Guiso L (2016) The right amount of trust. Journal of European Economic Association. 14(5):1155–1180
Cohn A, Fehr E, Marechal MA (2014) Business culture and dishonesty in the banking industry. Nature 516 (4 December): 86–89.
Croson R, Buchan N (1999) Gender and culture: International experimental evidence from trust games. Am Econ Rev 89(2):386–391
Das A (2022) U.S. soccer and women's players agree to settle equal pay lawsuit. New York Times. Available at: https://www.nytimes.com/2022/02/22/sports/soccer/us-womens-soccer-equal-pay.html. Accessed on 2 July 2025
Department of Justice (2019) United States Attorney's Office Northern District of Iowa. Field of schemes fraud results in over a decade in federal prison for leader of largest organic fraud case in U.S. history. https://www.justice.gov/usao-ndia/pr/field-schemes-fraud-results-over-decade-federal-prison-leader-largest-organic-fraud. Accessed on 6 Sept 2025
Dohmen T, Falk A, Huffman D, Sunde U (2012) The intergenerational transmission of risk and trust attitudes. Rev Econ Stud 79(2):645–677
Evensky J (2005) Adam Smith's theory of moral sentiments: On morals and why they matter to a liberal society of free people and free markets. Journal of Economic Perspectives 19(3):109–130
Fehr E, Fischbacher U, Kosfeld M (2005) Neuroeconomic foundations of trust and social preferences: Initial evidence. American Economic Review 95(2):346–351
Fischbacher U, Gächter S, Fehr E (2001) Are people conditionally cooperative? Evidence from a public goods experiment. Econ Lett 71:397–404
Gambetta D (2000) Can we trust. In: Gambetta, Diego (ed), Trust: making and breaking cooperative relations, electronic edition, Department of Sociology, University of Oxford, chapter 13, pp. 213–237, http://www.sociology.ox.ac.uk/papers/gambetta213-237.pdf.
Goldin C (2025) How underpaid are W.N.B.A. players? It's embarrassing. New York Times, 6 June.
Guiso L, Sapienza P, Zingales L (2006) Does culture affect economic outcomes? Journal of Economic Perspectives 20(2):23–48
Han X, Ma Y (2024) Oxytocin in human social network cooperation. The Neuroscientist. 1–16.

Hernandez J (2022) The U.S. men's and women's soccer teams will be paid equally under a new deal. https://www.npr.org/2022/05/18/1099697799/us-soccer-equal-pay-agreement-women#:~:text=The%20U.S.%20Soccer%20Federation%20announced%20Wednesday%20that%20it,pay%20gap%20that%20saw%20female%20players%20earning%20less. Accessed on 30 Aug 2025

Kasper C et al. (2017) Genetics and developmental biology of cooperation. Molecular Ecology. Available at: https://onlinelibrary.wiley.com/doi/epdf/https://doi.org/10.1111/mec.14208. Accessed on 16 March 2022

Maccoby EE (1980) Social development. Harcourt, San Diego

McKenzie RB (1987) The fairness of markets. Lexington Books, Lexington, MA

Ostrom E (2000) Collective action and the evolution of social norms. Journal of Economic Perspectives 14(3):137–158

Thaler RH (1992) The winner's curse: Paradoxes and anomalies of economic life. Free Press, New York, NY

Thaler RH (2016) Behavioral economics: Past, present, and future. American Economic Review 106(7):1577–1600. https://doi.org/10.1257/aer.106.7.1577

Thomas RP (1981) Microeconomic applications: Understanding the American economy. Wadsworth, Belmont, CA

Transparency Internation (n.d.). Corruption perceptions index. https://www.transparency.org/en/cpi/2021. Accessed on 6 Sept 2025

Tu Q, Bulte E (2010) Trust, market participation and economic outcomes: Evidence from rural China. World Dev 38(8):1179–1190

Tzieropoulos H (2013) The trust game in neuroscience: A short review. Soc Neurosci 8(5):407–416

Worm B, et al. (2006) Impacts of biodiversity loss on ocean ecosystem services. Science 314(5800).

Zak PJ (2017) The neuroscience of trust management behaviors that foster employee engagement. Harvard Business Review, January-February.

Zak PJ, Borja K, Matzner WT, Kurzban R (2005) The neuroeconomics of distrust: Sex differences in behavior and physiology. American Economic Review 95(2):360–363

Zethraeus N, Kocoska-Maras L, Ellingsen T, von Schoultz B, Linden Hirschberg A, Johannesson M (2009) A randomized trial of the effect of estrogen and testosterone on economic behavior. PNAS 106(16):6535–6538

CHAPTER 16

Written Rules: Religion

> Not only do two-thirds of evangelical Protestants think the government is carrying out functions better left to religious groups and other private charities, but religiously committed Americans of nearly all faiths see less need for government services and government intervention than do most citizens of other high-income countries.[1]

> The religious atmosphere of the country was the first thing that struck me in the United States [in the 1830s]. For the Americans the ideas of Christianity and liberty are so completely mingled that it is almost impossible to get them to conceive of the one without the other.[2]

> Remember the sabbath day, to keep it holy.[3]

Game five of the 1929 World Series between the Chicago Cubs and Philadelphia Athletics was postponed from Sunday to Monday because of prohibitions of Sunday games in Pennsylvania. In fact, prior to the 1920s, many teams were prohibited from playing Sunday games by local or state law. Prior to 1932, Massachusetts forbade Sunday games within

[1] Benjamin M. Friedman in Friedman (2021), p. 411.

[2] Alexis de Tocqueville, from 1830, quoted in Matthews (1991).

[3] Third (or Fourth) Commandment.

L. Hadsell, *Social Economies*,
https://doi.org/10.1007/978-3-032-21916-9_16

a thousand feet of a church, forcing the Boston Red Sox to play their Sunday games at Braves Field rather than at Fenway Park.[4] Not until 1934 did the Pennsylvania legislature and voters repeal their law prohibiting Sunday games.[5] So-called "blue laws" like these prohibiting certain business activity on the Christian Sabbath were once common in the U.S., restricting not just Sunday sporting events but commerce of a wide variety.

Blue laws had religious origins, as recognition of a day of rest in the Christian faith, but later achieved mostly secular purposes—such as providing a day of rest for weary workers. While blue laws are now generally an historical artifact, some remain. Many states still prohibit selling alcohol on Sunday, including Arkansas, where thirty-nine of 75 counties prohibit the sale of alcohol on any day.[6] Until deemed unconstitutional in 1982, Massachusetts law allowed churches to challenge liquor sales within 500 feet of the church.[7] Most blue laws today regulate liquor sales, but others go further. Maine, for example, currently prohibits stores with more than 5000 square feet from opening on Easter and Christmas.[8] Until 1985, Texas, blue laws prohibited selling housewares such as pots, pans, and washing machines on Sunday, and car dealerships in the state still operate under blue-law prohibitions.

Religious beliefs also affect individual and business choices quite separately from any legal constraints. For example, while observance of a "day of rest" has waned considerably in the U.S., a few companies still honor such views. The popular fast food chain Chick-fil-A, for instance, is closed Sundays, much to the irritation of weekend travelers on the New York State thruway, where, in 2022, the company became the lead restaurant at nine of the 27 rest stops between New York City and Buffalo. Arts and crafts store Hobby Lobby is similarly closed on Sundays; noted for using Christian principles to guide business decisions, it also gained Supreme Court approval in 2014 to deny insurance coverage for contraceptive care

[4] Menendez (2007). The American Association began as a result, in part, of the National League president William Hulbert banishing the Cincinnati team from that league in 1880 for playing games on Sunday and selling alcohol in the stands.

[5] Upheld by the Pennsylvania Supreme Court in 1927.

[6] Alcohol Problems and Solutions (n.d.). Comen (2019).

[7] Tribe (2024).

[8] Dineen (2019).

to employees, despite requirements in the Affordable Care Act to do so.[9] The U.S. Supreme Court has generally upheld the right of businesses to apply their religious beliefs to business practices, as in the 2018 case of Masterpiece Cakeshop v. Colorado Civil Rights Commission, in which the Court upheld the right of the cake shop to refuse to create a cake for a same-sex wedding celebration because of the cake shop owner's religious opposition to same-sex marriage, noting that he was a devote Christian. The Court held that "religious and philosophical objections to gay marriage are protected views and in some instances protected forms of expression."[10]

Religion also influences economic behavior in pro-market ways, originating with sacred religious writings and viewpoints of religious leaders. Incentives related to salvific merit are among the most prominent incentives derived from religious beliefs. "If people believe in the possibility of salvation through their own efforts, it makes sense that they are likely to perform the actions that contribute to attaining such an end. Therefore, religious beliefs have implications for behavior, such as work effort, saving, and charity."[11] These effects manifest themselves from the individual to national levels. Religion creates and enforces norms and customs, including such things as a strong work ethic and conceptions of fairness and reciprocity. Emphases on thrift and careful investment promote formation of physical capital. Human capital is encouraged through education. And, as a social as well as spiritual endeavor, religion enhances community, particularly bonding social capital (as described in Chapter 19).[12]

Compared to other developed countries, a higher share of Americans identify with a religion (mostly Christian), with about half saying that religion is "very important" to them.[13] Americans also pray and attend religious services more often. At the same time, affiliation and religiosity has been declining in the U.S. for decades, with a sharp shift in recent

[9] Rutman (2014).

[10] Supreme Court of the United States (2017).

[11] McCleary (2007).

[12] It will be noted in Chapter 19 that bonding social capital has both positive and negative elements, both of which show up in the religious sphere.

[13] Gallup (2024).

years, so that about one in five say they do not follow any particular religion. Given the influence of religion on individuals in economic settings, the high levels of religiosity in the U.S. and its recent sharp decline foreshadows important implications for the U.S. economy.

16.1 A Sometimes Complicated and Hidden Relationship

To begin our look at the effects of religion on economic activity, complete the nearby survey before continuing. It is one my colleagues and I developed and complements other surveys such as the World Values Survey (WVS), administered worldwide every five years to more than 400,000 people, the General Survey of Social Sciences (GSS) administered in the U.S., and several other country-specific surveys.

Religiosity Index

Statements 1–4: Use the following rating scale to indicate how strongly you agree or disagree with each statement.

Neither						
Strongly Disagree 1	Disagree 2	Slightly Disagree 3	Agree nor Disagree 4	Slightly Agree 5	Agree 6	Strongly Agree 7

1. I believe in God.
2. I believe in an afterlife.
3. I believe that some persons will go to an unpleasant afterlife (i.e., Hell, Hades, etc.)
4. I make an effort to apply my spiritual/religious beliefs to the way I live my life.

5. How often do you attend organized worship services?

Never	*rarely*	*Only during holidays*	*During hard times in my life*	*Some Scheduled*	*Most scheduled*	*All*
1	2	3	4	5	6	7

6. How often you spend time in individual prayer.

Never	*rarely*	*During special times*	*Some days*	*Most days*	*Every day*
0	1	2	3	4	5

7. How often do you read (outside of church) the holy books or writings associated with your spiritual or religious beliefs.

Never	*rarely*	*During special times*	*Some days*	*Most days*	*Every day*
0	1	2	3	4	5

The Religiosity Index is created by summing responses to the seven statements.

Source Jones, Hadsell, and Burrus (2019).

The survey provides one measure of an individual's religious beliefs and actions by summing responses to the seven statements to create the Religiosity Index. When my colleagues and I surveyed nearly 2300 individuals in the U.S. in 2016, the average score on the index was 22, with, and here's the key, individual totals highly correlated with support for free markets (as captured by the Capitalism Index, CI, described in Chapter 3). That is, more religious individuals tended to be more supportive of free markets. Further, religiosity and support for markets varies substantially by affiliation, as shown in Fig. 16.1. Perhaps surprisingly, given the limitations on economic activity via blue laws noted at the beginning of the chapter, religiosity and support for free markets generally go hand-in-hand.

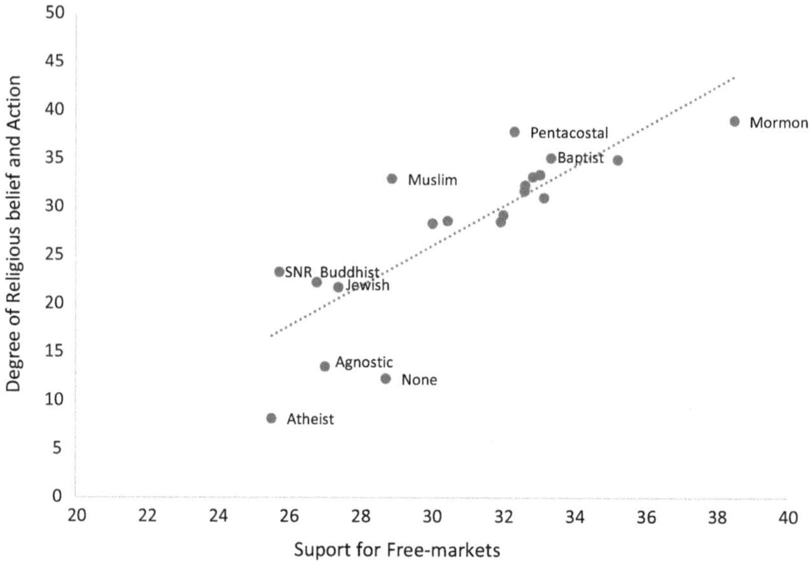

Fig. 16.1 Religion and support for Capitalism (Average scores on the Religiosity Index survey [earlier in this chapter] is shown on the vertical axis, while average scores on the capitalism Index [Chapter 3] is shown on the horizontal axis. Self-reported affiliations/denominations represented by dots in the graph are Catholic, Baptist, Episcopal, Lutheran, Methodist, Nondenominational Protestant, Pentecostal, Presbyterian, Mormon, Buddhist, Jewish, Orthodox, Muslim, Hindu, Spiritual-But-Not-Religious, Agnostic, None, Atheist. Based on Jones et al. [2019])

While various Protestant denominations and Catholics generally had high levels of religiosity and support for markets, Mormons had both very high religiosity and were the strongest supporters of markets.[14] Although not nearly as numerous as other denominations, Mormons, with a well-known emphasis on tithing, volunteerism, and abstinence, represent an interesting case.[15] Economic historian Leonard Arrington,

[14] White Baptists in the sample were more pro-market than other Protestants (though black Baptists were not).

[15] Mormons number about 15 million adherents worldwide, including about six million in the U.S., compared to more than 1 billion members worldwide each for Catholics, Hindus, and Muslims and nearly 1 billion Protestants.

in a history of the Mormon Church, documents how economics was incorporated into the religion, noting that nearly 80% of the sermons of Mormon founder Joseph Smith focused either partly or entirely on economic issues, including arguments for property rights and wealth creation, strongly connecting the religious and economic aspects of the movement.[16] Suggestive of this legacy, the state seal and flag of Utah, where Salt Lake City is headquarters of the Mormon church, features the beehive, symbol of industriousness—and the state motto is, simply, "Industry."

At the other end of the religiosity scale, we see that those with no strong religious beliefs—the spiritual-but-not-religious and atheists—expressed the lowest average support for markets. In sum, being more likely to believe in God and Hell, and to pray and attend services, correlates strongly with greater support for markets and with less government intervention.

The main Christian religions, such as Protestantism, with its "Protestant work ethic" linking labor and moral duty, have historically had significant impact on economic choices, especially in America.[17] Hard work and accumulation of wealth are "expressions of God's grace," and activities promoting idleness, for example, are "at times outright condemned for going against God's will."[18] An affinity for markets has been particularly strong at times in the U.S., where, for instance, mid-nineteenth-century Protestant churches "were among the most vehement voices in American Society in favor of laissez-faire economic policies."[19] Today, certain cross-denominational groups of Protestantism, such as Evangelicals, are well-known for their active support of conservative economic policies. Baptists have a particularly strong emphasis on separation of church and state and high support for free markets.[20]

Of course, not all religious pronouncements are so favorable to free markets, as the Sunday blue laws demonstrate. One might consider recent Catholic Social Teaching (as seen in, for example, Pope Francis' 2015 encyclical letter Laudato Si) which emphasizes principles such as the

[16] Arrington (2005). Jones et al. (2019).

[17] Hayward and Kemmelmeier (2011). Keely (2003).

[18] McCleary (2007), p. 67.

[19] Bateman and Kapstein (1999).

[20] Southern Baptist Convention. (1967). Maples (2007). Norman (2005).

dignity of work and the rights of workers, a preferential option for the poor, the care of God's creation, and the common good—values which ostensibly call for individuals to act a certain way, in addition to potentially lending support for government intervention to limit market forces. In this view, "the imperative of religion is not to banish self-interest but to limit and regulate it. The self-love to which a Christian spirit was contrary was only 'an inordinate self-love,' what amounted to selfishness."[21]

The "Social Gospel Movement" of the late 1800s and early 1900s is an example of less than favorable views toward unfettered markets. In fact, the leading organization today for professional economists, The American Economic Association, was co-founded in 1910 by Richard Ely, on Social Gospel principles which emphasized social justice, labor reforms, and active government oversight of markets:

> The one common element identifying the American economics profession at the time was its ethical, or social, concern. [The] new ethical economics had a real impact on American society and politics. Social Gospelers like Ely and [economist John R.] Commons were instrumental in the Progressive movement in the first two decades of this century and they could claim at least partial credit for a whole host of reforms that were once unthinkable in the American political context, from unemployment insurance to worker safety and child labor laws. In such laws we see the first glimmers of America's postwar welfare state, and the institutionalization of social safety nets for the most vulnerable members of society.[22]

Religion continues to play a complicated role in economic affairs, in the U.S. and around the world. To give you an idea of the subtle and often surprising influence of religious beliefs on individuals, consider research based on responses from around the world to surveys such as the one earlier in this chapter. Countries whose inhabitants have a strong belief in Hell tend to have higher rates of economic growth just as individuals who have a strong belief in Hell are also more likely to support free-market capitalism; and, more generally, the more religious an individual or country is the greater their support for markets.[23] More religious individuals have, on average, more savings, higher levels of trust, more positive

[21] Friedman (2021).

[22] Bateman and Kapstein (1999), pp. 255–256.

[23] Barro and McCleary (2003).

attitudes toward work, and different risk tolerance (and investment decisions).[24] Even businesses in more religious areas tend to have more ethical business practices (fewer accounting irregularities, more accurate earnings reports). And government regulation and taxes tend to be lower in countries and states within the U.S. with more religious populations.

Religion shapes many economic attitudes and actions, through at least four channels:

1. Physical capital formation—through an emphasis on thrift
2. Human capital formation—through education
3. Social norms, such as effort (through labor-force participation and productivity) and trust
4. Social capital formation—by building a community network.

Most efforts to identify religious influences on economic-relevant variables concentrates on Christian religions. Protestantism, with its emphasis on individual responsibility, industriousness ("idle hands do the devil's work"), and salvation through actions, clearly emphasizes qualities that are valuable in markets. Trust and attitudes toward risk are important elements of market transactions, as well. In multi-country surveys, those attending services are found to be more trusting, an effect that is especially strong for Protestants.[25] Dutch survey data show that religious households save more.[26] Other research suggests that religion affects risk preference.[27] Because tolerance for risk is necessary for entrepreneurship, this may influence views of capitalism and success in markets. Survey data show that Christians generally tend to show greater support of private ownership of property and believe poverty is the result of laziness and lack of will power.[28]

[24] Jones et al. (2019).

[25] Guiso et al. (2003). Renneboog and Spaenjers (2012).

[26] Renneboog and Spaenjers (2012)

[27] Halek and Eisenhauer (2001). Though Catholics were more tolerant of speculative risk, leading researchers to conclude that the greater tolerance for speculative risk "may reflect differences in religious teachings regarding gambling in general; whereas some Protestant denominations view gambling as sinful, many Catholic parishes employ games of chance to raise funds for church use."

[28] Guiso et al. (2003).

In America, the roots of capitalist thought are intertwined with religion, from the time the first Europeans arrived seeking religious freedom to the widespread revivals in the mid-1800s and again a century later, with Billy Graham crusades, to the outsize role in political and economic life of current-day evangelicals. The 1950s Cold War environment is captured by a quote from President Eisenhower's secretary of state, John Foster Dulles: "For us there are two kinds of people in the world. There are those who are Christians and support free enterprise, and there are the others."[29] Evangelist Billy Graham, influential icon of the post-WWII Christian revival in America who preached salvation and economic freedom, likewise was a prominent member of the anti-communist crusade, attracting crowds of tens of thousands at rallies, millions of television viewers, and advising prominent public officials, including presidents. Christianity, especially Protestantism, fused with politics to strongly promote individual economic freedom and an anti-government ethos. The influence remains strong: As economist Benjamin Friedman notes, the U.S. is in many ways an outlier when it comes to influence of religious thinking on economic thinking.[30] Friedman points to religion as a factor in many Americans' steadfast stance against economic policies that have no direct negative effect on them (and sometimes would have a positive impact), such as taxes on very high incomes and multi-million dollar estates and subsequent redistribution via an enhanced social safety net.[31] Policies that tax economic success are often seen as taxes on divine grace. Taxing wealth is taxing God.

16.2 Non-Christian Religions

One consistent finding of researchers looking at survey data, in the U.S. and worldwide, is that followers of other religions, such as Judaism, Buddhism, Hinduism, and Islam, tend to view markets less favorably than do followers of Christianity. The reasons are numerous and often subtle.

[29] As told in Friedman (2021), p. 379.

[30] Friedman (2021), p. 390.

[31] Friedman (2021), pp. xii, 391. The current tax exclusion on estates exceeds $15 million.

For example, whereas Christianity tends to emphasize individual responsibility, Islam stresses communal enforcement.[32] Key features of Islamic economics principles are prohibition of interest, redistribution through taxes on wealth to finance poverty relief, and norms that "command good" and "forbid evil," encouraging individuals to work hard, charge fair prices, and pay others their due.[33] Based on international surveys, Hindus and Muslims tend to view competition less favorably and are on average less trusting of secular government than are adherents of other religions, though Hindus tend to prefer more private ownership whereas Muslims want less.[34] Of course, these are averages with a wide distribution and should not be taken to mean conformity of views for any group. Yet economic growth rates and use of market-based economic systems are empirically connected to religion—with non-Christian countries tending to grow more slowly and relying less on markets.

16.3 Religion and the State

Individual beliefs can have an influence beyond individual choice, for instance affecting government policies that either support or constrain economic choices, with some examples noted at the beginning of the chapter. Our research finds that U.S. states with greater shares of voters who hold strong Christian religious beliefs tend to have less overall government regulation, taxing, and spending. Conversely, less religious and therefore less pro-market states tend to have more government intervention. Internationally, we see that the share of the population in a country that is Protestant is positively associated with less government intervention in markets, while the shares of Catholics and Muslims are unrelated to government taxing and regulation.[35]

Some research suggests that greater government regulation and spending crowd out church charitable activity. That is, increased government regulation and spending are associated with less private giving, suggesting the existence of the view that in the absence of religion, government will be expected to support actions otherwise performed by

[32] McCleary (2007).

[33] Kuran (1995).

[34] Guiso et al. (2003).

[35] Hillman and Potrafke (2018).

religious organizations.[36] For the active Christian, faith and the church are the safety net, whereas for the not-religious, government provides that safety net. Strong religious beliefs can act as a constraint on behavior that might otherwise be constrained by the state through regulations and other policies restricting choice. In short, strong religious faith acts as a substitute for activist government. In other words, less belief in the ability of religion and religious institutions to limit market forces implies a greater reliance on government programs.

16.4 Religion and Business

Individual religious attitudes translate into real differences in market activity and can carry over to business practice at the firm level. For example, a religious emphasis on saving and thrift suggests pursuit of a conservative business philosophy. Such a restraint on excesses in business activity is apparent in recent research findings: Firms located in geographic areas with strong religious influence exhibit lower incidences of financial reporting irregularities, are less likely to practice aggressive earnings management (e.g., by reporting revenue earlier than it should or delaying reporting of expenses, either of which raises current profit), are less prone to shareholder lawsuits, and have more modest management compensation packages and more generous worker pay.[37] One study finds that the number of churches in a U.S. county has a strong negative association with senior corporate executive pay of businesses headquartered in that county. The authors note that the effect is particularly strong for Protestant denominations, while the effect of number of Catholic churches is not significant. They speculate that the mechanism leading to the lower compensation reflects "the extent the corporate board (and possibly the CEO) is influenced by the community's concept of fairness." Another study finds higher employee compensation and smaller pay disparity between executives and employees in Chinese companies located in more religious areas (employing Buddhist principles).[38]

[36] Gruber and Hungerman (2007).

[37] Grullon et al. (2009); McGuire et al. (2012), Dyreng et al. (2012). Kanagaretnam et al. (2015).

[38] Zhao et al. (2022).

Other studies find that firms headquartered in U.S. counties with higher levels of religiosity are more conservative in investment and growth strategies.[39] That is, the firms require higher expected rates of return before undertaking new investment in projects, ranging from new equipment to research and development. Essentially, managers in such firms are more risk averse. The same researchers find that when CEOs switch employers, they are more likely to join firms with a similar religious environment as their prior firm.[40]

16.5 Concluding Comments

Religion has important effects on cultural norms which restrain the worst vices of capitalism while at the same time promoting its best aspects.[41] As conservative social commentator William F. Buckley once noted, "religion must guide the individual when he faces such questions as what are honorable and what are dishonorable means of amassing wealth, and what are responsible and irresponsible means of disbursing this wealth."[42]

An agreed-upon set of acceptable actions can reduce uncertainty, increase trust and efficiency, and thus increase economic value.[43] Religion appears to serve such a purpose. While religious beliefs sometimes proscribe certain market activity, such as Sunday commerce, significant empirical evidence suggests that Christian religious beliefs encourage individual and collective action that is conducive to prosperous markets. Other religions similarly influence economic actions, though adherents tend to be less pro-market than Christians.

An under-appreciated outcome of waning religious affiliation and practice in the U.S., given the positive correlation between religiosity and support for free markets, is the implied declining support for free-market economics it may imply. If secularization, which has picked up speed since 2000, continues, we might expect a desire for greater substitution of government intervention for market forces. Whether that is a good thing or not depends on your perspective.

[39] Hilary and Hui (2009).

[40] Hilary et al. (2009).

[41] McGuire et al. (2012).

[42] Buckley (1951), p. 330.

[43] McKenzie (1987), p. 20.

References

Alcohol Problems and Solutions (n.d.) Alcohol Blue Laws. https://www.alcoholproblemsandsolutions.org/Controversies/Alcohol-Blue-Laws.html. Accessed on 30 Aug 2025

Arrington LJ (2005) Great Basin Kingdom: An economic history of the latter-day saints, 1830–1900. University of Illinois Press, Urbana and Chicago

Barro RJ, McCleary RM (2003) Religion and economic growth across countries. Am Sociol Rev 68(5):760–781

Bateman BW, Kapstein EB (1999) Between God and the market: The religious roots of the American Economic AssociationXE "American economic association." Journal of Economic Perspectives 13(4):249–258

Buckley WF (1951) [2004] God and Man at Yale. ISI Conservative Classics.

Comen E (2019) These 9 states still have dry counties. https://247wallst.com/special-report/2019/12/12/states-that-still-have-dry-counties/. Accessed on 30 Aug 2025

Dineen H (2019) 'Blue Laws' prevent many stores from being open on Thanksgiving Day. https://www.newscentermaine.com/article/life/blue-laws-prevent-many-stores-from-being-open-on-thanksgiving-day/97-67d216e0-70bc-415f-88d1-4fd8378e1cf4#:~:text=Furthermore%2C%20blue%20laws%20prohibit%20many%20large%20stores%20from,on%20Easter%20Day%2C%20Thanksgiving%20Day%20and%20Christmas%20Day. Accessed on 30 Aug 2025

Dyreng D, Mayew WJ, Williams CD (2012) Religious social normsXE "Social norms" and corporate financial reporting. J Bus Financ Acc 39(7–8):845–875

Friedman B (2021) Religion and the rise of capitalism.

Gallup (2024) How religious are americans? https://news.gallup.com/poll/358364/religious-americans.aspx. Accessed on 30 Aug 2025

Gruber J, Hungerman DM (2007) Faith-based charity and crowd-out during the great depression. J Public Econ 91:1043–1069

Grullon G, Kanatas G, Weston J (2009) Religion and corporate (mis)behavior. Available at: https://doi.org/10.2139/ssrn.1472118

Guiso L, Sapienza P, Zingales L (2003) People's opium? Religion and economic attitudes. J Monet Econ 50:225–282

Halek M, Eisenhauer JG (2001) Demography of risk aversion. Journal of Risk and Insurance: 1–24.

Hayward RD, Kemmelmeier M (2011) Weber revisited, a cross-national analysis of religiosity, religious culture, and economic attitudes. J Cross Cult Psychol 42(8):1406–1420

Hilary G, Hui KW (2009) Does religion matter in corporate decision making in America? J Financ Econ 90:455–473

Hillman A, Potrafke N (2018) Economic freedom and religion: An empirical investigation. Public Finance Review 46(2).

Jones AT, Hadsell L, Burrus RT (2019) Capitalist views and religion. East Econ J 45:384–414

Kanagaretnam K, Lobo GJ, Wang C (2015) Religiosity and earnings management, international evidence from the banking industry. J Bus Ethics 132(2):277–296

Keely L (2003) Comment on, people's opium? Religion and economic attitudes. J Monet Econ 50:283–287

Kuran T (2018) Islam and economic performance: Historical and contemporary links. Journal of Economic Literature 56(4):1292–1359

Maples J (2007) The point of the Southern Baptists' departure from the doctrines of Calvinism. Master's thesis, Reformed Theological Seminary.

Matthews J (1991) Toward a new society: American thought and culture 1800–1830. Twayne Publishers, Boston

McCleary RM (2007) Salvation, damnation, and economic incentives. J Contemp Relig 22(1):49–74

McGuire ST, Omer TC, Sharp NY (2012) The impact of religion on financial reporting irregularities. Accounting Review 87(2):645–673

McKenzie RB (1987) The fairness of markets. Lexington Books, Lexington, MA

Menendez AJ (2007) The battle for sunday baseball. Liberty Magazine September/October. https://www.libertymagazine.org/article/the-battle-for-sunday-baseballAccessed on 30 Aug 2025

Norman RS (2005) The Baptist way, distinctives of a Baptist church. Broadman and Holman, Nashville, TN.

Renneboog L, Spaenjers C (2012) Economic attitudes and household finance. Oxf Econ Pap 64(1):103–127

Rutman L (2014) The hobby lobby decision: imposing religious beliefs on employees. https://aclu-wa.org/blog/hobby-lobby-decision-imposing-religious-beliefs-employees Accessed on 30 Aug 2025

Southern Baptist Convention (1967) Resolution on separation of church and state. Available at: http://www.sbc.net/resolutions/943.

Supreme Court of the United States (2017) Masterpiece Cakeshop, Ltd., et al. v. Colorado Civil Rights Commission et al. https://www.supremecourt.gov/opinions/17pdf/16-111_j4el.pdf. Accessed on 30 Aug 2025

Tribe LH (2024) Where freedom ends. New York Review of Books, November 7.

Zhao G, Liang S, Zhang J, Huang HH (2022) Religious tradition and employee compensation. J Int Account Res 21(3):169–185

CHAPTER 17

Family Structure: Marriage and Children

Oh, the Family! The imperfect Economy.
Often demanding more than we can supply.[1]

In 1900, the average number of children per family in the U.S. was 3.5, and the average age at first marriage was 21 years. By 1955, the typical household consisted of a married couple with 2.2 children, with marriage entered into by age 23.[2] The husband typically worked outside the home (engaged in paid market labor) while the wife cared for the home and children (engaged in unpaid non-market labor). Although women may have worked outside the home prior to marriage social custom meant they often stopped upon marriage or with the birth of a child; women with young children seldom worked outside the home. Divorce was uncommon (though how happy marriages were is not cataloged). Six decades later, much has changed. The typical U.S. household in 2020 is likely to be comprised of cohabitating (unmarried) individuals. Marriage is delayed—age at first marriage in the U.S. is now 31. Marriage is also much less common, as the fraction of married 25–44-year-olds is now just a bit over 70%. Divorce rates are higher, too, though remarriage is

[1] Christine Hadsell

[2] For couples with children under 18.

L. Hadsell, *Social Economies*,
https://doi.org/10.1007/978-3-032-21916-9_17

less common now than it used to be. And 40% of children are born to unmarried parents. Each of these changes has important economic causes as well as a wide array of consequences, from impacts on housing markets to wealth accumulation.

Birth rates have declined, in the U.S. and most other industrialized countries, such that the average is now below replacement level—the number of children per woman required to maintain current population, about 2.1. The resulting decline in population, absent sufficient replacement immigration, leads to an aging population and to a series of social and economic problems including labor shortages, inflation, lower tax revenue and higher spending for major government programs such as social security and Medicaid (paid for by taxes on a shrinking workforce), and a shortage of old-age caregivers and care homes.

Other developed economies are seeing similar changes. The average age of first marriage is 34 in Germany, 35 in Italy, 38 in South Korea, 39 in Japan (though in the U.K. it is just 30, and in China it is 27). Birthrates in developed economies as a whole fell below 2.1 in 1982 and continued to decline, to an average 1.6 in 2022. The current rate in Japan is 1.3, where population peaked in year 2000, and in South Korea it is 0.8, where population has been declining since 2020 (South Korea delayed population decline through immigration whereas Japan allows much less immigration). Italy's population has declined slightly since 2011, while Germany's has been stagnant since 2000.

Combined with rapid growth in retirement age population due to the Baby Boom generation and generally longer lives, each of these countries is experiencing, among other maladies, school closings, labor shortages, and difficulty funding social services, especially for the elderly. The U.S. has been spared of the worst effects so far, the result of substantial immigration. Still, with an aging population the cost of elder care is a financial timebomb in the U.S., just as it is elsewhere.

While the forces leading to changes in marriage and childbearing are myriad, dramatic shifts in family structure in the U.S. and other industrialized countries have as much to do with economic forces as they do with social change, and the two cannot be separated anyway. Changes to marriage and childbearing, rather than being a product solely of more liberal social policies and increased availability of contraception, also resulted from changing economic incentives. In all economically developed and advanced developing economies around the world, declining birth rates go hand-in-hand with increases in wages and the lifting of social and legal restrictions on women in the workforce. Rising wages for women entice more women into the workforce and increase the opportunity cost of caring for children: children become more expensive in terms of forgone wages if a parent stays home to care for them. The rise in labor-force participation among women is also facilitated by greater cultural acceptance of women in professional roles not previously open to them. Both allowed financial independence among women that further shaped marriage and child-rearing patterns.

In this chapter, I outline the dynamic between family and economy. This dynamic is two-way: family structure is deeply affected by economic forces, and family structure has an important influence on economic systems and the individuals comprising those systems. By far the biggest impacts are related to labor markets and choices regarding time allocation. Fewer children, and a rising return to human capital, i.e., education, means that parents spend more time nurturing each child and invest more in improving each child's future economic circumstances through education, from toys to tutoring. To investigate this dynamic is to investigate a fundamental aspect of all economic systems: what happens in the home cannot be separated from what happens in markets. This should not be surprising. After all, the word "economics" comes from the Greek *Oikonomia*, meaning household management.

17.1 Social, Technological, and Legal Changes

The historical connection between family structure and economic activity is well-documented. Before markets developed, when production was mainly based in the home, economic concerns were the primary consideration regarding marriage and child-rearing. Children were important to the production of food, clothing, and so on in the home, making marriage economically essential. The link between work and home was weakened during the Industrial Revolution, by technological changes, further specialization, and the spread of labor markets, placing an emphasis on work performed outside the home. Overwhelmingly, the husband became the wage earner, and the wife worked at home. Children became less integral to economic survival, and the number of children per household declined.[3]

[3] The decline in births was also facilitated by medical advances that meant more children survived into adulthood.

By the 1950s in the U.S., as new technologies introduced labor-saving household devices, more women began entering formal paid markets, if mostly on a limited basis, in limited roles and typically only until marriage or childbirth, with vastly unequal opportunities and treatment compared to men. Review of the employment advertisements in the 1920s, as shown in Fig. 17.1, illustrates how starkly different gender discrimination was tolerated just a few generations ago. (Similarly discriminating ads appeared throughout the 1950s and 60s.) Yet, as household appliances became ever more affordable and wages rose, more women entered labor markets, with female labor-force participation rising from 35% in 1950 to 60% by 1980 (see Fig. 17.2).[4] Increasing acceptance of women in the labor force and rising wages further increased the opportunity cost of having and caring for children. Public policies such as Social Security (1930s) and Medicaid (1960s) additionally reduced the need to have children who could care for elderly parents, even as lifespans were increasing.

These changes were accompanied in the 1960s and 1970s by significant reductions to legal barriers for participation by women in labor and financial markets, especially in banking, credit, and home ownership. By 1968, placing help-wanted ads specifying gender became illegal in the

HOUSEWORK, wanted, a woman for housework in the country. Italian, Spanish or French. Telephone 197-J-6, Newtown, Pa.

HOUSEWORK—Girl for general housework. Apply 1814 Greenwood Avenue.

HOUSEWORK — Middle-aged woman for housework; plain cooking. Possibly could use woman with small child. Three miles from city. Take Hopewell trolley get off at home of Robert Brophy, or 'phone 12-R12, Pennington.

HOUSEWORK — White girl for general housework at shore immediately. Apply this evening or Thursday. 11 Perdicaris' Place.

LADIES (young) for demonstrating and canvassing a necessity in life. $1.50 a day. Address Albert A. Miller, 75 Ferrier Ave.

MAID, white, wanted for general housework; reference required. Phone 4942-W.

Fig. 17.1 1920s employment advertisement (*Source* Trenton Evening Times (Trenton, New Jersey), 13 July 1921, page 18)

[4] Greenwood et al. (2016), p. 8.

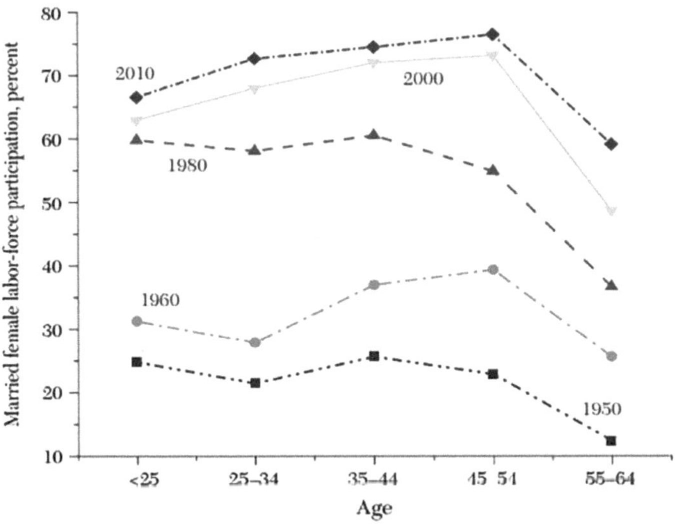

Fig. 17.2 Female labor-force participation, 1900–2010 (*Source* Greenwood et al., 2016)

U.S.[5] The Equal Credit Opportunity Act became law in 1974, allowing single, widowed, or divorced women, regardless of their income, to get a loan without a man as co-signer. Before this act, banks could refuse an unmarried woman credit; and if the woman was married, could require that her husband cosign. And beginning in 1978, women could not legally be dismissed from their job for becoming pregnant. Of course, gender discrimination (and sexual harassment) continued, despite the legal restrictions, but women's economic opportunity expanded greatly. To illustrate the remarkable shift in female labor market participation, consider that a woman with a six-month-old child in 2003 was more likely to work outside the home than a woman in 1970 with a sixteen-year-old. (Interestingly, we have no similar data on the likelihood of a man with a child working.) (Fig. 17.3).

With these social, technological, and legal changes, individuals had less need to marry for economic reasons. Women were no longer relegated to home production, having children was no longer an economic necessity,

[5] And in the U.K. Guardian (2014).

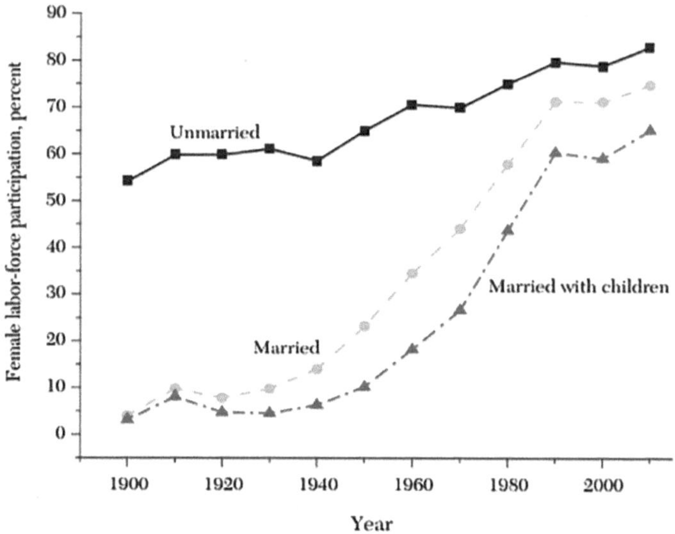

Fig. 17.3 Female labor-force participation (*Source* Greenwood et al., 2016)

and women in unhappy marriage could more easily divorce and support themselves.[6] The economic effects were profound.

With the movement of women into formal, paid labor markets, their work formerly done outside of markets now counted toward gross domestic product (GDP), the official economic measures of economic activity.[7] This by itself raised measures of economic growth, by up to 25% according to one estimate. Women's earnings now counted toward social security benefits and pensions, further lessening a need for marriage and children. Greater access to employment also allowed women to use talents that were previously neglected, benefiting not only themselves but society.

[6] Greenwood et al. (2016). See also Horwitz (2007). Women also had more control of their reproductive rights, with medical and legal changes regarding contraception and abortion in the 1960s and 1970s.

[7] Even today, only work that occurs in formal, paid markets is counted toward GDP, meaning a lot of non-market work, such as home childcare and eldercare, housework, and meal production, all typically performed by women, is not counted.

Marriage was delayed, for some, due to education requirements in an ever more advanced economy. In the U.S., most high school graduates now attend college, and most college students are female (currently around 57%). The need to establish a career after college graduation further delayed marriage. Yet, the decline in marriage rates in the U.S. in the last few decades has disproportionately affected those without a college education. Economists Courtney Coile and Mark Duggen note that marriage rates were nearly identical across all education groups in 1980, but by 2017 had dropped by 20 percentage points among all groups with less than a college education, while dropping only slightly for college graduates.[8] As suitable matches for women seeking marriage became scarcer, median age at first birth for mothers with a college education rose from 24 to 30, between 1960 and 2010, while it remained unchanged for low education mothers.[9] Further, as much as one-third of the decline in marriage among low-income individuals is attributable to incarceration of men.[10] And Men with less education are "now less likely to ever get married, more likely to get divorced, and less likely to remarry than their counterparts with more education."[11] Women with less formal education "are more likely [than college graduates] to enter into cohabiting partnerships early and bear children while cohabiting, are less likely to transition quickly into marriage, and have much higher divorce rates."[12] Combined with an increase in assortative mating (choosing a partner with a similar level of education) the economic implication is a widening gulf, economically and socially, between households with a college education and those without, and between married and not married.

The decline of manufacturing employment—a result as much from technological changes as international trade—has also affected marriage rates. Economists David Autor and colleagues show that areas with trade-induced declines in manufacturing employment experienced increases

[8] Coile and Duggan (2019).

[9] Putnam (2015), p. 65.

[10] Gould Werth (2018), Schneider et al (2018). Federal and state imprisonment rates increased dramatically beginning around 1980: for decades prior the rate was 100 per 100,000 of the population; after a steady climb between 1980 and 2000, the rate now hovers around 500 per 100,000.

[11] Coile and Duggan (2019)

[12] Lundberg et al. (2016).

in idleness among prime-age men and that these men were also less likely to marry or to have children.[13] Correspondingly, these same areas experienced increases in the proportion of children living with just one parent and in the fraction of children living in poverty. Others find that the decline in manufacturing employment has led to lower marriage rates as well as a larger gap in marriage rates by race and education. The economic implications are profound. Consider income and wealth inequality: median wealth for unmarried householders is only about 15% of the median for married householders (less than $50,000 vs $269,000, in 2021). Unmarried female head of households had the lowest (at just 75% of the level of unmarried men).[14]

For children, the effects of these changes in marriage can be long-lasting. Economists Pablo Mitnik and colleagues report an intergenerational continuation: in the U.S., children raised in higher (lower) income households are more (less) likely to marry by their late 30s. This appears to be so for both men and women. And children from one parent households are less likely to complete college and have worse health.[15]

17.2 Two More Considerations: Time with Children and Housing Costs

Even though women were having fewer children, time spent with children rose, with hours per week rising one-third for women between 1965 and 2011 and rising three-fold for men.[16] Even so, by 2011, women still devoted nearly twice as much time as men did to childcare, but the gap was closing, slowly, as women worked more hours outside the home. (During this period, hours spent on housework doubled for men and halved for women.) A 2011 Pew Research Center poll found that 49% of parents said they spent more time with their children than their parents did with them. Fewer children and a rising return to human capital (i.e., wage premium for education) meant that not only could parents spend more time nurturing each child but could invest more in each child's future economic circumstances, spending more on education.

[13] Autor et al. (2016).

[14] Bennett et al. (2022).

[15] Ziol-Guest et al. (2015).

[16] Pew Research Center (2013).

Housing is a significant expense of modern households.[17] Thus, housing costs indirectly shape family decisions through the timing of transitions into home ownership.[18] Choice of where to live and whether to buy versus rent are closely connected to family structure. Adult children are delaying moving from their parents' home, triggering a "domino effect," in which later exit from parental home leads to later marriage and later childbearing. Reasons for later exit are not hard to fathom: the cost of housing is a large lift at the same time that wages, even for college graduates, have generally stagnated. These delays naturally lead to fewer births.

17.3 Other Developed Economies

Similar changes to marriage and childbearing are taking place in most developed economies, where, in aggregate, the age at first marriage increased from 25 years for women and 28 for men in 1990 to 32 and 34 years, respectively, in 2021.[19] Birth rates are falling, as detailed earlier. Excluding immigration, population is declining in 25 of 28 developed countries.[20] Japan provides an extreme illustration: the average age to first marriage is nearly 39 for women and 31 for men, increases of 13 and 14 years, respectively, since 1970. Marriage is not only being delayed but often forgotten: The proportion of 50-year-old Japanese who have never married tripled in that time. The reasons are familiar: Among them, women are working more outside the home and have less social pressure to marry. Because Japan severely restricts immigration, population is declining (expected to be halved by the end of the century) and average age is rising dramatically, creating a host of economic and social problems that are common among most developed economies, as discussed later.

In terms of social and legal limitations and economic incentives for women, we see in other countries changes similar to what has been witnessed in the U.S. Figure 17.4 shows that women have entered the

[17] Housing costs are a significant portion of child-rearing expenses: around 30 percent in the U.S.

[18] Flynn (2016).

[19] OECD (2025a).

[20] OECD countries. Turkey, Mexico, and Israel are the exceptions.

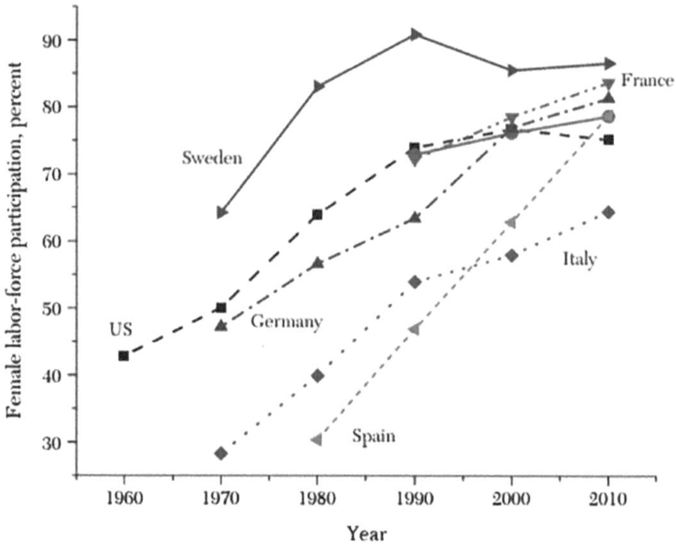

Fig. 17.4 Female labor-force participation, multiple countries (*Source* Greenwood et al., 2016)

paid labor *en masse* across developed economies. The U.S. was by no means an exception.

17.4 In Developing Economies

The patterns of change in marriage and childbearing we see in developed countries are also seen in emerging economies. In China a similar pattern has been occurring in recent decades as workers—especially younger ones—move from rural areas to cities to participate in the burgeoning industrial production, where pay is higher and living standards presumably better. In 2015, China's one-child limit, implemented in 1980 as population was expanding faster than desired, was abandoned, as rising wages, evolving labor markets, and fast-growing incomes led to the same kinds of changes to family structure as seen in the U.S. and other developed

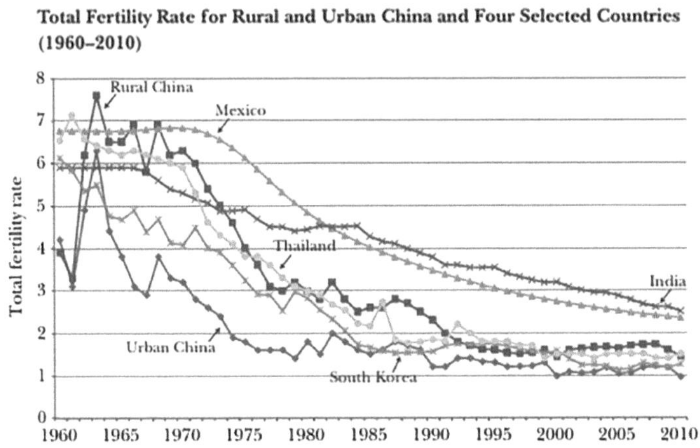

Fig. 17.5 Fertility rates, selected countries 2017 (*Source* Zhang [] [© American Economic Association. Used with permission])

economics.[21] Figure 17.5 shows the 50-year progression in fertility for several countries with developing economies. All follow a similar, familiar path. Regardless of the type of economic system, increasing opportunity cost of having children (i.e., higher incomes and greater reliance on markets) is associated with fewer children—independent of particular social norms or legal restrictions on women and birth. Powerful economic forces are universal.

17.5 Economic and Social Implications

New economic and social challenges develop as a population ages, as many older, more experienced workers retire and fewer young workers replace them. Strains on publicly funded social care (pensions, health care) and labor markets appear. We are beginning to see some of those implications, with worker shortages and increased wages and prices. Current projections for the Social Security program are that large tax increases,

[21] "Given China's extremely high economic growth after 1979 and the fertility transition experienced in other East Asian countries, China's further decline of fertility after 1979... cannot be fully or even mainly attributed to the effect of the one-child policy." Zhang (2017, p. 156).

large benefits reductions, or a combination of the two, will be needed by the early 2030s to sustain the system: there are simply fewer and fewer workers paying into the pay-as-you-go system, in which taxes paid today are immediately transferred to retirees, to maintain current tax rates and benefits.[22] Medicare—the government provided healthcare program for older Americans—is another financial timebomb, with medical costs continuing to rise faster than inflation compounding the effects of a rapidly aging population. Again, with fewer workers paying taxes, current benefit levels can be sustained only with much higher taxes.

Caring for the elderly has additional implications for labor market participation. One in 16 workers leave the labor force to care for an elderly relative, while one in 10 remain in the labor force but reduce their hours, and four in five miss some work. One in 10 lose a job because of elder care problems. As a result, incomes fall for caregivers and achievable market opportunities such as professional advancement decline—burdens that disproportionately affect women, one reason for declining female labor-force participation in the U.S. since 1997.[23] The reduced labor-force participation and the resulting lower income leads to lower future social security benefits and lower pensions for those caregivers.

We also see a significant income hit for women around childbirth.[24] After birth of their first child, women in the U.S. and U.K see their earnings decline by 30–45% while earnings stay roughly the same for men. Women reduce their hours worked (in labor markets) and experience reduced wage rates. The disparity persists ten years after birth. As economist Henrik Kleven and colleagues note, these "child penalties," as they term it, are a pervasive problem, though the impacts vary greatly by country. Declines in earnings are much smaller for women in some countries, such as Sweden or Denmark, where it is around 21–27%, while the penalty is larger, 51–61%, in others, such as Germany and Austria. Parental leave and childcare policies appear to have little effect on the gap. The primary driver of this decline in earnings appears to be gender norms: the greater the share of a population that thinks "women with children under school age should stay at home" the larger the decline in post-birth income for women.

[22] Committee for a Responsible Federal Budget (2024).

[23] Montgomery (2023). Federal Reserve Bank of Minneapolis (n.d.).

[24] Kleven et al. (2019).

Intermixed with these financial implications are some very real social ones. Cohabiting relationships (individuals living together who are not married), for instance, which are more common among individuals with less formal education, are much less stable than marriages—with lower barriers to, and stigma associated with, leaving. Children in such relationships "are more likely to experience instability in ... household income, and parental presence," leading to elevated inequality across generations.[25] Single-parent households often provide a precarious environment for children. Compared to children from two-parent households, children in "single-parent households are more likely ... to drop out of high school (15% vs. 9%), be idle (26 vs. 12%), experience a birth before age 20 (33 vs. 21%), and are less likely to complete college (15% vs. 24)," according to economists Jeremy Greenwood and colleagues.[26] Other research suggests that individuals raised in single female-headed households are more receptive to government intervention in markets than those who were raised by two parents.[27] One implication concerns support for free markets as an approach to organizing economic activity: will support for free markets decline as single parenthood increases?

17.6 Policy Responses

One may get the impression that high fertility and women working are at odds. According to economist Olivier Thevenon, this is not necessarily so. He notes that countries with the highest fertility have been those where a high percentage of women perform paid work, due mainly to policy and cultural differences.[28] The key for sustainable families and market-based economic systems, with equal opportunity for all, is a gender-equal culture and appropriate social support for families and child development.

Governments across the globe have responded to declining birth rates with various social and economic policies designed to affect family size

[25] McLanahan and Percheski (2008).

[26] Greenwood et al. (2016).

[27] Jones et al. (2019). That is, those children score lower on the Capitalism Index (as adults) compared to children raised on two-parent households.

[28] Thevenon (2011).

and structure and counteract the noted market forces.[29] This support, with examples from around the world, includes -

1. Entitlements such as paid parental leave or mandated flex time:

    - Nearly all countries have mandated maternal leave, and now more than half have mandated paternal leave (up from 20% in 1995).[30] The U.S. remains one of the very few that does not have mandated leave as a national policy, although several states do.
    - In Sweden, parents are entitled to receive full income for 390 days after birth, followed by an additional 90 days at roughly $20 per day.[31] Norway has similar benefits.
    - In Norway, mothers are entitled to time at work to breast-feed or pump.[32]

2. Tax credits and cash transfers such as "baby bonuses" and ongoing child allowances:

    - In Italy, parents are paid up to $2,300 for each child born.[33]
    - In Singapore, couples get $6,125 each for the first and second child, and $7,500 for subsequent children.[34]

3. Provision of services such as publicly funded childcare and education.

    - Public spending on childcare and early education in developed economies is around $6,000 per child.[35]
    - The figure in the U.S. is about half the average. Denmark, Norway and Sweden spend more than $11,000 per child.

[29] Economist (2015), Thevenon (2011).

[30] Unicef (2019).

[31] Olsen (2024).

[32] Delaney (2024), who quotes demography researcher Trude Lappegard, "The government's goal has never been explicitly to encourage people to have more children, but instead to make it easier for women to balance careers and children."

[33] The Italian Times (2019).

[34] Ministry of Social and Family Development (2021). Figures as of 2022, based on September 9, 2024 exchange rates.

[35] OECD (2025b).

- The Japanese government sponsors events where singles can meet. They hope to soon launch a dating app.[36]

Each policy is designed to provide incentives for parents to have children and to ease the financial burden of what is an increasingly costly endeavor that has wider social and economic implications. Such policies raise government and business costs (taxes), at least in the short run. They also provide benefits to parents, children, and to society. And in the long run, costs to government and business may be lower, once those children become adults and join the formal economy. One may even argue that such spending is more of an investment in market systems as much as it is in children or families. At the same time, old-age social programs such as social security and Medicare act as substitutes for financial support and care from children. In other words, with these programs there is less need to have children for insurance against destitution in old age. The question remains, though: will policies meant to encourage more babies be effective? The short answer for many is probably not. The most significant factors boil down to opportunity cost: many people simply would rather spend their time and money on other things.

17.7 Concluding Comments

Family structure and activity affect economic outcomes of family members in numerous ways. A later chapter explores the specific role of parents, and another examines the influence of (and on) community. The presentation here just scratches the surface of the family-economy connection. Family influences are deep and sometimes surprising, often neglected or ignored. Explicitly recognizing the connection between family and economy, and the bidirectionality of it, greatly adds to our understanding of economic and social dynamics.

References

Autor DH, Dorn D, Hanson GH (2016) The China shock: Learning from labor market adjustment to large changes in trade. Annual Review of Economics 8:205–240

[36] Wall Street Journal (2024).

Bennett N, Hays D, Sullivan B (2022) Wealth inequality in the U.S. by household type. U.S. Census Bureau (2022) https://www.census.gov/library/stories/2022/08/wealth-inequality-by-household-type.html.

Committee for a Responsible Federal Budget (2024) https://www.crfb.org/papers/cbos-february-2024-budget-and-economic-outlook#:~:text=Over%20the%20FY%202025%20to%202034%20budget%20window%2C,decade%20and%20spending%20will%20exceed%20revenue%20by%20one-third.

Coile CC, Duggan MG (2019) When labor's lost: Health, family life, incarceration, and education in a time of declining economic opportunity for low-skilled men. Journal of Economic Perspectives 33(2):191–210

Delaney C (2024) Worldwide efforts to reverse the baby shortage are falling flat. October 13. https://www.wsj.com/world/birthrate-children-fertility-europe-perks-family-04aa13a0?mod=Searchresults_pos8&page=1. Accessed on 30 Aug 2025

Flynn L (2016) Delayed and depressed: from expensive housing to smaller families. Int J Hous Policy 17(3):374–395

Gould-Werth A (2018) Marriages in the US are on the decline. Here's why. World Economic Forum. https://www.weforum.org/agenda/2018/11/what-upticks-in-u-s-economic-inequality-and-incarceration-mean-for-marriage/. Accessed on 30 Aug 2025

Greenwood J, Guner N, Vandenbroucke G (2016) Family economics writ large. FRED Working Paper 2016–026A. http://research.stlouisfed.org/wp/2016/2016-026.pdf.

Guardian (2014) https://www.theguardian.com/money/us-money-blog/2014/aug/11/women-rights-money-timeline-history.

Horzitz S (2007) Capitalism and the family: The market economy is responsible for ever-changing family structures. https://fee.org/articles/capitalism-and-the-family/.

Jones AT, Hadsell L, Burrus RT (2019) Capitalist views and religion. East Econ J 45:384–414

Kleven H, Landais C, Posch J, Steinhauer A, Zweimüller J (2019). Child penalties across countries: evidence and explanations. NBER Working Paper # 25524. http://www.nber.org/papers/w25524.

Lundberg S, Pollak RA, Stearns JE (2016) Family inequality: Diverging patterns in marriage, cohabitation, and childbearing. NBER Working Paper 22078.

McLanahan S, Percheski C (2008) Family structure and the reproduction of inequalities. Annual Review of Sociology 34(1): 257–276, p. 81.

Ministry of Social and Family Development (2021) Baby bonus scheme. October 22. https://www.msf.gov.sg/what-we-do/help-those-in-need/article/programmes/baby-bonus-scheme. Accessed 30 Aug 2025

Montgomery DH (2023) Who's not working? Behind the full-time caregivers leaving the workforce. Federal Reserve Bank of Minneapolis. https://www.minneapolisfed.org/article/2023/whos-not-working-behind-the-full-time-caregivers-leaving-the-workforce.

OECD (2025a) Family database. https://webfs.oecd.org/Els-com/Family_Database/SF_3_1_Marriage_and_divorce_rates.pdf. Accessed on 30 Aug 2025

OECD (2025b) Family database. https://www.oecd.org/content/dam/oecd/en/data/datasets/family-database/pf3_1_public_spending_on_childcare_and_early_education.pdf#:~:text=On%20a%20per%20child%20basis%2C%20total%20public%20spending,again%20this%20varies%20considerably%20across%20countries%20%28Child%20PF3.1.B%29. Accessed on 30 Aug 2025

Olsen JM (2024) Sweden launches groundbreaking new childcare law. Independent. https://www.independent.co.uk/news/world/europe/sweden-childcare-grandparents-pay-allowance-b2572331.html.

Pew Research Center (2013) Modern parenthood roles of moms and dads converge as they balance work and family. https://www.pewresearch.org/social-trends/2013/03/14/chapter-5-americans-time-at-paid-work-housework-child-care-1965-to-2011/.

Putnam R (2015) Our Kids. Simon & Schuster, New York

Schneider D, Harknett K, Stimpson M (2018) What explains the decline in first marriage in the United States? Evidence from the Panel Study of Income Dynamics, 1969 to 2013. J Marriage Fam. https://doi.org/10.1111/jomf.12481

The Italian Times (2019) Bonus bebè 2019 Inps: novità nel Decreto Crescita requisiti e importi. TheItalianTimes.it. May 26.

Thevenon O (2011) Family policies in OECD countries: A comparative analysis. Population and Development Review 37(1): 57–87. https://www.jstor.org/stable/23043262.

Unicef (2019) Paid parental leave and family-friendly policies. https://www.unicef.org/media/95086/file/UNICEF-Parental-Leave-Family-Friendly-Policies-2019.pdf. Accessed on 30 Aug 2025

Wall Street Journal (2024) City Hall prepares its own dating app. 7 June, p. A6.

Zhang J (2017) The evolution of China's one-child policy and its effects on family outcomes. Journal of Economic Perspectives 31(1):141–160

Ziol-Guest KM, Duncan GJ, Kalil A (2015) One-parent students leave school earlier. Education Next. https://www.educationnext.org/one-parent-students-leave-school-earlier/. Accessed on 30 Aug 2025

CHAPTER 18

Parents: Nature and Nurture

> Twin studies suggest that economic outcomes and preferences… appear to be about as heritable as many medical conditions and personality traits.[1]

> Parents who are more involved in the upbringing of their children have children with more favorable attitudes and traits…. that further their success in life.[2]

In the early morning hours of April 26, 1986, operators at the Chernobyl nuclear plant, a two-hour drive north of Kyiv, Ukraine, experienced a catastrophic event. The reactor meltdown that night sent radioactive material high into the atmosphere, where prevailing winds took it north and west. In Sweden, expectant mothers were unaware that they would provide a "natural experiment" (in the language of economists): though they were more than 500 miles away, they would soon intake some of the radioactive cesium fallout that floated their way. Their babies would be irreparably harmed, though the damage would take years to show. As economist Douglas Almond and colleagues report, students today who were in utero during this time in regions of Sweden with higher fallout

[1] Benjamin et al. (2012).
[2] Zumbuehl et al. (2021).

L. Hadsell, *Social Economies*,
https://doi.org/10.1007/978-3-032-21916-9_18

performed worse in secondary school (mathematics in particular).[3] The effects were particularly impactful for children born to parents with low levels of formal education, though the reasons for this are not clear. Children of mothers in Hiroshima and Nagasaki pregnant in August 1945, when the atomic bombs exploded, experienced similar outcomes. These two examples demonstrate what is now well-known: excessive radiation can change cell structure and DNA, leading to outcomes ranging from miscarriage to slower than normal fetal growth. They also help to explain why epigenetics, the study of how genes react to external stimuli, is of growing interest to economists.

Genes react to a wide array of external stimuli.[4] Research finds outcomes similar to those above for children in utero during periods of high stress for the mother, such as famine or death of a close relative of the mother and, perhaps of greatest interest to us in this post-COVID world, for children in the womb during the 1917–18 flu pandemic. In each case, individuals who were in utero during that period exhibited adverse health and educational outcomes in adulthood, with long-term economic effects such as reduced employment and income.

In Chapter 2, I introduced genoeconomics, an overlap of economics with human biology which studies the human genome's impact on economic outcomes, as a relatively new sub-field in economics.[5] Later, in Chapters 13 and 14, I discussed one of those economic outcomes: inequality of income and wealth. We saw that the household into which you were born says a lot about the economic circumstances for you as an adult. People who were raised in the poorest households tend to be poor as adults, and those who are at the other end of the ladder likewise tend to stay close to home. Economist Mary Daley calls this the "parental pull." What explains this pull? Why do parents seem to make such a large difference in the lives of their children? The answer is rather clear, even if the details are complicated and not easy to discern. It's partly that parents provide the right (or wrong) environment for the growth of that child. Even more importantly, parents provide genetic material, DNA, so influential to their child's adult economic success. An added layer consists of

[3] Almond et al. (2009).

[4] Weihrauch-Blüher et al. (2018).

[5] "Genoeconomics" following the nomenclature of Benjamin et al. (2012). It may also be called neuroeconomics or behavioral genetics.

random events such as those described above. Economists have known for some time through studies of twins and adopted children of the importance of genetics to economic outcomes. The mapping of the human genome in the year 2000, and subsequent research based on it, provides more insight into the power of nature.

Thus, the connection between parents and children has two pathways: nature and nurture; that is, biological, covering both genes and hormones, and environmental. While the genetic connection is strong, it is not immutable. As the Chernobyl experience illustrates, environmental forces can have lasting effects, which can be positive or negative. Genetic advantages can be muted in a poor environment and disadvantages can be mitigated in a favorable one, with early-life support, for example. The implications for economics are profound. How we think about inequality and opportunity, even the structure of economic systems themselves, is based on our understanding of the origin of individual ability, effort, choice, preferences, and a host of other traits. And that understanding is changing.

18.1 Biological Connections

If you tell someone that their height, chances of having schizophrenia, or possibility of getting breast cancer have a strong genetic basis, you are not likely to get much pushback. The hereditary connection to each is well-documented and, most significantly, widely accepted as true. As evidence of the widespread belief in the connection, consider the aftermath of actor Angelina Jolie's revelation in 2013 that she had had a preventative double mastectomy after she learned she was carrying the BRCA1 gene, putting her at elevated risk of developing breast cancer. In the succeeding weeks, genetic testing for BRCA at commercial DNA companies jumped 64 percent.[6] Just as well-documented as the health impacts of DNA, though not nearly as widely known, is that certain factors critical to economic outcomes also have a genetic basis, though in a way that is much more complicated than with BRCA (in that rather than a single gene, we are talking about aggregating hundreds together). Those factors, ranging from educational attainment to risk tolerance, play a role in shaping adult economic outcomes of offspring, such as employment

[6] Igoe (2016).

and wealth. In short, a strong connection between genes and economic success is present between parents and offspring, with some arguing that this connection is as strong as the connection between genes and physical attributes or health.

Economic research has described how physical attributes such as attractiveness, height, weight, and voice are small but relevant factors influencing one's income. More attractive, taller, slimmer, and lower-pitched individuals earn higher income, on average. (See Chapter 14 for details.) These physical characteristics are heritable to varying degrees—genes explain three-quarters of height differences, for example. Personality, covering attributes such as confidence and sociability, is nearly half heritable. Intelligence, often gauged by IQ score, another measure strongly related to educational attainment and income, appears to be about two-thirds heritable. By comparison, breast cancer is about one-third heritable.[7]

Still, the environment interacts with one's genetic makeup, sometimes enhancing, sometimes mitigating those genetic effects through the process of epigenetics: as gene expression (that is, whether a particular gene is "turned on" or "off") can be activated by certain enzymes that can be triggered by the environment—stressful events or pollution, or choices we each make such as to smoke or drink, for example. Epigenetic changes may occur in the womb or after birth, and is why identical twins, though they start with 100% of their DNA in common, are, in fact, different. Post-birth environment, whether nurturing or neglectful, also alters genetic predispositions. Genes are not deterministic.

Elevated stress is one cause of epigenetic change, even before birth. One example is individuals in the womb during the 1918 influenza pandemic, who were significantly less likely to graduate high school and more likely to be poor as adults, among other effects, compared to children born just before or just after.[8] Similar findings hold for the Dutch "Hunger Winter," the period from late 1944 to early 1945, when food supplies in western Netherlands were disrupted by German blockade: months of famine ensued and decades later, long-term effects on the children in utero at the time became evident, as they experienced lower

[7] Harden (2021).

[8] Almond and Mazumder (2005).

employment and poorer health outcomes.[9] In another example, a mother's prenatal exposure to the death of a close maternal relative is associated with the child's greater use of ADHD medications during childhood and anti-anxiety and depression medications in adulthood.[10]

Such findings are important in that they suggest that limiting prenatal stress can lead to large improvements in health and economic outcomes for the child. We know, for instance, that unemployment can be very stressful, suggesting public policies designed to minimize this stress. With the 2020 Covid pandemic, we have reason to believe that softening the economic fallout of mass unemployment by distributing government payments to expectant mothers (among others) will have long-term beneficial effects for children, even those who were in utero. Another implication of such epigenetic effects is that greater stress exposure among the poor may partially explain the intergenerational persistence of poverty.[11] People living in poverty experience a range of economic and social stressors not common to those with higher income, ranging from financial stress to fear of physical harm. Each may work in small ways to turn on or off genes that either assist or negate genetic advantages or genetic disadvantages.

18.2 Genetic Influences

Early research into the relationship genes have with economic and social outcomes relied on studies of twins, which attempt to isolate genetic effects from environmental by comparing outcomes between siblings with genetic similarity. Twins can be either from the same ovum, monozygotic (identical), or from two ova, dizygotic (fraternal). Identical twins have nearly 100 percent of genes in common while fraternal twins have about half, the same as any other sibling.[12] In addition to twins and other birth siblings, such studies may also include non-birth (adopted) siblings—who share the least percentage of genes, reflecting an individual randomly selected from the population.

[9] Scholte et al. (2012).

[10] Persson and Rossin-Slater (2016).

[11] Persson and Rossin-Slater (2016). Borghol et al. (2012).

[12] Shared DNA for siblings can range from 38 to 61 percent, given randomness of transmission from parents to child.

A common assumption in twin studies is that the environment for each child is the same. To the extent that this assumption is accurate, the common environmental component can be netted out, with only the varying genetic component remaining to explain differences between siblings. Of course, "identical environments" is a big assumption, as many with siblings will recognize, and it is a contention among researchers. Nonetheless, the evidence of genetic heritability of a multitude of economic outcomes is becoming clear. Identical twins have highly correlated incomes as adults, substantially more so than for fraternal twins.[13] Interestingly, the correlation appears to be markedly stronger for identical males than for identical females. In other words, genetics plays a role, though environmental (social) factors are present as well: economic and social opportunities are generally more uniformly available for men (or, in other words, women face more cultural-based impediments). Several generally accepted facts follow from decades of such research:

1. Substantial heritability exists for personality traits, cognitive abilities, and income.[14]
2. Common family environment is less important than genes.[15]
3. A substantial portion of the variance of income is unexplained. That is, much remains unknown.

Risk tolerance is an example of a market-important personality quality that twin studies have revealed as having a strong genetic component. Risk tolerance or preference affects a wide range of individual economic choices, from affinity for entrepreneurship and self-employment to job-switching to investing.[16] As such, risk-taking is a factor affecting individual success in market economies (the classic risk-return tradeoff), as some people have a high tolerance while others have much less. Research suggests that 20 to 50 percent of the variation in risk preference

[13] Benjamin et al. (2012).

[14] Cognitive abilities correlate at about 0.40 to 0.60; height at about 0.80; income at around 0.50.

[15] Benjamin et al. (2012).

[16] Caliendo et al. (2024).

is genetically based.[17] Given the culturally accepted association between risk and reward, such findings have important implications for how we understand the risk–return trade-off.

Completion of the human genome sequencing in 2001, development of new technologies, and falling costs have opened new lines of inquiry for social scientists in this area. Recent studies compare polygenic scores, based on groups of related genes, with economic outcomes of interest, called a phenotype (more generally, a set of observable characteristics of an individual). A particular polygenic score might consist of summation of the genetic information in 100 genes that are found to be, as a group, correlated in a large sample of individuals with certain economic outcomes, the phenotype, which could be educational attainment or income or a particular health indicator. Individual polygenic scores differ depending on the particular copies of each gene that one gets from parents, allowing us to identify genetic similarities between individuals much more comprehensively. No longer do we have to rely on an assumption of shared percentage of genes of twins or siblings to gauge genetic influence on certain outcomes. Everyone will have a polygenic score, with wide variation between individuals. Polygenic scores confirm many of the prior findings, explaining meaningful portions of the variance between individuals' educational attainment, income, wealth, and a host of other economically relevant variables. The task of relating polygenic scores to phenotypes is not straightforward though. Consider a polygenic score that correlates with educational attainment. The set of genes that comprise the polygenic score will include genes that influence multiple factors that lead to success in education, such as intelligence and personality (self-control, motivation, ambition). Additionally, the polygenic score might be related to personal characteristics that are affected by environmental factors, such as racism, in the attainment of education (or whatever outcome is of interest). And in the end, we have no idea exactly why those particular genes are associated with those particular economic outcomes.

Genome-based analysis represents an advance in our ability to understand the bases for individual differences in economic outcomes. In part they confirm prior findings from twin studies, but they also broaden

[17] Nicolaou and Shane (2019). Cesarini et al. (2009).

studies beyond twins and provide deeper insight into the complicated role of genes.

18.3 Environment and Gene Interaction

Part of the complicated nature of genes is that biological and environmental influences interact in their transmission of economically valuable attributes from parent to child. Economist Bruce Sacerdote cautions against misinterpreting the findings that relate genes to economic outcomes, arguing that saying a "variation in a given outcome for some population has a large genetic component is very different from saying that the outcome is predetermined or cannot be changed by interventions."[18] The effect that environment has on genes is a particularly contentious issue, though it seems clear that an individual growing up in a different environment would likely have a different outcome.[19] For instance, the relationship between polygenic score and rates of college graduation is strong but it is substantially stronger for individuals who grew up in households with higher socioeconomic status relative to those who grew up in poorer households, raising concerns about wasted potential arising from limited household resources.[20] Others similarly find that polygenic effects on health and health behaviors are enhanced by high parental socioeconomic status (SES).[21] We also know that some polygenic scores are more strongly related to various outcomes for men than for women, or for whites than for Blacks, strongly implying a social or cultural influence on expression of genetic tendencies.

In short, genes are not immutable, and related outcomes are not predetermined. Epigenetics further tells us that "different genes react to external stimuli, such as toxins, environmental factors, physical exercise, pharmacological treatment or even influencing socioeconomic factors or nutrition."[22] In a study of colorectal cancer, which has a small heritable component, for instance, researchers found that lifestyle also mattered: individuals with an unfavorable lifestyle had a 47% higher risk of colorectal

[18] Sacerdote (2011).

[19] Meyer et al. (2020).

[20] Papageorge and Thom (2020).

[21] Bolyard and Savelyev (2024).

[22] Weihrauch-Blüher et al. (2018).

cancer. This was so regardless of genetic predisposition.[23] We expect similar observations when it comes to economic outcomes, with environmental effects ranging from negative (such as stress while in utero) to positive (early education programs), including any number of epigenetic changes as described in the prior section.

18.4 Environment

Environmental factors, quite apart from their impact gene expression, also play a role in the development of children and their economic success later in life, although direct parental influences appear to be less important than once thought, prior to the mounting evidence of the impact of genes. Still, parents play an important role in selecting the environment their child grows up in. Environmental factors include family and neighborhood effects, encompassing both physical and social aspects. They affect a child's academic and social development and, later in life, a wide range of economic outcomes, including employment and income. They can take the form of role modeling (i.e., setting an example that children learn and follow), reading to children, or influence on schooling through parents' choice of where to reside. A primary channel is through human capital accumulation: basically, academic and social knowledge and skills important in market settings. Some effects have short-term impacts though many are much more far-reaching. Parents assist their children with (1) academic/cognitive support, (2) by providing a healthy and safe environment, (3) building social networks, and (4) instilling non-cognitive attributes.

1. Academic/cognitive support. The support children receive at home regarding their academic development includes things like the number of books in the home, whether the parents read to their children, and interest shown in academic progress. Something as simple as providing books can give a child a boost:

> Children growing up in homes with many books get 3 years more schooling than children from bookless homes, independent of their

[23] Though it must be noted, the differences were small, 1.29% compared to 2.07%, in a 10-year period. Shen et al. (2024).

> parents' education, occupation, and class. This is as great an advantage as having university educated rather than unschooled parents, and twice the advantage of having a professional rather than an unskilled father. It holds equally in rich nations and in poor; in the past and in the present; under communism, capitalism, and apartheid; and most strongly in China.[24]

(Keep in mind that most of the studies cited in this section neglect the role of genes, thereby muddying the conclusions. In the above example, is it access to the books that provides a boost or the parents' genes that lead to the books being provided in the first place?).

A child raised in a higher socioeconomic-status home will hear three times as many words by age four as a child in a lower socioeconomic-status home. This leads to wide variation in language ability at an early age that persists throughout the child's schooling. More broadly, we observe that parental involvement and hence child development vary by socioeconomic status.[25] Parents also play a direct role in setting expectations and attitudes of children. And once again, we observe differences by socioeconomic status. College-educated parents, for example, tend to value self-reliance more and obedience less than parents with no more than a high school education.[26] In one study,

> Two groups of ten-year-old boys were selected, equated for social class and intelligence test score, but differing in their level of their achievement need; one was high, the other was low. The investigators visited the boys' homes and asked the parents to watch while their sons tried to perform a rather difficult task. They had to build a tower of irregularly shaped blocks while blindfolded and restricted to the use of one hand. The parents were told that they could do or say whatever they wanted but that they could not touch the blocks. They were also told the height of the tower the "average boy" would erect and were asked to predict (confidentially) how well their own son would do.

[24] Evans et al. (2010).

[25] Hart and Risley (1995); Schwab and Lew-Williams (2016). Hemmerechts et al. (2017). Redding (2000): "Students with a lower SES also have lower reading literacy and reading attitudes than students with a higher SES. We also find that children with a lower SES experience more late parental involvement in literacy activities (during the fourth year of formal schooling) than children with a higher SES...."

[26] Putnam (2015), p. 119.

> The parents of the two groups of boys behaved quite differently. To begin with, parents of high-scoring boys predicted a better level of performance than did the other parents. This is probably what they do in general, setting high standards of excellence for the child to strive for. Further differences showed up while the boy was busy piling block upon block. The parents of sons with high achievement needs were more encouraging and more likely to reward accomplishment with warm praise. An interesting further difference concerns the fathers. Fathers of high-achievement-oriented boys were warm and friendly while their sons were working but remained in the back seat. They left their sons free to make their own decisions, perhaps giving a hint or two, but rarely telling them how to do it. The fathers of the low-achievement-oriented sons were more domineering. They gave specific directions from the sidelines and were more likely to show irritation when things went awry.[27]

Academic support by parents comes in myriad ways, including setting high expectations, communication between parents and children regarding school, and between parents and school representatives, each of which supports academic achievement.[28] Monetary resources are of course often an important element of parents' contribution to children's academic achievement, and not just for college. K-12 achievement also is enhanced with financial resources. As little as an extra $1000 financial assistance to families adds small amounts to math and reading scores, and later adult income, with the largest gains going to children from disadvantaged families.[29] Financial assistance for low-income households, such as the Earned Income Tax Credit, provides such a boost.

2. Healthy environment. Parents affect the physical and mental health of their children through choices they make regarding where they live, what they eat, and how often they are seen by a doctor. The link between poor physical health during childhood and adult health and economic outcomes later during adulthood is well established,

[27] Based on the research of Rosen and D'Andrade (1959).

[28] Boonk et al. (2018).

[29] Dahl and Lochner (2012), Barr et al (2022).

with the effects accumulating over children's lives.[30] Sicker children miss more days of school, attain lower levels of schooling, and earn lower incomes as adults. We know, too, that household income negatively affects children who have chronic conditions, with particularly dire long-term consequences of mental health crises. Studying nearly 20,0000 individuals born in early 1958, epidemiologist Anna Goodman finds,

> First, childhood psychological problems have a significant negative impact on economic outcomes, producing 14–28% lower incomes or wages from early adulthood into middle age. Second, a significant part of the estimated negative effects of childhood psychological problems are present at the beginning of adulthood. So the impact measured in one's early 20s is similar to the impact at age 50.[31]

Attention by medical professionals and better diet might stem the negative consequences of poor childhood health. Also important are clean air and water, and an environment free of violence. Consider the latter: Analyzing shootings at Texas public schools that occurred between 1995 and 2016, economist Marika Cabral and colleagues report that students exposed to shootings "have an increased absence rate and are more likely to be chronically absent and repeat a grade in the two years following the event..." with negative "long-term impacts on the likelihood of high school graduation, college enrollment and graduation, as well as employment and earnings at ages 24–26."[32] While school shootings are perhaps an extreme case, the negative impact of childhood violence is reality enough for many children living high-crime neighborhoods to be taken seriously as a concern. Economist Raj Chetty and colleagues show that differences in childhood environments shape gender gaps in adulthood, contending that childhood disadvantage is especially harmful for boys as evidenced by lower adult employment for men raised in areas of

[30] Case et al. (2002), Goodman et al. (2011), Case et al. (2005), Currie and Stabile (2003), Currie et al. (2010).

[31] Goodman et al. (2010), Smith (2009), Jayakody et al. (1998), Smith and Smith (2010).

[32] Cabral et al. (2020), Marcotte (2017).

concentrated poverty and crime versus women with similar neighborhood backgrounds.[33]

3. Social networks. Upwards of 50% of jobs are found through social ties created by both parents and their children.[34] Social networks form through one's life in a multitude of settings: school, neighborhood, and work among them. Parents choose the neighborhood in which the child will live and the primary and secondary school, and they have a big say in college choice. Through coworkers and social acquaintances, parents play a large role in social network possibilities for their children. The economic value of networks/friends/connections in labor markets is that they address the problem of information asymmetry. In the employment case, the information problem is bi-directional:

   - On the prospective employee side: where is a (good) place to work?
   - On the prospective employer side: who might be a good employee?

Job seekers rely on their network to provide information about prospective employers. Employers rely on their networks or current employees for information on applicants.[35] Workers recommended through networks tend to be more valuable employees: referred candidates are more likely to be hired (lowering employer hiring costs), experience an initial wage advantage, and have longer tenure in the firm (again lowering employer costs and raising productivity).[36]

Social networks also affect economic success through peer effects. More about peer effects, and social groups more generally, will be discussed in Chapter 19. For now, know that economists—and other social scientists—are keenly aware of the potential for individuals around us—fellow students, workers, friends—to influence our choices and performance. Capable students and workers have the ability to lift those

[33] Chetty et al. (2016).

[34] Gee et al. (2017) place the number at over 50%. Blau and Robins (1990) report about 30%.

[35] Hellerstein et al. (2008).

[36] Brown et al. (2014).

around them. Their greater ability rubs off onto those nearby, in situations ranging from classrooms to grocery stores—where, for example, cashiers who are faster scanners have a positive impact on the productivity of nearby cashiers.[37]

4. Non-cognitive attributes. The last of the four environmental connections to be discussed here is non-cognitive attributes. These include difficult to measure qualities that accrue from social interactions and societal expectations: motivation, persistence, self-esteem, and social skills, among others.[38] Some economists believe that non-cognitive attributes outweigh cognitive ability in their impact on personal achievement, challenging the view of cognitive ability's dominant role.[39] In a study where workers were randomly assigned to teams, economists Ben Weidmann and David Deming identify "team players" who consistently cause their team to exceed its predicted performance. They suggest that social skills are responsible, helping to improve team performance about as much as IQ seems to. Non-cognitive skills affect schooling, work experience, and productivity, all of which ultimately affect wages.[40] Non-cognitive traits may explain why many who would appear to financially benefit from college do not pursue it—with low motivation and self-esteem acting as roadblocks.[41]

As an example of the direct economic implications, research has reported that men's stronger hope for success, lower fear of failure, and "lower agreeableness" partially explains the higher average wage for men.[42] Or consider locus of control: People who believe in their own ability to affect change—an internal locus of control—are more likely to change jobs, and reap the benefits of higher wages and promotions as a result.[43] Parental shaping of such non-cognitive skills appears to be

[37] Griffith and Rask (2014).

[38] Heckman et al. (2006).

[39] Heckman et al. (2006).

[40] Weidmann and Deming (2020).

[41] Heckman et al. (2006).

[42] Risse et al. (2018).

[43] Ahn (2015), Schnitzlein and Stephani (2016), McGee and McGee (2016).

crucial. As one example, a trio of economists examining a large set of German parents and children find a strong connection between parental involvement in child-rearing and several non-cognitive skills, such as agreeableness, locus of control, trust, and risk preference, adding to our understanding of cultural transmission of values.[44] While instructive, the study does not account for the role of genes in transmitting some of the qualities they study, leaving unresolved the contribution of environment separate from genes.

In fact, while many studies find that parents play an important environmental role, sizeable environmental effects associated with parents should be taken with some caution, as studies typically do not control for genetics. Households with lots of books or parents who read and talk to their children, both correlated with higher child achievement, are also likely to be households in which the parents have genetic predisposition to such things, and those parents passed along that genetic predisposition to their child. So is it the books, reading, and talking, or the genetics in the child that are responsible for their higher achievement? Likely it is some of both. Truly randomized studies that might sort out the differences are rare, though twin studies indicate that identical twins have amazingly similar outcomes, irrespective of most environment factors. Studies relying on the human genome further strengthen the conclusion that genes play an important role. The right environment certainly helps children but it is only part of the story.

18.5 Concluding Comments

An understanding of the role parents play in the development of their children and their later economic success provides insight into interpersonal differences in market-related outcomes and our assessment of market systems themselves. One result of an improved understanding is better public policy. One such policy might be investment in prenatal care and early childhood, given that early intervention can have long-term effects on child educational attainment, health, social life, and adult economic outcomes. As one noted economist concluded, "Early interventions, such as enriched childcare centers coupled with home visitations, have been successful in alleviating some of the initial disadvantages of children born

[44] Zumbuehl et al. (2021).

into adverse family environments. The success of these interventions is not attributable to IQ improvements of children, but rather to their success in boosting non-cognitive skills."[45] Even before birth, easing pregnancy for the mother—by reducing stress of unemployment, for instance—can have lasting effects on the child decades later.

In terms of understanding economic systems and phenomenon such as intergenerational persistence of inequality, having an appreciation of the origins of factors underlying that inequality can certainly inform views of fairness and opportunity in economic systems. Genetic differences are an important determinant of economic success. But caution is in order. Do genes cause certain economic outcomes? No, the connection between genes and economic outcomes are time and place specific. Economic and social outcomes "can and do reflect racism, sexism, or other prejudices, as well as more benign environmental factors."[46] Change the environment and any particular individual will very likely have a different outcome. We are finding correlations, and it is early in our understanding. And remember, the correlation is far less than 100%. Even a correlation of 0.8 (as it is for height) leads to a wide distribution of outcomes. That is, a person's height can be estimated from their parents' but take it with a grain of salt because deviations from a simple formula connecting the two is not deterministic—too many other factors beyond the measurable genetics are in play. One can be 5′10″ as an adult with parents who are both under 5′4," it's just not very likely. Beyond simple genetic chance, environmental factors can alter the outlook for any individual. Two people can have similar cognitive test scores and end up in different places as adults because of vastly different childhood. "These findings suggest an important role for policies that invest in poor children and, more generally, provide some support that such investments could mitigate inefficiently low investments in human capital."[47]

The most important result of studying the connection between genes and economic outcomes is the caution it provides for those who wish for simple answers to why some people are rich and others are poor. Get an education, work hard, choose wisely, are all well-meaning and good advice. But to say only this is to say next to nothing, since we know that

[45] Heckman et al. (2006)

[46] Meyer et al. (2020).

[47] Papageorge and Thom (2020), p. 1394.

this very reasonable advice is not followed by a large fraction of the public and another large fraction follows the advice and yet does not prosper. The influence of genes on economic outcomes is complicated but worth studying because doing so provides insight into *why* some people get a college degree and some do not, *why* college degree completion is so strongly correlated with parents' education, *why* some people are wealthy, and some are not.

One conclusion might be that economic success is, to a large extent, a matter of luck. Luck in the DNA you start with, luck in the environment your mother encountered while you were in her womb, luck in the environment that you encounter as a child, luck in the society in which you live.

References

Ahn T (2015) Locus of control and job turnover. Econ Inq 53(2):1350–1365

Almond D, Mazumder B (2005) The 1918 influenza pandemic and subsequent health outcomes: an analysis of SIPP data. American Economic Review 95(2).258–262

Almond D, Edlund L, Palme M (2009) Chernobyl's subclinical legacy: prenatal exposure to radioactive fallout and school outcomes in Sweden. Q J Econ 124(4):1729–1772

Barr A, Eggleston J, Smith AA (2022) Investing in infants: the lasting effects of cash transfers to new families. Q J Econ 137(4):2539–2583. https://doi.org/10.1093/qje/qjac023

Benjamin DJ et al (2012) The promises and pitfalls of genoeconomics. Annual Review of Economics 4:627–662

Blau DM, Robins PK (1990) Job search outcomes for the employed and unemployed. J Polit Econ 98(3):637–655

Bolyard A, Savelyev PA (2024). Understanding the educational attainment polygenic index and its interactions with SES in determining health in young adulthood. IZA – Institute of Labor Economics, discussion paper no. 17056. https://www.econstor.eu/bitstream/10419/300952/1/dp17056.pdf.

Boonk L, Gijselaers HJM, Ritzen H, Brand-Gruwel S (2018) A review of the relationship between parental involvement indicators and academic achievement. Educ Res Rev 24(June):10–30

Borghol et al (2012) Associations with early-life socio-economic position in adult DNA methylation. Int J Epidemiol 41:62–74

Brown M, Setren E, Topa G (2014) Do informal referrals lead to better matches? Evidence from a firm's employee referral system. Institute for the Study of Labor. IZA DP No. 8175.

Cabral M, Kim B, Rossin-Slater M, Schnell M, Schwandt H (2020) Trauma at school: The impacts of shootings on students' human capital and economic outcomes. NBER Working Paper 28311.

Caliendo M, Fossen Fand Kritikos AS (2024) Personality characteristics and the decisions to become and stay self-employed. Small Bus Econ 42:787–814. https://doi.org/10.1007/s11187-013-9514-8

Case A, Fertig A, Paxson C (2005) The lasting impact of childhood health and circumstance. J Health Econ 24:365–389

Case A, Lubotsky D, Paxson C (2002) Economic status and health in childhood: the origins of the gradient. American Economic Review 92:1308–1334

Cesarini D, Dawes CT, Johannesson M, Lichtenstein P, Wallace B (2009). Genetic variation in preferences for giving and risk taking. The Quarterly Journal of Economics May: 908–842.

Chetty R, Hendren N, Lin F, Majerovitz J, Scuderi B (2016) Childhood environment and gender gaps in adulthood. American Economic Review 106(5):282–288

Currie J, Stabile M (2003) Socioeconomic status and child health—why is the relationship stronger for older children? American Economic Review 93:1813–1823

Currie J, Stabile M, Maniyong P, Roos L (2010) Child health and young adult outcomes. Journal of Human Resources 45:517–548

Dahl GB, Lochner L (2012) The impact of family income on child achievement: evidence from the earned income tax credit. American Economic Review 102(5):1927–1956

Evans MDR, Kelley J, Sikora J, Treiman DJ (2010) Family scholarly culture and educational success: books and schooling in 27 nations. Research in Social Stratification and Mobility 28:171–197

Gee LK, Jones J, Burke M (2017) Social networks and labor markets: how strong ties relate to job finding on Facebook's social network. J Law Econ 35(2):485–518

Goodman A, Joyce R, Smith JP (2011) The long shadow cast by childhood physical and mental problems on adult life. Proc Natl Acad Sci 108(15):6032–6037

Griffith AL, Rask KN (2014) Peer effectsXE "Peer effects" in higher education: A look at heterogeneous impacts. Econ Educ Rev 39:65–77

Harden KP (2021) The genetic lottery. Princeton University Press

Hart, B., & Risley, T. R. (1995). Meaningful differences in the everyday experience of young American children. Paul H Brookes Publishing.

Heckman JJ, Stixrud J, Urzua S (2006) The Effects of Cognitive and Noncognitive Abilities on Labor Market Outcomes and Social Behavior. NBER Working Paper 12006.

Hellerstein JK, McInerney M, Neumark D (2008) Neighbors and co-workers: the importance of residential labor market networks. NBER Working Paper 14201.

Hemmerechts K, Agirdag O, Kavadias D (2017) The relationship between parental literacy involvement, socio-economic status and reading literacy. Educ Rev 69(1):85–101

Igoe K (2016) The "Angelina Jolie" effect. Harvard Medical School, News and Research, 14 December.

Jayakody R, Danziger S, Kessler R (1998) Early-onset psychiatric disorders and male socioeconomic status. Soc Sci Res 27:371–387

Marcotte DE (2017) Something in the air? Air quality and children's educational outcomes. Econ Educ Rev 56:141–151

McGee A and McGee P (2016) Search, effort, and locus of control. Journal of Economic Behavior & Organization 126(A): 89–101.

Meyer MN, Turley P, Benjamin DJ (2020) Response to Charles Murray on polygenic scoreshttps://medium.com/@michellenmeyer/response-to-charles-murray-on-polygenic-scores-e768cf145cc.

Nicolaou N, Shane S (2019) Common genetic effects on risk-taking preferences and choices. J Risk Uncertain 59(261–279):265

Papageorge NW, Thom K (2020) Genes, education, and labor market outcomes: evidence from the health and retirement study. J Eur Econ Assoc 18(3):1351–1399

Persson P, Rossin-Slater M (2016) Family ruptures, stress, and the mental health of the next generation. NBER Working Paper No. 22229.

Putnam R (2015) Our Kids. Simon & Schuster, New York

Redding S (2000) Parents and learning. International Academy of Education; International Bureau of Education.

Risse L, Farrell L, Fry T (2018) Personality and pay: do gender gaps in confidence explain gender gaps in wages? Oxf Econ Pap 70(4):919–949

Rosen BC, D'Andrade R (1959) The psychosocial origins of achievement motivation. Sociometry 22:185–218

Sacerdote B (2011) Nature and nurture effects on children's outcomes: what have we learned from studies of twins and adoptees? Handbook of Social Economics 1:1–30

Schnitzlein DD, Stephani J (2016) Locus of control and low-wage mobility. J Econ Psychol 53:164–177

Scholte RS, van den Berg GJ, Lindeboom M (2012) Long-run effects of gestation during the Dutch hunger winter famine on labor market and hospitalization outcomes. Institute for Evaluation of Labour Market and Education Policy. Working Paper 2012:15.

Schwab JF, Lew-Williams C (2016) Language learning, socioeconomic status, and child-directed speech. Wiley Interdisciplinary Reviews: Cognitive Science 7(4):264–275

Shen Y, et al. (2024) Polygenic risk score, healthy lifestyle score, and colorectal cancer risk: a prospective cohort study. Cancer Epidemiology, Biomarkers & Prevention, OF1-OF8.

Smith JP, Smith GC (2010) Long-term economic costs of psychological problems during childhood. Social Science Medicine 71:110–115

Weidmann B, Deming DJ (2020). Team players: How social skills improve team performance. Working Paper #27071. https://doi.org/10.3386/w27071

Weihrauch-Blüher S et al (2018) Body weight regulation, socioeconomic status and epigenetic alterations. Metabolism 85:109–115

Zumbuehl M, Dohmen T, Pfann G (2021) Parental involvement and the intergenerational transmission of economic preferences, attitudes and personality traits. Econ J 131:2642–2670

CHAPTER 19

Community

> If I am not for me, who will be? And if I am only for me, what am I?[1]

> Designing many economic policies requires a deep understanding of social structure.[2]

In his essay "Does Community Have a Value?" essayist Wendell Berry tells the story of an Amish farmer. When asked, what does community mean to him, the farmer explains that,

> when he and his son were plowing in the spring he could look around him and see seventeen teams at work on the neighboring farms. He knew those teams and the men driving them, and he knew that if he were hurt or sick, those men and those teams would be at work on his farm.[3]

Berry describes how, for the Amish, "economy is not merely a function of community; the community and the economy are virtually the same." The Amish have created a social norm built on an expectation

[1] Rabbi Hillel

[2] Matthew O. Jackson et al. (2016).

[3] Berry (1987).

L. Hadsell, *Social Economies*,
https://doi.org/10.1007/978-3-032-21916-9_19

of reciprocity, one that emerges as the result of membership in the local community. Admittedly, the Amish represent a special case, and the interaction between community and economic activity is complicated and varies from place to place and over time, but economists have long recognized the importance of connectedness to the functioning of economies. The special relationship among the Amish described above represents an example of such connectedness, a form of social capital—the ties that provide support in times of need.

In every economic system, even in markets, where self-interest is paramount, the relationships individuals have with others influence choices in myriad ways. Community creates the culture in which economic activity takes place, creating expectations and enforcing norms of acceptable behavior. Community provides information about jobs and other opportunities and promotes the trust that is so important in market (and social) exchanges. Community provides restraint on self-interest, allowing individuals to work toward common goals (in providing public goods, for example). High levels of social capital lead to higher economic growth, stimulate financial markets, and lower loan default risk and hence lower interest rates.[4] Individuals with high social capital obtain more education and earn higher incomes. Even rates of Covid-19 infection and death were lower in areas with high levels of social capital: evidence suggests that public acceptance of and compliance with COVID control measures were based on trust and norms, a substantial part social capital.[5] Unfortunately, we will see that while community in its many forms has served an important role in containing the excesses of self-interest, this valuable resource is declining, with considerable implications for social and economic health.

19.1 Community and Social Capital

Social capital is one typical measure of the more elusive concept of community. Similar in a way to physical and human capital, "social capital refers to features of social organization such as networks, norms, and social trust that facilitate coordination and cooperation for mutual

[4] Hasan et al. (2020).

[5] Bartscher et al. (2021).

benefit."[6] Measures of social capital, as used by economists and sociologists, typically includes metrics such as rates of marriage and habitation, religious participation, volunteering, attendance at public meetings, helping neighbors, membership in social and business organizations, and voting. Quantifying social capital allows us to more precisely connect community to economic and social outcomes of interest. More social capital—more supportive interactions among members of society—leads to greater cooperation and trust and information flow, among other outcomes, which in turn grease the wheels of markets, leading to economic development, greater productivity, and other economic benefits.

Social capital can be bonding or bridging.[7] Bonding occurs with people who are similar to you and with whom you typically associate, where something is shared: neighbors, family, coworkers, military veterans. Bridging social capital occurs with people who are not normally in your orbit: they may be different by class, race, age, income, religion, or geographic area. Peers are one source of bonding social capital. Peer groups set boundaries and expectations for members, enforce codes of conduct with threat of ostracism when those codes are abrogated, share information, and provide support. Peer effects—how those around you affect your performance at work, in school, and as a consumer—are the aspect of community that is perhaps most studied by economists and other social scientists. Because we typically self-select our groups, choosing others who are like us, it is hard to tell what effect individuals have on each other. But research provides support for the intuition that who you hang out with affects who you become and what you do, and the choices you make. Research clearly shows that adolescent peers influence smoking, drinking, and drug usage of those around them. According to one study, for example, "moving a high-school student from a school where no children smoke to a school where one quarter of the youths smoke is found to increase the probability that the youth smokes by about 14.5 percentage points."[8] Peers also influence the amount of (and success in) schooling and a host of economic-related choices, from consumer purchases to productivity and employment, with effects which

[6] Putnam (1995), p. 67.

[7] Putnam (2000). Claridge (2018).

[8] Powell et al. (2005).

can be particularly strong for some groups. For instance, economists from Northwestern and Stanford identified social connections with female peers as a primary driver improving women's chances of becoming a senior-level manager, as peers provide emotional support, information, and job referrals.[9]

Economists Ayako Kondo and Masahiro Shoji look at peer effects on employment rates of evacuees of the area surrounding the Fukushima Daiichi nuclear power plant after the accident there in 2011. The evacuees were randomly assigned to new areas, with new peers not of their choosing, solving the self-selection problem. They find that higher employment rates of the new peers increase the probability of employment of the relocated individual as well, suggesting that social norms are a driving force in peer effects.[10]

Peer groups, and bonding social capital more generally, can also facilitate persistence of inequalities.[11] U.S. high school students represent a typical case of separation into distinct peer groups. Few will be surprised that students' self-reported close friendships are strongly related to ethnicity, with students of the same ethnicity being significantly more likely to be connected to each other than students of different ethnicities. Much is true for the rest of us. Census data show that Americans are more racially and economically segregated today than decades earlier, in their schools, neighborhoods, and workplaces.[12] Consider the flow of information—of a job opening, say—which passes from person to person, when there are two separate groups. When the number of members common to both groups is few (low bridging capital), information stays exclusive to one group longer, providing an information advantage to members of that group. More broadly, if the separation is sufficiently strong, each group will develop different behaviors, norms, and expectations that can persist, with consequences for education and career choices.[13] The implication for persistence of income and wealth inequality will be revisited

[9] Hampole et al. (2023).

[10] Kondo and Shoji (2019).

[11] Jackson et al. (2017).

[12] Workplace racial segregation is being driven by segregation between establishments rather than segregation within. A primary driver is that new businesses tend to be less diverse than existing ones. See Ferguson and Koning (2018).

[13] Jackson et al. (2017), p. 4.

later in this chapter. These and similar observations on information flow provide a foundation for understanding the emphasis many put on social and professional networks. The same principles of information flow can be applied to the diffusion of new technologies or methods, an important aspect of economic growth and development.

Among the direct economic outcomes affected by peers is productivity. Economists Natalia Emanuel, Emma Harrington, and Amanda Pallais examine whether proximity to coworkers—specifically, working in the office versus from home—affects worker productivity.[14] They find that "being near coworkers has tradeoffs: proximity increases long-run human capital development at the expense of short-term output." That is, in the short term, workers got less done but participated in more collaboration and mentoring which showed up in the long run as gains in productivity. The impacts were more pronounced for women, "who both do more mentoring and receive more mentorship when near their coworkers."

Beyond information and productivity boosts (or drags, depending on the peers), other benefits of social value accrue from group membership. Of course, there's the benefit when experiencing difficult times of direct support from other members (as in the Amish example). Group membership also often confers status, either within the group (as a leader) or as a member vis-à-vis non-members. That status provides psychological benefits which can act as a buffer against losses in other areas of life, such as job loss or financial stress. According to researchers:

> [c]onnectedness has the power to narrow the well-being gap that exists between times of financial struggle and times of relative comfort. It suggests that the psychological benefits of social integration have the capacity to displace money as a source of status and self-worth, and similarly that the importance of money may be exaggerated where these psychological gains are not available through other domains of life.[15]

Group membership is based on, and at the same time provides, identity, reinforcing boundaries and expectations for members. Sometimes this identity is a hindrance, as individuals respond to a perceived competence commonly associated with the group to which they identify, either "living

[14] Emanuel et al. (2023).

[15] Richards (2016).

up" or "living down" to one's perceived ability based on group affiliation—"social identity threat" in the parlance of psychologists. Group membership in this case might be based on gender, race, or socioeconomic background. Countless studies demonstrate the impact, both negative and positive, depending on the situation, on individual performance when their group association is made salient. In one representative study by psychologist Toni Schmader, women with high levels of gender identity who were "reminded" that women tend to do less well in math compared to men, performed worse than men, while women who had low levels of gender identity performed just as well as men. When no mention of gender identity was made, women performed equally to men, regardless of the importance they placed on gender identity.[16] In another, when researchers reminded employees of a large international bank of their professional identity as bank employees, they became more dishonest, on the whole, compared to when they were not reminded.[17]

As these studies suggest, identifying with a group and then being reminded of cultural expectations for members of that group can have real economic consequences, ranging from educational attainment to employment choices and productivity at work. Economist Roland Fryer relates how for him, as a young black student, doing well in school, earning high grades, was considered "acting white" by many of his black peers and risked his being ostracized.[18] Demonstrating this, Fig. 19.1, from Fryer, plots student achievement (GPA) and a measure of popularity for a large sample of students. It shows that minority popularity lags that of whites as GPA increases. Being smart wins few friends in the case of blacks and loses friends for Hispanics. Fryer summarizes: "a black student with straight As is no more popular than a black student with a 2.9 GPA, but high-achieving whites are at the top of the popularity pyramid." For Hispanics, it is even more discouraging. The consequences of such stereotyping and group enforcement are captured not only in lower academic performance, but subsequent lower wages. While we may argue that popularity is not the end goal, so these findings are of little consequences, we have to

[16] Schmader (2002).

[17] Cohn et al. (2014).

[18] Fryer (2006).

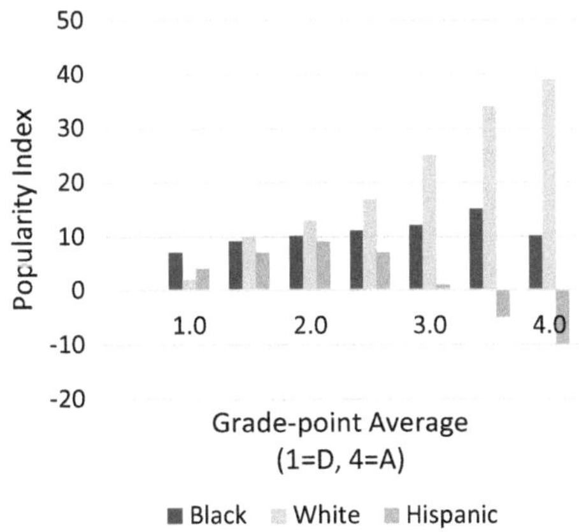

Fig. 19.1 GPA and popularity (Based on Fryer [2006])

remember that social acceptance is a basic social need and can influence educational attainment along with a full range of other choices and outcomes.

Similar effects on worker productivity can be seen in the results of a study by economists Karla Hoff and Priyanka Pandey.[19] Subjects were young boys in rural India from opposite ends of the caste system. Although officially outlawed, a strong caste system persists in tacit form, with corollary cultural norms and expectations. The boys were placed in groups of six; some groups were homogeneous—all members were the same caste, while others had an even mix of high and low caste. In the control groups, subjects were anonymous—caste membership was not revealed (caste could be hidden since caste membership had no outward markers). In the other groups, each boys' caste membership was revealed. Individuals in each group were asked to solve simple mazes by themselves in a set period of time (and were paid based on their performance). The findings:

> low-caste subjects in the anonymous condition did not perform significantly differently from high-caste subjects; but when caste identity was publicly revealed in a mixed caste group, a significant caste gap emerged. The caste gap was due to a 20 percent decline in the average number of mazes solved by the low caste.

[19] Hoff and Pandey (2006).

Even though caste membership was irrelevant to the task at hand, publicly revealing this social identity of an individual affected that individual's performance. Identity is valuable and must be protected, sometimes even at a cost to oneself. Hoff and Pandey's findings align with other research of the effects of stereotype threat more generally. People perform down to expectations just as they sometimes perform up.

In sum, we see that group membership can have desirable as well as undesirable effects. But on the whole, being connected—having social capital—is associated with a wide range of positive outcomes. To the extent that these can be encouraged, and the less desirable outcomes discouraged, economic and social outcomes can improve.

19.2 When Social Capital Declines

Social capital has declined dramatically since peaking in the 1960s.[20] Drops in group membership and community participation, evidenced by a range of measures, from union membership to changes in pronoun usage ("I" rather than "we"), suggests we are less connected. Such a decline has several ramifications. It ostensibly represents a weakening of commitment to each other and greater emphasis on ourselves, correlating with such things as a decline in social spending on the poor, reduced financial market regulation, increased income inequality, and a decline in corporate and individual tax rates. Either promoting or responding to a new emphasis on individualism led by conservatives such as Ayn Rand and Milton Friedman, the new ethos has changed how many of us think about markets and government intervention in markets.

The decline in social capital also appears to have contributed to an epidemic of loneliness in America, as highlighted by U.S. Surgeon General Vivek Murthy in 2023.[21] Loneliness is associated with a greater risk of cardiovascular disease, dementia, stroke, depression, anxiety, and premature death. Murthy notes, "The mortality impact of being socially disconnected is similar to that caused by smoking up to 15 cigarettes a day, and even greater than that associated with obesity and physical inactivity." Work productivity also suffers—workplace loneliness lessens employees' commitment to their organizations, with accompanying decline in job

[20] Putnam (2000 and 2015).

[21] Murthy (2023).

performance, according to one recent paper.[22] Because loneliness implies low social connection, we can presume (though this has not been extensively researched) that loneliness goes hand-in-hand with such things as less information about job opportunities and less social and financial support in times of need, with implications for subsequent income and wealth.

19.3 What Explains the Decline of Social Capital?

Given so much of our social capital is built around employment, loss of employment can be particularly hard on individuals and communities. The combination of trade with low-wage countries and technological change has led to seismic shifts in employment, especially in manufacturing. Job losses tend to be geographically concentrated, with long-lasting economic and social effects. Unemployment increases and wages fall, along with tax revenue for local governments and schools; marriage rates also decline, and mortality rises.[23] Economists Anne Case and Angus Deaton, as detailed elsewhere in this book, have warned of an epidemic of "deaths of despair," closely tied to social and economic isolation and dissatisfaction.[24] Other researchers report that the largest increases of such deaths were evidence of economic distress and diminished social capital.[25] Economist David Autor suggests that trade effects, especially with China, contributed to widening political polarization over the last three decades.

Changes to family structure also play a role. Fewer children and delayed or forgone marriage are factors contributing to declining participation in a whole range of community-oriented events, including attendance at school sporting events, concerts, and parent-teacher conferences. Parents are often the most involved with their community because good parenting requires it—meetings with teachers, PTA meetings, booster clubs, school sporting events, holiday concerts, spring soccer leagues, summer camps, scouts, birthday parties, baptisms, bat mitzvah, confirmations, weddings,

[22] Ozcelik and Barsade (2018).

[23] Autor and Hanson (2018).

[24] Case and Deaton (2020), p. 166.

[25] Woolf and Schoomaker (2019), p. 11.

attendance at religious services, and so on. Fewer children, more single-parent households, and more employment outside the home as women entered the labor force in greater numbers, all contributed to constrain time available for socialization.

The extent of the contribution of online activity—from social media to video streaming—to the decline of social capital is an open question. Putnam argues that new technology trends "are radically 'privatizing' or 'individualizing' our use of leisure time and thus disrupting many opportunities for social-capital formation."[26] Putnam explains how "electronic technology enables individual tastes to be satisfied more fully, but at the cost of the positive social externalities associated with more primitive forms of entertainment." While online technologies have benefits, especially for some individuals (e.g., introverts), evidence suggests a link between overuse of certain technologies and a variety of social and psychological maladies, with unknown long-term economic consequences.

19.4 Contributing to Inequality and Immobility

Lack (or loss) of good social capital exacerbates economic inequality. Insufficient bridging capital limits access to opportunities outside one's primary relationships. Poor bonding capital—such as a bad neighborhood or friends without connections themselves—leads to a sort of lock-in or myopia, perpetuating limited opportunities. Sociologists Robert Manduca and Robert Sampson find in their studies that poor children's exposure to neighborhood violence, incarceration, and lead combine to independently predict their later incarceration as adults, teenage motherhood, lower income, and lower social mobility.[27] Excessive bonding capital may have negative social and economic consequences such as limiting access to new ideas and knowledge of opportunities outside one's circle, leading to a certain inward-looking mindset, a conformity that is antithetical to individual and community development. One needs the right kind, in the right amount.

The influence of community on opportunity is becoming more pronounced as U.S. schools become even more racially segregated in

[26] Putnam (1995), p. 75.

[27] Manduca and Sampson (2019).

the U.S. According to data from the Educational Opportunity Project at Stanford University, segregation between Black and white students increased 64% between 1988 and 2020 in the country's 100 largest school districts and segregation between lower income and higher income students increased by 50% since 1991.[28] This has occurred even while cities generally are becoming less racially segregated, although segregation by income is also rising in cities.[29]

Data show that educated affluent parents have more close friends and that more educated parents have broader social networks—they know more people and more types of people (by profession) than less educated, less affluent parents.[30] Having fewer connections means, among other things, less information about job or educational opportunities, even know-how necessary to navigate complex processes such as applications for college and financial aid. Along these lines, economist Raj Chetty and colleagues examined 21 billion friendship connections of 70 million Facebook users, representing 82% of 25–44-year-olds in the U.S., seeking to measure "the extent to which people with low and high socio-economic status (SES) are friends with each other," a form of bridging capital, what they call social connectedness.[31] Their findings support prior research: social capital helps mobility, even just knowing the right people helps. Low SES individuals with high connectedness to high SES individuals improves the chances of the low SES of moving up the socioeconomic ladder, in large part because "high-SES individuals make more friends than low-SES individuals do on average." They also report that where a low SES child grows up is important. "If children with low-SES parents were to grow up in counties with economic connectedness comparable to that of the average child with high SES parents, their incomes in adulthood would increase by 20% on average." Thus, one of the key benefits of "connectedness" appears to be economic mobility.

Robert Putnam has extensively studied the separation by SES and the consequent reduction in bridging social capital. In "the 1950s, affluent kids and poor kids lived near one another, went to school together, played and prayed together, and even dated one another...." Today this

[28] Potter (2024).

[29] Meixell et al. (2020).

[30] Putnam (2015), pp. 208–209.

[31] Chetty et al. (2014). Also Chetty and Hendren (2018a, 2018b).

is much less likely. Even married couples are more likely to segregate by education today than decades ago. That is, high school graduates tend to marry other high school graduates and college graduates tend to marry other college graduates. This assortative mating has tended to reinforce economic and social inequality. In fact, scholars are finding that "social networks are collapsing inward, and now consist of fewer, denser, more homogeneous, more familial (and less non-kin) ties."[32] Access to new technologies such as the Internet and the connective possibilities there, on LinkedIn, Facebook, and so on, with so much information available free of charge, does not appear to narrow the gap between low and high SES individuals, partly because connections in "real-life" tend to carry over to online, reinforcing but not expanding existing ties. And low and high SES individuals tend to use the technologies differently, reinforcing previous inequalities.[33]

19.5 Creating Social Capital

Public policies and economic approaches can either build up community or tear it down. Of the latter, consider the social capital destroyed in the 1960s and 1970s by neighborhood-clearance and highway building policies common across America. Or the consolidation of rural post offices and small school districts meant to save money but again at a potential loss of social capital, as group membership, identity, and participation decline. Of policies that build social capital, consider community colleges, tax deductions for charitable contributions, and community-wide activities such as festivals, parades, and "fun-runs" that encourage people to gather and interact.[34]

Based on the Chetty study noted earlier, encouraging bridging capital between low SES and high SES individuals and groups is likely to improve social and economic mobility. Note that this benefits not only the individual but society, as those previous underused resources—human talent—are better employed, providing value for the individual and everyone with whom s/he interacts. Increasing safety and resources available at the neighborhood level similarly has great potential, as suggested

[32] Putnam (2015), p. 211.

[33] Putnam (2015), pp. 211–2.

[34] See Putnam (1995), pp. 76–77.

by one study that found that a range of outcomes improved for young children who changed peer groups by moving to a less poor area.[35] In another, young kids moving to less disadvantaged neighborhoods, with assistance from public housing (Sect. 8) vouchers, were less likely to drop out of school, earned higher incomes decades later as adults, and committed fewer violent crimes.[36] Such examples demonstrate the strong influence of surroundings, and thinking back to Chapter 18, the importance of environment.

Trade policy, discussed earlier in this chapter, also can either support or destroy social capital. Unfettered trade, especially with countries having very different economic, social, and legal frameworks (e.g., in terms of wages, working conditions, and pollution controls), leads to lower social capital in the area with higher restrictions, as employment moves elsewhere. Managed trade with partners with similar frameworks, and government financial support for displaced workers and their community organizations can at least mitigate short-term social capital loss, with potential for long-term gains. In this way, trade policy with substantial barriers (e.g., high tariffs) may be good policy; even though it will lead to domestic price increases and declines in efficiency, it also has the potential to shore up social and economic institutions that support social capital, which enhances social and economic well-being.

New technologies can similarly add or subtract. Artificial Intelligence is the next big test: if its adoption quickly leads to massive job rearrangement, or even unemployment, we could see large declines in social capital, along with all the other maladies associated with unemployment. Managed well, AI can enhance work and social capital rather than harm it.

Bottom line, if you want to help people succeed economically and socially, invest in developing social capital. Promote clubs, organizations, groups, and connections that promote social and financial support. Early-age development is especially impacted by social connection, as building social and human capital are fundamentally social activities.[37] Economic development initiatives are more likely to succeed when they include policies that promote social capital formation.

[35] Agostinelli et al. (2020).

[36] Chyn (2018).

[37] List et al. (2020).

19.6 Concluding Comments

Every economic system, whatever form it takes, closely depends on social institutions. The nature and extent of community ties greatly affect economic activity, just as economic activity impacts community. Rather than a sideline interest of economists, social capital is another key component in understanding how economic systems function. Improving social capital improves both quality of life and economic well-being.

A caveat is in order. While the decline of measured social capital in the U.S. is well-documented, keep in mind that many of the peaks of social engagement identified by researchers were in the 1960s, hardly a time of social and political togetherness. One might note that strife may be as likely as agreement to stoke participation. We also know that a high degree of bonding capital resulting from close associations may breed conformity, stasis, and bad decisions, sparking a backlash—as in the 1950s and 1960s political, environmental, social, and economic scenes. The 1970s was a period of declining social capital but it also saw great changes for the better: greater concern with the political system, environment (EPA, Earth Day, and the Clean Water Act all originated in the 1970s), and women's legal, social, and economic rights.

Fundamentally, investment in social capital is investing in people, and their potential. Economists hate wasted resources—more and better social and human capital can lessen some of the most egregious wastes.

References

Agostinelli F, Doepke M, Sorrenti G, Zilibotti F (2020) It takes a village: the economics of parenting with neighborhood and peer effects. NBER Working Paper 27050. https://doi.org/10.3386/w27050

Autor D, Dorn D, Hanson G (2018) When work disappears: manufacturing decline and the falling marriage-market value of young men. NBER Working Paper 23173. https://doi.org/10.3386/w23173.

Bartscher A-K, Seitz S, Siegloch S, Slotwinski M, Wehrhöfer N (2021) The effect of contact restrictions on social contact and economic activity during the COVID-19 pandemic: evidence from Germany. CESifo Working Paper 8926. https://doi.org/10.2139/ssrn.3632834

Berry W (1987) Home economics. North Point Press, San Francisco

Case A, Deaton A (2020) Deaths of despair and the future of capitalism. Princeton University Press, Princeton

Chetty R, Hendren N, Kline P, Saez E (2014) Where is the land of opportunity? The geography of intergenerational mobility in the United States. Quart J Econ 129(4):1553–1623. https://doi.org/10.1093/qje/qju022

Chetty R, Hendren N (2018a) The impacts of neighborhoods on intergenerational mobility I: childhood exposure effects. Quart J Econ 133(3):1107–1162. https://doi.org/10.1093/qje/qjy007

Chetty R, Hendren N (2018b) The impacts of neighborhoods on intergenerational mobility II: county-level estimates. Quart J Econ 133(3):1163–1228. https://doi.org/10.1093/qje/qjy006

Chyn E (2018) Moved to opportunity: the long-run effects of public housing demolition on children. American Economic Review 108(10):3028–3056. https://doi.org/10.1257/aer.20161512

Claridge T (2018) Functions of social capital—bonding, bridging, linking. Social Capital Research. Available at: https://www.socialcapitalresearch.com/functions-social-capital-bonding-bridging-linking/.

Cohn A, Fehr E, Maréchal M (2014) Business culture and dishonesty in the banking industry. Nature 516(7529):86–89. https://doi.org/10.1038/nature13977

Emanuel N, Harrington E, Pallais A (2023) The power of proximity to coworkers: training for tomorrow or productivity today? NBER Working Paper 31880. http://www.nber.org/papers/w31880

Ferguson JP, Koning R (2018) Firm turnover and the return of racial establishment segregation. Am Sociol Rev 83(3):445–474. https://doi.org/10.1177/0003122418761778

Fryer RG (2006) The social price paid by the best and brightest minority students. Harvard University. Available at: https://scholar.harvard.edu/files/fryer/files/acting_white.pdf

Hampole M, Truffa F, Wong A (2023) Peer effects and the gender gap in corporate leadership: evidence from MBA students. 2023 ASSA annual meetings: Gender Gaps session. January 8.

Hasan I, He Q, Lu H (2020) The impact of social capital on economic attitudes and outcomes. J Int Money Financ 108:102206. https://doi.org/10.1016/j.jimonfin.2020.102206

Hoff K, Pandey P (2006) Discrimination, social identity, and durable inequalities. American Economic Review 96(2):206–211. https://doi.org/10.1257/000282806777212373

Jackson MO, Rogers BW, Zenou Y (2017) The economic consequences of social-network structure. Journal of Economic Literature 55(1):49–95. https://doi.org/10.1257/jel.20151218

Kondo A, Shoji M (2019) Peer effects in employment status: evidence from housing lotteries. J Urban Econ 113:68–86. https://doi.org/10.1016/j.jue.2019.03.006

List JA, Momeni F, Zenou Y (2020) The social side of early human capital formation: using a field experiment to estimate the causal impact of neighborhoods. NBER Working Paper 28283. https://doi.org/10.3386/w28283

Manduca R, Sampson RJ (2019) Punishing and toxic neighborhood environments independently predict the intergenerational social mobility of black and white children. Proc Natl Acad Sci 116(16):7772–7777

Meixell B, Plerhoples Stacy C, Hariharan A (2020) Residential segregation is declining. How can we continue to increase inclusion? The Urban Institute. Available at: https://www.urban.org/urban-wire/residential-segregation-declining-how-can-we-continue-increase-inclusion

Murthy V (2023) Our epidemic of loneliness and isolation. The U.S. Surgeon General's advisory on the healing effects of social connection and community. Available at: https://www.hhs.gov/sites/default/files/surgeon-general-social-connection-advisory.pdf

Ozcelik H, Barsade SG (2018) No employee an island: workplace loneliness and job performance. Acad Manag J 61(6):2343–2366. https://doi.org/10.5465/amj.2017.1347

Potter H (2024) How a Fifty-Year-Old Supreme Court Decision Fuels School Segregation Today. The Century Foundation. Accessed August 30, 2025 at https://tcf.org/content/commentary/how-a-fifty-year-old-supreme-court-decision-fuels-school-segregation-today/#:~:text=Data%20from%20the%20Segregation%20Explorer%2C%20an%20interactive,students%20increased%20by%2050%20percent%20since%201991

Powell LM, Tauras JA, Ross H (2005) The importance of peer effects, cigarette prices and tobacco control policies for youth smoking behavior. J Health Econ 24(4):950–968. https://doi.org/10.1016/j.jhealeco.2004.12.003

Putnam R (1995) Our Kids. Simon & Schuster, New York

Putnam R (2000) Bowling alone: America's declining Social Capital. Springer, New York, NY

Putnam R (2015) Our kids. Simon & Schuster, New York

Richards L (2016) For whom money matters less: social connectedness as a resilience resource in the UK. Soc Indic Res 125(2):509–535. https://doi.org/10.1007/s11205-015-0923-7

Schmader T (2002) Gender identification moderates stereotype threat effects on women's math performance. J Exp Soc Psychol 38(2):194–201. https://doi.org/10.1006/jesp.2001.1491

Woolf SH, Schoomaker H (2019) Life Expectancy and Mortality Rates in the United States, 1959–2017. JAMA. 2019 November 26; 322(20): 1996–2016. https://doi.org/10.1001/jama.2019.16932.

CHAPTER 20

And Lastly—Concluding Comments

James Thurber once said that it's better to know some of the questions than all of the answers. Perhaps a comforting thought for someone like me, who is sure there are a lot of answers I don't know. But there's a lot of truth in Thurber's observation, too, because one does not know what one doesn't know—and therefore which questions to ask. Asking questions is the path to knowing. If you know all the answers then you haven't asked enough questions. Knowing which questions to ask is especially important in an age of artificial intelligence, when the key to its use is asking the right questions. But even AI cannot answer the most important and basic questions. Even AI cannot know the right questions to ask. *Social Economics* has been about asking the right questions—along with providing some answers from recent research in economics and related disciplines. Which of course only leads to more questions.

a. Context and Questions

This book has also been about context, with an overarching argument that too narrow a view of economies leads to a myopia that harms the economy, individuals, society, and our environment. Multiple perspectives are to be welcomed, as they increase our understanding of economies and their impacts on other facets of life. This book has stressed that economies

L. Hadsell, *Social Economies*,
https://doi.org/10.1007/978-3-032-21916-9_20

are social constructs, best examined with insights from a variety of disciplines, enriching our understanding of the economic choices we make as individuals and collectively as a society. A broader perspective also helps us ask better questions.

Individuals and societies decide how to structure economic activity, what rules to apply, and what goals to aim for. Deciding what is fair and acceptable reflects individual and cultural preferences that have been formed over time with results seen in variation between individuals and countries, in their views of appropriate economic activity and their economic systems. Our goals reflect our values. Recognizing the origins of individual and societal preferences—for growth vs sustainability, or profits vs purpose, for example—and that each goal has an opportunity cost, allows us to better appreciate views of others and make better choices together.

Successfully dealing with economic challenges of the twenty-first century will require a broad understanding of the interplay between economies, society, and nature. And that requires the kind of interdisciplinary approach many economists are pursuing today. Questions concerning artificial intelligence and climate change head that list of challenges. Both are linked to a third set of big questions, concerning inequality. And the three are connected in some form or other to most of the topics discussed in this book. AI will affect not just employment, but climate (through massive energy use), inequality, and culture. Climate change (and more generally, our environmental impact) calls into question our economic goals and poses challenges for businesses and consumers as they evaluate their roles. In turn, these first round effects will lead to changes in family structure, health, and community.

AI will garner the most immediate attention, with its sudden impact on labor markets and productivity. The double-edged sword of AI is that it brings both the threat of job loss and the promise of abundance, as a result of vastly increased productivity. AI will likely replace many white-collar workers, much as robotics in factories replaced blue-collar workers previously. An earlier response to threats to blue-collar jobs was to increase human capital—more education—followed by a move into the white-collar world. What is the response when AI replaces white-collar work? When AI is smarter than any human, so that no amount of college education will guarantee employment, what will a large fraction of the population do? The most optimistic answer is that they will find other work, much as has happened with earlier technological change, work that humans can do better than AI. Still, the adjustment will not be easy, for individuals directly affected and their families, or for communities, as we have witnessed before with the decline in manufacturing. We have seen from abundant research that absence of work hurts more than family finances. A future in which AI reduces the need for work could very well see more economic and social unrest. The recent political upheavals in many economically developed countries may be just the beginning.

How we think about work will be challenged. Mainstream (or neoclassical) economics views work as a disutility, something to be minimized, but at the same time it recognizes in its research findings that work has value beyond income. How to square the two? An alternative perspective of the meaning and value of work, from Buddhist economics, is instructive: work is necessary not primarily for money, though that is important, but for purification of the human character. Absence of work is not desirable, even if sufficient income is provided from other sources (i.e., asset ownership or government transfer). Marxists, on the other hand, might emphasize the widening power gulf between owners of capital (investors in AI) and workers. With fewer employment options available to white-collar workers they will no doubt be less empowered, and more at the mercy of others. Increased inequality seems inevitable.

But democratic societies have choices. As we consider the impacts of AI we can think deeply about the meaning of work and the role our economy has in supporting social and environmental life. In the end, the question comes down to this: is the primary goal of economies simply to produce more and more stuff? Or do we want our economic systems to support individual, social, and environmental health?

Society could decide, for example, that workers should receive ownership rights in the new AI technology if their job is impacted, ensuring a steady stream of income for that person. Without such a guarantee, the share of national income going to workers will continue to shrink, just as the share going to owners/capital will rise. After holding steady around 63 percent from 1950 to 2000, labor's share declined to 59 percent by 2010, where it stands today. While 4 percent may seem small, that's a decline of more than a trillion dollars annually. In the absence of ownership sharing, the recent decline will continue. A reasonable conclusion of a further weakening of the bargaining power of workers is that it will inevitably lead to more social and political strife. Ensuring a fair distribution of the benefits from business use of AI is good not only for individuals and society as a whole, it is good for the economy.

Are a replacement job or ownership rights and guaranteed income enough? Perhaps not. Research shows that an absence of meaningful work leads to lower life satisfaction, lower productivity, and more job-switching; and unemployment is associated with less life satisfaction, higher divorce rates, and increased risk of death—63% higher risk of death for unemployed persons in one study. Loss of a job means loss of identity and connections (to place, coworkers, purpose) as well as a loss of income. So neo-classical economics seems to be wrong and Buddhist economics right: work is not best thought of as a disutility. We will see the implications in the coming years as AI seeps throughout the economy.

The second major challenge is our impact on environmental sustainability, including climate change. Here the task is well-known and long-standing. Living within ecological limits, locally and globally, is nothing new and is a basic feature of any economy. This is not an "existential crisis" as many say. The earth will survive. Humans will survive. But the adjustment—to new climates, fewer pollinators, and so on—will likely be as destructive to economic and social institutions as anything we've seen before. Technological change and international trade with low-cost, low-regulation countries may be seen as cakewalks by comparison. Newer pollutants—microplastics, PFAS, and others—are replacing older ones—lead, sulfur dioxide, nitrogen oxides, which have been greatly reduced through effective regulation, though some well-known problems continue: lead poisoning, for example, afflicts as many as a quarter of poor children in some areas, more than a half century after it was banned from gasoline and household paint.

Of course, many other challenges confront us. Two of the biggest are healthcare and public debt. Healthcare tests our ability as a society to deal with collective problems. Ensuring a right to basic healthcare will be particularly difficult in a pluralistic society that places great emphasis, as the U.S. surely does, on individual economic freedom. Already consuming nearly 20 percent of economic resources, and already inadequate for many, healthcare costs are set to rise dramatically as the Baby Boom generation continues to age. The tension between those who prefer more economic freedom and those who prefer less will only exacerbate the conflict, making compromise more difficult. Public debt is a problem of similar nature: already costly and about to become even more problematic. Rising commitments to the elderly—via Social Security and Medicare—and national defense are the largest components of current spending—and are set to become much larger in coming decades. Add rapidly increasing interest costs on the national debt and a reckoning is not far in the future. Few answers exist, and none are palatable to a large fraction of the population: raise taxes, reduce spending, print money (drastically raising inflation), default. We may be at a crossroad.

Economic and social inequality makes each challenge worse, more intractable Those who have, want to retain; those who don't have, want their fair share. Rawls' thought experiment (Chapter 14) provides a path to a solution, but implementation is impractical. All we know with near certainty is that a widening gulf between those with and those without will not end well. The good news is that society can, theoretically, take collective, democratic action to avert crisis. Unfortunately, the very system we hope to save is a primary force stroking the social and political division that makes consensus so difficult.

Additional questions will have to be addressed. Some come from within—we need to ask them. Others will be asked of us. Of the former, we must consider how to deal with excessive self-interest and encroachment of market principles. No better example exists to illustrate the potential harm to individuals and society of excessive self-interest than social media. We see the damage now, to mental health, relationships and community involvement (social capital), and democratic institutions. What is particularly disturbing is that these harms are, essentially, intentional: major social media companies have made well-documented efforts to maximize profit by maximizing social strife. It's a recipe for huge profits... and a fractured society. Will we, as a society, curtail such behavior by deciding that the purpose of business is much greater than maximizing profits? That businesses have a responsibility to stakeholders other than shareholders? Society already places limits on self-interest—through norms and customs, social institutions, and laws. As economic forces are ever-changing the current limits are not enough; the conversation needs to continue.

A set of related questions revolves around the extent to which we allow market principles to creep into our lives. Should we encourage a market in which we can buy and sell human kidneys? (Proposed.) Buy a fast-track path to citizenship? (Allowed.) Sell votes? (Not allowed, yet. At least not directly.) Markets tend to efficiently allocate resources, but they also can erode other values worth having—from self-worth to civic duty. A key concept in economics is that of opportunity cost. It seems natural that we should apply it when we choose a method of allocation of resources. Economists are engaging with ethicists to sort through these sticky questions. Ultimately, the questions come down to, what are economies for?

Near the front of the pack of the questions that will be asked of us, because there is little (nothing?) we can do that forestall it, is how we will deal with the economic and social implications of population decline. Implications for economies and society of a continued decline in fertility are many, from fiscal impacts for governments to consequences for labor markets, families, and communities. One labor market effect as populations age is a shortage of care workers. Perhaps those made unemployed by AI will be redirected to caring fields, which will sorely need more people in the coming decades.

Additional big questions will arise from study of the human genome. Genoeconomics has already uncovered genetic and epigenetic connections with economic outcomes, changing how we think about inequality, opportunity, and economic and social mobility, as economic outcomes and preferences appear to be as heritable as many medical conditions and personality traits. Yet, as important to economic success as genes appear to be, plenty of room remains for social and environmental factors to affect outcomes. Social policy can complement or complicate the hand each of us are dealt. One challenge in the coming decades will be to provide support structures that enhance positive genetic traits and mitigate negative ones.

b. As the Future Goes

Good luck seeking answers to these questions from AI. Though AI may provide reasoned responses, it's still artificial. AI is not able to weigh our values or decide what questions to ask next. While AI may guide us, our most important questions are not something AI can ask, nor are they ones AI can answer for us, it's something we have to figure out for ourselves.

Congressman Tip O'Neill is noted for saying that all politics is local. If I could paraphrase: all economics is local. That is, it begins at the individual, family, and community levels. Will we allow a diversity of views to guide us to the right questions?

Author Index

L. Hadsell, *Social Economies*,
https://doi.org/10.1007/978-3-032-21916-9

Subject Index

L. Hadsell, *Social Economies*,
https://doi.org/10.1007/978-3-032-21916-9

FSC
www.fsc.org
MIX
Papier | Fördert gute Waldnutzung
FSC® C083411

Kolibri 360 GmbH
Ferdinand-Jühlke-Straße 7
99095 Erfurt, Deutschland
produktsicherheit@kolibri360.de